T0214203

Lecture Notes in Computer Science 11162

Commenced Publication in 1973
Founding and Former Series Editors:
Gerhard Goos, Juris Hartmanis, and Jan van Leeuwen

Editorial Board

More information about this series at http://www.springer.com/series/7412

Patrick Bourdot · Sue Cobb
Victoria Interrante · Hirokazu kato
Didier Stricker (Eds.)

Virtual Reality and Augmented Reality

15th EuroVR International Conference, EuroVR 2018
London, UK, October 22–23, 2018
Proceedings

 Springer

Editors
Patrick Bourdot (iD)
University of Paris-Sud
Orsay
France

Sue Cobb (iD)
University of Nottingham
Nottingham
UK

Victoria Interrante (iD)
University of Minnesota
Minneapolis, MN
USA

Hirokazu kato
Nara Institute of Science and Technology
Ikoma
Japan

Didier Stricker
University of Kaiserslautern and DFKI
Kaiserslautern
Germany

ISSN 0302-9743   ISSN 1611-3349 (electronic)
Lecture Notes in Computer Science
ISBN 978-3-030-01789-7   ISBN 978-3-030-01790-3 (eBook)
https://doi.org/10.1007/978-3-030-01790-3

Library of Congress Control Number: 2018958798

LNCS Sublibrary: SL6 – Image Processing, Computer Vision, Pattern Recognition, and Graphics

This Springer imprint is published by the registered company Springer Nature Switzerland AG
The registered company address is: Gewerbestrasse 11, 6330 Cham, Switzerland

Preface

We are pleased to present in this LNCS volume the proceedings of the Scientific and Technical papers of EuroVR 2018, the 15th annual EuroVR conference, which took place at the Savoy Place in London (UK) during October 22–23, 2018.

Previous EuroVR conferences were held in Bremen; Germany (2014), Lecco, Italy (2015), Athens, Greece (2016), and Laval, France (2017). This series was initiated in 2004 by the INTUITION Network of Excellence in Virtual and Augmented Reality, supported by the European Commission until 2008, and included in the Joint Virtual Reality Conferences (JVRC) from 2009 to 2013. The focus of the EuroVR conferences is to present, each year, novel virtual reality (VR) to mixed reality (MR) technologies, including software systems, display technologies, interaction devices, and applications, to foster engagement between industry, academia, and the public sector, and to promote the development and deployment of VR/AR technologies in new, emerging, and existing fields.

This annual event of the EuroVR association (https://www.eurovr-association.org/) provides a unique platform for exchange between researchers, technology providers, and end users around commercial or research applications. Along with the scientific and technical sessions representing the research papers of this LNCS volume, two keynote speakers were invited to EuroVR 2018, namely: Prof. Robert W. Lindeman (HIT Lab New Zealand at the University of Canterbury), and Brian Waterfield (National Automotive Innovation Centre at the University of Warwick). Moreover industry-oriented sessions were also organized to report on a number of applications of VR/AR technologies in multiple fields (automotive, medical, etc.), while poster and demo sessions allowed discussions to be held around several works in progress.

Since 2017, EuroVR has been collaborating with Springer to publish the papers of the scientific and technical track of our annual conference. To increase the excellence of this applied research conference, which is basically oriented toward new uses of VR and AR technologies, we have formed a set of committees including an International Program Committee (IPC).

This IPC selected 15 papers for the scientific/technical track of EuroVR 2018, which are gathered in this LNCS volume. Nine full papers and six short papers were selected from 39 submissions, resulting in an acceptance rate of 38%. Each paper was reviewed by three members of the IPC with the help of some external expert reviewers. From the review reports, the final decision was taken by the IPC chairs. The selected papers are organized in this volume according to five topical parts: Vision-Based Motion Tracking, 3D Acquisition and 3D Reconstruction, Haptics and 3D Audio, Perception and Cognition, and Interactive Techniques and Use-Case Studies.

Additionally, several submissions to the scientific/technical track were redirected to the industrial, poster, or demo tracks of the conference, based on the recommendation of the reviewers. The abstracts of these other tracks are not included in this LNCS volume.

We would like to thank the members of the IPC and the external reviewers for their insightful reviews, which ensured the high quality of the papers selected for the scientific/technical track. Furthermore, we would like to thank the industrial co-chairs, the poster/demo co-chairs, and the local organizers of EuroVR 2018.

We are especially grateful to Anna Kramer (Assistant Editor, Computer Science Editorial, Springer) and Volha Shaparava (Springer OCS Support) for their support and advice during the preparation of this LNCS volume.

September 2018

Patrick Bourdot
Sue Cobb
Victoria Interrante
Hirokazu Kato
Didier Stricker
International Program Committee Chairs
of EuroVR 2018 and Volume Editors

Mirabelle D'Cruz
Joe Gabbard
Chris Freeman
General Conference Chairs of EuroVR 2018

Organization

General Conference Chairs

Mirabelle D'Cruz — University of Nottingham, UK
Joe Gabbard — Virginia Tech, USA
Chris Freeman — Advanced Manufacturing Research Centre/High Value Manufacturing Catapult, UK

International Program Committee Chairs

Patrick Bourdot — VENISE/LIMSI, CNRS, France
Sue Cobb — University of Nottingham, UK
Victoria Interrante — University of Minnesota, USA
Hirokazu Kato — NAIST, Japan
Didier Stricker — DFKI, Germany

International Program Committee

Mariano Alcañiz Raya — Universidad Politécnica de Valencia, Spain
Toshiyuki Amano — Wakayama University, Japan
Angelos Amditis — ICCS, Greece
Ferran Argelaguet Sanz — Inria, France
Pierre Boulanger — University of Alberta, Canada
Guillaume Bouyer — IBISC, Université Evry, Université Paris-Saclay, France
Doug Bowman — Virginia Tech, USA
Annelies Braffort — ILES/LIMSI, CNRS, France
Marcello Carrozzino — Scuola Superiore Sant'Anna, Italy
Lucio De Paolis — University of Salento, Italy
Thierry Duval — IMT Atlantique, France
Alessandro Farnè — CRNL, INSERM, France
Vincenzo Ferrari — University of Pisa, Italy
Bernd Froehlich — Bauhaus-Universität Weimar, Germany
Kaj Helin — VTT Technical Research Centre of Finland Ltd, Finland
Eric Hodgson — Miami University, USA
Ioannis Karaseitanidis — ICCS, Greece
Alexander Kulik — Bauhaus-Universität Weimar, Germany
Nicolas Ladevèze — P2I/LIMSI, CNRS, France
Marc Erich Latoschik — University of Würzburg, Germany
Domitile Lourdeaux — Heudiasyc, CNRS, France
Katerina Mania — Technical University of Crete, Greece

Belen Masia	Universidad de Zaragoza, Spain
Daniel Mestre	Mediterranean Virtual Reality Center, CNRS, France
Luciana Nedel	Federal University of Rio Grande do Sul, Brazil
Anne-Hélène Olivier	University of Rennes 2, France
Jérôme Perret	Haption, Germany
Lorenzo Picinali	Imperial College London, UK
Alexander Plopski	Nara Institute of Science and Technology, Japan
Wendy Powell	University of Portsmouth, UK
Dirk Reiners	University of Arkansas, USA
James Ritchie	Heriot-Watt University, UK
Marco Sacco	ITA, CNR, Italy
Jose San Martin	Universidad Rey Juan Carlos, Spain
Hedi Tabia	ETIS, ENSEA, France
Daniel Thalmann	EPFL, Switzerland
Kiran Varanasi	DFKI, Germany
Jean-Louis Vercher	Institut des Sciences du Mouvement, CNRS, France
Jean-Marc Vézien	VENISE/LIMSI, CNRS, France
Krzysztof Walczak	Poznan University of Economics and Business, Poland
Manuela Waldner	TU Wien, Austria
Gabriel Zachmann	University of Bremen, Germany

Industrial Chairs

Jérôme Perret	Haption, Germany
Kaj Helin	VTT Technical Research Centre of Finland Ltd., Finland
Rab Scott	Advance Manufacturing Research Centre, UK
Christoph Runde	VDC, Germany
Martin Courchesne	CEA, France

Poster and Demo Chairs

Lorenzo Picinali	Imperial College London, UK
Richard Eastgate	University of Nottingham, UK
Ioannis Karaseitanidis	ICCS, Greece
Krzysztof Walczak	Poznan University of Economics and Business, Poland

Exhibition and Sponsor Chairs

Chris Freeman	Advanced Manufacturing Research Centre/High Value Manufacturing Catapult, UK
Fiona Killkenny	ImmerseUK, UK
Birgit Berktold-Schulze	BARCO, Belgium
Laurent Chretien	Laval Virtual, France
Angelos Amditis	ICCS, Greece

Publicity Chairs

Carrie Wooten	KTN, UK
Matthieu Poyade	The Glasgow School of Art, UK
Harshada Patel	University of Nottingham, UK
Tara Solebury	Arts and Humanities Research Council, UK
Francesca Sacchini	ITA, CNR, Italy
Daniele Spoladore	ITA, CNR, Italy

Organizers

Contents

Perception and Cognition

Interactive Techniques and Use-Case Studies

Vision-Based Motion Tracking

Structure-Aware 3D Hand Pose Regression from a Single Depth Image

Jameel Malik[1,2](✉), Ahmed Elhayek[1](✉), and Didier Stricker[1](✉)

[1] Department Augmented Vision, DFKI Kaiserslautern, Kaiserslautern, Germany
{`jameel.malik,ahmed.elhayek,didier.stricker`}@dfki.de
[2] NUST-SEECS, Islamabad, Pakistan

Abstract. Hand pose tracking in 3D is an essential task for many virtual reality (VR) applications such as games and manipulating virtual objects with bare hands. CNN-based learning methods achieve the state-of-the-art accuracy by directly regressing 3D pose from a single depth image. However, the 3D pose estimated by these methods is coarse and kinematically unstable due to independent learning of sparse joint positions. In this paper, we propose a novel structure-aware CNN-based algorithm which learns to automatically segment the hand from a raw depth image and estimate 3D hand pose jointly with new structural constraints. The constraints include fingers lengths, distances of joints along the kinematic chain and fingers inter-distances. Learning these constraints help to maintain a structural relation between the estimated joint keypoints. Also, we convert sparse representation of hand skeleton to dense by performing n-points interpolation between the pairs of parent and child joints. By comprehensive evaluation, we show the effectiveness of our approach and demonstrate competitive performance to the state-of-the-art methods on the public NYU hand pose dataset.

Keywords: Hand pose · Depth image
Convolutional Neural Network (CNN)

1 Introduction

Markerless 3D hand pose estimation is a fundamental challenge for many interesting applications of virtual reality (VR) and augmented reality (AR) such as handling of objects in VR environment, games and interactive control. This task has been extensively studied in the past few years and great progress has been achieved. This is primarily due to the arrival of low cost depth sensors and rapid advancements in deep learning. However, estimating 3D hand pose from a single depth image is still challenging due to self similarities, occlusions, wide range of articulations and varying hand shapes.

Hand pose estimation methods are classified into three main catagories namely learning based methods (discriminative), model-based methods (generative) and combination of the discriminative and generative methods (hybrid).

© Springer Nature Switzerland AG 2018
P. Bourdot et al. (Eds.): EuroVR 2018, LNCS 11162, pp. 3–17, 2018.
https://doi.org/10.1007/978-3-030-01790-3_1

Among these methods, CNN-based discriminative methods have shown the highest accuracy on the public benchmarks. Despite of the fact that these methods achieve higher accuracy, they do not well exploit the structural information of hands during the learning process [11,34,35]. Specifically, independent learning of sparse joint positions with no consideration to joint connection structure and hand skeleton constraints leads to coarse predictions. This is the main reason these methods still generalize poorly on unseen hand shapes [34] and consequently, not directly usable in practical VR applications.

Therefore, our main contribution for this paper is a novel structure-aware CNN-based discriminative approach which incorporates the structural constraints of hand skeleton and enhances the loss function for better learning of 3D hand pose. Our main idea is to jointly learn the 3D joint keypoints and the hand structure parameters. Thereby, facilitating the CNN to maintain a structural relation between the estimated joint keypoints. Our method is simple, efficient and effective. It optimizes a combined loss function of 3D joint positions and simple structural constraints of the hand skeleton. The constraints comprise of fingers lengths, fingers inter-distances and distances of joints in the kinematic chain of the hand skeleton (kinematic distances). These constraints are easy to learn and guide the optimization process to estimate more refined and accurate 3D hand pose. Another contribution which helps to improve the accuracy is to convert the sparse joints keypoints to dense representation. To this end, we perform n-points interpolation between the pairs of parent and child ground truth joint positions along the kinematic chain of hand skeleton. These simple strategies can be easily used to improve the accuracy of any CNN-based discriminative method without additional cost.

Existing hand pose estimation methods assume already segmented hand region from a raw depth image as input to their algorithms. The hand segmentation approaches are mainly based on heuristics or ground truth annotation which make them difficult to use in practical applications. The problem of hand segmentation is not well addressed in the existing works. Hence, our second contribution is a new CNN-based hand segmentation method to extract the hand region from a raw depth frame. For training over images with varying backgrounds and camera noise, we combine several existing hand pose datasets including a new dataset which we capture to include more variation in hand shapes. The combined dataset will be public.

By performing exhaustive evaluation of our algorithm, we show the effectiveness of our hand segmentation algorithm, n-points interpolation strategy and learning the structural constraints jointly with the 3D hand pose. Experiments show that our method performs better than several state-of-the-art hand pose estimation on the NYU public benchmark. The main contributions for this paper are:

1. A novel structure-aware CNN-based algorithm for 3D hand pose estimation including the structural constraints of hand skeleton; see Sect. 4.2.
2. A novel CNN-based algorithm to effectively segment the hand region from a raw depth image; see Sect. 4.1.

3. A simple and effective interpolation strategy for improved hand pose estimation; see Sect. 4.2.

2   Related Work

3D hand pose estimation using a depth sensor has been widely studied in the past few years. For detailed overview, we refer the reader to the survey papers [24,34]. Here we limit our discussion to the most related works.

Depth-Based Hand Segmentation Methods: Tompson et al. [27] introduce a per-pixel classification of the hand region using random decision forest (RDF) based method. However, the per-pixel manual labeling of large number of training frames is cumbersome. Oberweger et al. [16] apply depth-thresholding thereby, computing the center of mass of hand region. Then, crop the hand using the center of mass. Recently, [15] propose a CNN-based refinement network to further refine the segmented hand depth image by [16] to achieve better localization. In contrast, we convert the raw depth image to RGB by applying simple JET colormap and use a CNN to predict the 2D position of the hand palm center. Then, using the predicted palm center, depth value can easily be obtained from input depth frame. The proposed approach is simple and effective.

Discriminative Methods: RDF-based discriminative works [10,20,23,30,32] are lagging behind recent CNN-based methods such as [1,5,6,12,19,31] in accuracy of the estimated hand pose. Some works have employed either RGB or RGB-D data to estimate 3D joint positions [13,18,21,36]. In [5], Ge et al. effectively regress 3D pose using a single 3D-CNN. Recently, [12] propose a voxel-to-voxel pose predictor which takes voxelised input depth image and outputs 3D joint heatmaps. [6,31] introduce a region ensemble (REN) strategy which concatenates features from multiple networks to regress the 3D pose. Chen et al. [1] extend [31] by an iterative pose-guided REN strategy. All of the above methods optimize only for the 3D pose without incorporating any structural relations between the joint positions. In contrast, we extend the loss function defined on the joint positions only by including several hand structural constraints. Thereby, improving the accuracy of the estimated pose.

Hybrid Methods: [27] predict 2D heatmaps using a single CNN. After that they use inverse kinematics to recover the 3D pose. Ge et al. [4] use a 3D-CNN for 2D heatmaps estimation and then recover 3D joint positions. Oberweger et al. [17] train a complex feedback loop to regress 3D joint positions. Wan et al. [28] learn a shared latent space, between an encoder and a decoder, to reconstruct the depth image using generative adversarial network(GAN) and refine the 3D pose. The above mentioned works optimize only for the joints positions and do not explicitly account for the hand geometric constraints. Dibra et al. [3] propose a complex end-to-end framework to indirectly recover the 3D pose from reconstructed depth image. Zhou et al. [35] implement a forward kinematics layer inside the CNN and train an end-to-end pipeline. Malik et al. [11] extend this work to generalize over varying hand shapes. However, these methods suffer from low accuracy because regressing joint angles (for rotation matrices) is cumbersome.

3   Method Overview

The goal of our pipeline is to estimate more stable and accurate 3D joint positions J, given a raw depth input D_o. To this end, we simultaneously optimize for J, fingers lengths FL, fingers inter-distance FD and kinematics distances KD to facilitate the learning of 3D joint positions in a structured manner. Our pipeline is shown in Fig. 1. D_o is resized and then colorized (using the JET colormap) by a function g. The output RGB image D_i is of size $227 \times 227 \times 3$. D_i is passed as input to the PalmCNN to directly regress hand palm center (u,v) in image coordinates. Then, a cropping function f is applied to segment the 3D hand region D_s from the raw depth frame D_o. The colorization step is simple and helps to improve the accuracy; see Sect. 5.2. Finally, the PoseCNN takes D_s as input and estimates 3D joint positions J, fingers lengths FL, fingers inter-distance FD and kinematics distances KD. The PoseCNN comprises of a CNN and a regressor; see Sect. 4.2 for details. The PalmCNN and the PoseCNN are trained separately.

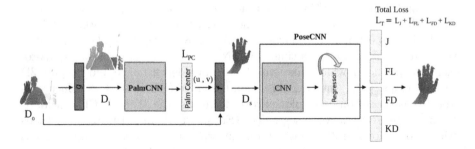

Fig. 1. Our pipeline for hand segmentation and pose estimation. The raw depth frame D_o is given as input to a function g which resizes D_o to $227 \times 227 \times 3$ dimension and colorizes it using the JET colormap. The output of g (D_i) is fed to the PalmCNN to regress 2D hand palm center (u,v). L_{PC} is the loss for the PalmCNN. The function f crops the hand region D_s given (u,v). D_s is fed to PoseCNN which outputs 3D joint positions J, fingers lengths FL, fingers inter-distances FD, and kinematic distances KD.

4   Hand Segmentation and Pose Estimation

In this section, we explain the individual components of the pipeline shown in Fig. 1. The function g, the PalmCNN and the crop function f are described in

Sect. 4.1. In Sect. 4.2, we explain the main component of our pipeline i.e. the PoseCNN.

4.1   CNN-Based Hand Segmentation

The function g simply resizes and colorizes D_o to be fed as input to the Palm-CNN. The output D_i of g is an RGB image of size $227 \times 227 \times 3$. The task of the PalmCNN is to estimate the pixel coordinates of the center of the hand region i.e. palm center (u,v). The CNN architecture of the PalmCNN is similar to the AlexNet [9] except that the final fully connected layer regresses the palm center. The softmax loss layer is replaced by euclidean loss layer. The euclidean 2D palm center loss is given as:

$$L_{PC} = \frac{1}{2}\|PC - PC_{GT}\|^2 \qquad (1)$$

where L_{PC} is the palm center loss and PC_{GT} is the ground truth palm center. To train the PalmCNN, we combine four of the publicly available hand pose datasets (i.e. NYU [27], ICVL [26], MSRA-2015 [23] and Dexter-1 [22]) with a new dataset which we captured using creative senz3D camera [2]. This additional small scale dataset is captured because the public datasets lack in hand shape variation [11]. To obtain the ground truth palm center, we employ the generative method proposed by [25]. We captured depth images from five different subjects. Our dataset contains 8000 original depth images. Notably, the variation in hand position should cover the whole image space. Therefore, we create around 10 augmented copies of every depth frame in the combined dataset by translating it around the whole image using the ground truth hand palm center position. The total number of training and testing frames are $4.55M$ and $200K$ respectively. We fine-tune the AlexNet (pre-trained on ImageNet dataset) with the combined dataset. The crop function f takes the estimated (u,v) and D_o as inputs and segments the 3D hand region; see Sect. 5.1 for details about f. The resultant image D_s is of size 224×224.

4.2   Structure-Aware 3D Hand Pose Estimation

In our pipeline, the PoseCNN aims to jointly estimate the hand joint keypoints J and additional constraints (i.e. fingers lengths FL, fingers inter-distance FD, kinematic distances FD). During training, these constraints help to maintain a structural relation between the joints positions. The ground truth for the constraints can easily be obtained from the ground truth joint positions. The euclidean 3D joint positions loss L_J is given as:

$$L_J = \frac{1}{2}\|J - J_{GT}\|^2 \qquad (2)$$

where $J_{GT} \in \mathbb{R}^{P \times 3}$ is a vector of 3D ground truth joint positions. P is the number of joint keypoints. The constraints are explained as follows:

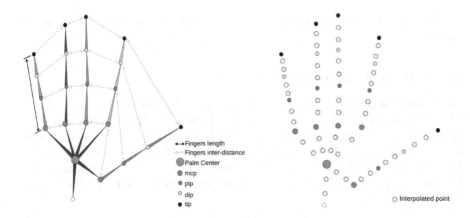

Fig. 2. The left figure shows the graphical representation of two of the structural constraints i.e. Fingers lengths and Fingers inter-distances. The hand skeleton on the right shows the interpolated points ($n = 2$) between the sparse ground truth joint positions.

Fingers Lengths: We first calculate J-1 hand bone-lengths from the ground truth joint positions using the standard 3D euclidean distance formula. To obtain a finger's length fl, we add the bone-lengths from the base joint (mcp) to the finger-tip joint (tip) as shown in Fig. 2. The equation for fl can be written as:

$$fl = bl_{mcp-pip} + bl_{pip-dip} + bl_{dip-tip} \tag{3}$$

where bl_{x-y} is the bone-length from a parent joint x to a child joint y. Therefore, a set FL_{GT} is represented as:

$$FL_{GT} = \{fl_{pinky}, fl_{ring}, fl_{middle}, fl_{index}, fl_{thumb}\} \tag{4}$$

The euclidean fingers lengths loss L_{FL} is:

$$L_{FL} = \frac{1}{2}\|FL - FL_{GT}\|^2 \tag{5}$$

where FL is the vector of estimated fingers lengths.

Fingers Inter-distances: The distances between the mcp joints of consecutive fingers for a particular hand mostly remain fixed. However, the distances between pip, dip and tip joints between fingers can vary depending on the pose of the hand. The inter-distances between neighboring fingers can easily be obtained by calculating 3D euclidean distances between respective joints of the fingers; see Fig. 2. For example, the inter-distances between $index$ and $middle$ fingers are evaluated as:

$$fd(index, middle) = \{d(mcp_{index}, mcp_{middle}), d(pip_{index}, pip_{middle}),$$
$$d(dip_{index}, dip_{middle}), d(tip_{index}, tip_{middle})\} \tag{6}$$

where $fd(.)$ is a set of inter-distances between the joints of two adjacent fingers and $d(.)$ represents 3D euclidean distance between two joints. Likewise, inter-distances for remaining finger pairs i.e. $(middle, ring)$, $(ring, pinky)$ and $(thumb, index)$ can be obtained using Eq. 6. Hence, a set FD_{GT} can be expressed as:

$$FD_{GT} = \{fd(index, middle), fd(middle, ring), \\ fd(ring, pinky), fd(thumb, index)\} \tag{7}$$

The fingers inter-distances loss L_{FD} can be written as:

$$L_{FD} = \frac{1}{2}\|FD - FD_{GT}\|^2 \tag{8}$$

where FD is the vector of estimated fingers inter-distances.

Kinematic Distances: Hand skeleton bears an inherent kinematic structure which should not be ignored in the pose estimation task. Otherwise, the resultant pose could be kinematically unstable [11,35]. In this work, we add a much needed loss function which incorporates kinematic distances of all the joints in the hand skeleton. Given the set of parents joints S_{p_j} of a joint p_j in J_{GT}, the kinematic distance kd_j from the root joint to p_j can be calculated as:

$$kd_j = \sum_{i=0}^{M-1} d(J_{GT_i}, J_{GT_{i+1}}) \tag{9}$$

where $i \in S_{p_j}$ and M is the size of the set S_{p_j}. Using Eq. 9, the kinematic distances of each joint in J_{GT} can be obtained. Hence, the loss L_{KD} can be written as:

$$L_{KD} = \frac{1}{2}\|KD - KD_{GT}\|^2 \tag{10}$$

where KD and KD_{GT} are the vectors of estimated and ground truth kinematic distances.

Total Loss: Including the additional constraints (mentioned above) help to improve the accuracy of hand pose estimation task and maintain the structure of the hand skeleton; see Sect. 5.2. The final loss equation for the PoseCNN can be written as:

$$L_T = L_J + L_{FL} + L_{FD} + L_{KD}. \tag{11}$$

Interpolation: In order to get a dense representation of hand skeleton, we linearly interpolate n joints between each pair of parent and child joints in the kinematic hierarchy of the hand skeleton; see Fig. 2. We try different number of interpolated points n and study their effects on the accuracy of the estimated pose; see Sect. 5.2. As an example, the formulas for interpolating two 3D points $P1$ and $P2$ between two 3D points P_a and P_b are:

$$P1 = 0.7 * P_a + 0.3 * P_b, \quad P2 = 0.3 * P_a + 0.7 * P_b \tag{12}$$

Architecture and Iterative Regression : The architecture of CNN in the PoseCNN is similar to the ResNet-50 [7] except that final fully connected (FC) layer which outputs the features $\varphi \in \mathbb{R}^{1024}$. The features φ are concatenated with an initial estimate of $E = \{J, FD, FL$ and $KD\}$ i.e. $\phi = \{\varphi, E\}$. Initial estimate of E is obtained using the mean values of $\{J, FD, FL$ and $KD\}$ from the NYU ground truth annotations. This estimate is kept fixed during the training and the testing. ϕ is fed to a regressor which comprises of two FC layers with 1024 neurons each. Both the FC layers use dropout layers with ratio of 0.3. The last FC layer contains M neurons. Where $M = 2P(n + 1) + 10n + 21$. The regressor aims to refine E in an iterative feedback manner i.e. $E_{t+1} = E_t + \delta E_t$. In our implementation, we use at least three iterations. Directly regressing E is challenging therefore, we observe that inclusion of the regressor is beneficial.

5   Experiments

In this section, we provide the implementation details, evaluation of our framework and comparison with the state-of-the-art hand pose estimation methods. The evaluation metrics are 3D joint location error and number of frames within certain thresholds. All the error metrics are reported in mm.

5.1   Implementation Details

We use Caffe [8], an open-source deep learning framework, to train the PalmCNN and the PoseCNN in our pipeline (see Fig. 1). The networks run on a desktop using Nvidia Geforce GTX 1080 Ti GPU. The PalmCNN is trained on the combined dataset; see Sect. 4.1. The learning rate is set to 0.0001 with a batch size of 256 and 0.9 SGD momentum. One forward pass in the PalmCNN takes 4.5 ms. We train the PoseCNN on the NYU hand pose dataset [27]. The NYU dataset has 72,757 images for training and 8252 frames for testing. In order to segment the hand region from the raw depth input D_o, we use the estimated palm center from the PalmCNN. Given (u,v) and D_o, the hand region is cropped in 3D using a bounding box of size 300 and the camera focal length. The pre-processed image is of size 224 × 224 and the depth values are normalized to $[-1, 1]$. The 3D joints annotations J_{GT} in camera coordinates are also normalized to range $[-1, 1]$. We obtain FL_{GT}, FD_{GT} and KD_{GT} from the normalized J_{GT}. For training the PoseCNN, we use 0.001 learning rate with 0.9 SGD momentum and a batch size of 128. The forward pass for the PoseCNN takes 35 ms.

5.2   Method Evaluation

In this subsection, we comprehensively evaluate the PoseCNN and the PalmCNN. We first observe the effects of the proposed structural constraints on the accuracy of the estimated joint positions J. Second is to study the effects of interpolating n-points between the sparse joint positions.

Table 1. We evaluate five different implementations of our PoseCNN on the NYU hand pose dataset. The PoseCNN(J) is the *baseline* which is trained for estimating joint positions only. The PoseCNN($J \cup FL \cup FD \cup KD$) performs the best and shows an error improvement of 15.13% on the estimated J over the *baseline*.

Method implementations	3D joint location error
	J
PoseCNN(J)	15.2 mm
PoseCNN($J \cup FL$)	14.7 mm
PoseCNN($J \cup FD$)	13.6 mm
PoseCNN($J \cup KD$)	13.9 mm
PoseCNN($J \cup FL \cup FD \cup KD$)	**12.9 mm**

Table 2. We observe the effects of n-points interpolation between the pairs of parent and child joints in the kinematic hierarchy of the hand skeleton. The value of n varies from 1 to 5. 5-point interpolation shows 5.5% improvement in accuracy. For $n > 5$, we do not observe notable error improvement.

n-points interpolation	3D joint location error
	J
PoseCNN(1-point Interp.)	12.80 mm
PoseCNN(2-point Interp.)	12.63 mm
PoseCNN(3-point Interp.)	12.38 mm
PoseCNN(4-point Interp.)	12.17 mm
PoseCNN(5-point Interp.)	**11.9 mm**

Fig. 3. Qualitative evaluation of our PoseCNN. The top row shows the predicted hand joint positions overlaid on the preprocessed NYU depth images from our *baseline* implementation (i.e. PoseCNN(J)). The bottom row shows the corresponding images with corrected joint positions from our PoseCNN(*all*) implementation.

Structural Constraints: To this end, we train the following implementations of the PoseCNN on the NYU hand pose dataset which learns:

1. Joint positions J only.
2. Fingers lengths FL with J (i.e. $J \cup FL$).
3. Fingers inter-distances FD with J (i.e. $J \cup FD$).
4. Kinematic distances KD with J (i.e. $J \cup KD$).
5. KD, FD and FL with J (i.e. $J \cup FL \cup FD \cup KD$).

Table 3. Influence of hand segmentation: Our hand segmentation method without colorization (wo/colorization) improves the joints prediction error by more than 1 mm over center of hand mass (CoM) calculation method. Our method with colorization (w/colorization) further improves the accuracy by 19.75% over CoM.

Methods	3D joint loc. error	3D palm center loc. error
CoM	14.83 mm	28.1 mm
Ours (wo/colorization)	13.05 mm	15.1 mm
Ours (w/colorization)	**11.9 mm**	**10.2 mm**

Table 1 shows the quantitative results of the these implementations. In simplest form, the PoseCNN is trained to estimate 3D joint keypoints J only, we call this implementation as our *baseline* (PoseCNN(J)). On top of the *baseline*, we include the structural constraints one by one to observe the effects on the accuracy of estimated joints J. By including fingers lengths FL with J (i.e. PoseCNN($J \cup FL$)), we observe a small increase (3.28%) in accuracy of J. Inclusion of fingers inter-distances FD (PoseCNN($J \cup FD$)) and kinematic distances KD (PoseCNN($J \cup KD$)) improves the accuracy of the estimated J by 10.5% and 8.55% over the *baseline*, respectively. The best accuracy is achieved by the architecture which includes all the constraints (PoseCNN($J \cup FL \cup FD \cup KD$)). It shows 15.13% improvement over the *baseline*.

Dense Hand Pose Representation: We further experiment on the PoseCNN($J \cup FL \cup FD \cup KD$) by interpolating n-points between the pairs of parent and child joints in the kinematic hierarchy of the hand skeleton. Thereby, converting the sparse hand skeleton to dense representation. This leads to increase in number of joint positions depending on the value of n. Consequently, the size of the vectors FD and KD also increases. The quantitative results are summarized in Table 2. Our model (PoseCNN($J \cup FL \cup FD \cup KD$)) with 5-points interpolation performs the best among the others. The results show improvement in accuracy of the estimated J using the interpolation strategy. Therefore, dense hand skeleton representation is useful for improved hand pose regression. For notational simplicity, we call this model as PoseCNN(*all*). This model improves the accuracy over the *baseline* by 21.71%.

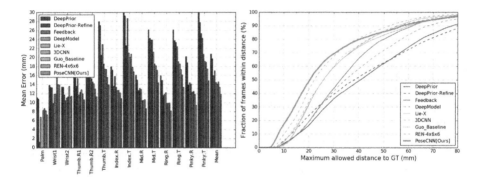

Fig. 4. Quantitative comparison on the NYU test set [27]. The right figure shows the fraction of frames within thresholds in mm. The left one shows the mean errors (mm) on individual joints of the NYU hand pose dataset. Our method PoseCNN(*all*) shows the average error of 11.9 mm which is better than several state-of-the-art methods.

The qualitative comparison of our *baseline* and PoseCNN(*all*) on the NYU dataset is shown in Fig. 3. The estimated joint positions J are displayed on the sample preprocessed depth images. The predicted hand skeleton from our *baseline* architecture (PoseCNN(J)) can be of incorrect size (i.e. shorter or longer) due to independent learning of joint keypoints. Whereas, PoseCNN(*all*) which incorporates all the constraints along-with interpolated points produces more stable and reliable results. These results clearly show the effectiveness of our

Table 4. Comparison with the state-of-the-art on the NYU test set [27]: Our proposed model (PoseCNN(*all*)) exceeds in accuracy over the state-of-the-art hand pose estimation methods.

Methods	3D joint location error
DeepPrior [16]	20.75 mm
DeepPrior-Refine [16]	19.72 mm
Crossing Nets [28]	15.5 mm
Neverova et al. [14]	14.9 mm
Feedback [17]	15.9 mm
DeepModel [35]	17.0 mm
Lie-X [32]	14.5 mm
GuoBaseline [6]	14.6 mm
3DCNN [5]	14.11 mm
REN [6]	13.3 mm
DeepPrior++ [15]	12.3 mm
PoseCNN(*all*) **[Ours]**	**11.9 mm**

novel strategies, namely, structural constraints and the dense hand pose representation.

Hand Segmentation: We evaluate our hand segmentation method (see Sect. 4.1) on the NYU dataset by studying the impact of colorization and comparing with the depth-thresholding followed by center of mass (CoM) computation method. The goal is to observe the effects of hand segmentation on the final 3D pose estimation accuracy. We train two different implementations of the PalmCNN. First, with colorized depth input (Ours(w/colorization)) and second, without colorization (Ours(wo/colorization)). Therefore, we get two different 3D palm centers for cropping the NYU depth images. Also, we obtain 3D palm centers from center of hand mass (CoM) calculation method; see Sect. 2. Using these three different palm centers, we obtain three distinct sets of pre-processed NYU training and testing frames. The PoseCNN(all) is trained for each of the three training sets. The effects on the accuracy of estimated J from the three PoseCNN(all) models are reported in Table 3. The best results are achieved by Ours(w/colorization) model. It shows an error improvement of 19.75% and 8.81% over the CoM and Ours(wo/colorization) methods; respectively.

Real-Time Demonstration: We test our complete framework in real-time using a single creative Senz3D depth camera [2]. The camera is placed on top of the display screen. Our framework tracks the hand movements with challenging poses as shown in Fig. 5. For better generalization, we train our PoseCNN(all) architecture on the *HandSet* dataset [11]. This dataset combines several public hand pose datasets (e.g. ICVL, NYU and MSRA-2015) in a single unified format. The PalmCNN successfully estimates the hand palm center. Thereafter, the PoseCNN reliably estimates the joint positions. The predicted hand skeleton is displayed on the input depth frame. The run-time of the pipeline is 42 ms.

Fig. 5. Real-time demonstration: We test our complete pipeline in real-time using the creative Senz3D depth camera [2]. The camera is mounted on top of the display screen. The predicted hand skeleton (yellow) is overlaid on the depth image. Our system successfully tracks various challenging hand poses from frontal camera view. (Color figure online)

5.3   Comparison with the State-of-the-Art

The state-of-the-art methods use either the ground truth palm center or the CoM localization approach to segment the hand region from a raw depth image. However, these approaches are not feasible for practical applications. In contrast, our CNN-based hand segmentation method automatically segments the hand region from a raw depth image and outperforms the commonly used CoM method (see Table 3). We compare our best performing model, PoseCNN(*all*), with the state-of-the-art hand pose estimation methods i.e. DeepModel [35], DeepPrior [16], DeepPriorRefine [16], Crossing Nets [28], Feedback [17], LieX [32], GuoBaseline [6], 3DCNN [5] and REN [6]. The quantitative results are shown in Table 4 and Fig. 4. Our algorithm exceeds in accuracy over these methods. The results clearly indicate the benefits of our hand segmentation approach, the interpolation strategy and simultaneous learning of the hand structural constraints with the joint positions.

6   Conclusion

In this paper, we present a novel structure-aware 3D hand pose regression pipeline from a single raw depth image. We propose two strategies which can be easily used to improve the hand pose estimation accuracy of any CNN-based discriminative method. To this end, a novel CNN-based hand segmentation method regresses the hand palm center which is used to segment the hand region from a raw depth image. Thereafter, a new CNN-based regression network simultaneously estimates the 3D hand pose and its structural constraints. Thereby, enforcing the hand pose structure during the training process. The proposed constraints help to maintain a structural relation between the estimated joint positions. Moreover, we study the effects of n-points interpolation between the pairs of parent and child joints in the kinematic chain of the hand skeleton. By performing extensive evaluations, we show the effectiveness of our approach. Experiments demonstrate competitive performance to the state-of-the-art hand pose estimation methods.

Acknowledgements. This work has been partially funded by the Federal Ministry of Education and Research of the Federal Republic of Germany as part of the research projects DYNAMICS (Grant number 01IW15003) and VIDETE (Grant number 01IW18002).

References

1. Chen, X., Wang, G., Guo, H., Zhang, C.: Pose guided structured region ensemble network for cascaded hand pose estimation. arXiv preprint arXiv:1708.03416 (2017)
2. Creative: Senz3D interactive gesture camera, March 2018. https://us.creative.com/p/web-cameras/creative-senz3d
3. Dibra, E., Wolf, T., Oztireli, C., Gross, M.: How to refine 3D hand pose estimation from unlabelled depth data? In: 3DV (2017)

4. Ge, L., Liang, H., Yuan, J., Thalmann, D.: Robust 3D hand pose estimation in single depth images: from single-view CNN to multi-view CNNs. In: Proceedings of the IEEE Conference on Computer Vision and Pattern Recognition, pp. 3593–3601 (2016)
5. Ge, L., Liang, H., Yuan, J., Thalmann, D.: 3D convolutional neural networks for efficient and robust hand pose estimation from single depth images. In: Proceedings of the IEEE Conference on Computer Vision and Pattern Recognition (2017)
6. Guo, H., Wang, G., Chen, X., Zhang, C., Qiao, F., Yang, H.: Region ensemble network: improving convolutional network for hand pose estimation. In: ICIP (2017)
7. He, K., Zhang, X., Ren, S., Sun, J.: Deep residual learning for image recognition. In: Proceedings of the IEEE Conference on Computer Vision and Pattern Recognition, pp. 770–778 (2016)
8. Jia, Y., et al.: Caffe: convolutional architecture for fast feature embedding. In: Proceedings of the 22nd ACM International Conference on Multimedia, pp. 675–678. ACM (2014)
9. Krizhevsky, A., Sutskever, I., Hinton, G.E.: ImageNet classification with deep convolutional neural networks. In: Advances in Neural Information Processing Systems, pp. 1097–1105 (2012)
10. Li, P., Ling, H., Li, X., Liao, C.: 3D hand pose estimation using randomized decision forest with segmentation index points. In: Proceedings of the IEEE International Conference on Computer Vision, pp. 819–827 (2015)
11. Malik, J., Elhayek, A., Stricker, D.: Simultaneous hand pose and skeleton bone-lengths estimation from a single depth image. In: 3DV (2017)
12. Moon, G., Chang, J.Y., Lee, K.M.: V2V-PoseNet: voxel-to-voxel prediction network for accurate 3D hand and human pose estimation from a single depth map. arXiv preprint arXiv:1711.07399 (2017)
13. Mueller, F., Mehta, D., Sotnychenko, O., Sridhar, S., Casas, D., Theobalt, C.: Real-time hand tracking under occlusion from an egocentric RGB-D sensor. In: Proceedings of International Conference on Computer Vision (ICCV), vol. 10 (2017)
14. Neverova, N., Wolf, C., Nebout, F., Taylor, G.W.: Hand pose estimation through semi-supervised and weakly-supervised learning. Comput. Vis. Image Underst. **164**, 56–67 (2017)
15. Oberweger, M., Lepetit, V.: Deepprior++: improving fast and accurate 3D hand pose estimation. In: ICCV Workshop, vol. 840, p. 2 (2017)
16. Oberweger, M., Wohlhart, P., Lepetit, V.: Hands deep in deep learning for hand pose estimation. In: CVWW (2015)
17. Oberweger, M., Wohlhart, P., Lepetit, V.: Training a feedback loop for hand pose estimation. In: Proceedings of the IEEE International Conference on Computer Vision, pp. 3316–3324 (2015)
18. Panteleris, P., Oikonomidis, I., Argyros, A.: Using a single RGB frame for real time 3D hand pose estimation in the wild. arXiv preprint arXiv:1712.03866 (2017)
19. Rad, M., Oberweger, M., Lepetit, V.: Feature mapping for learning fast and accurate 3D pose inference from synthetic images. arXiv preprint arXiv:1712.03904 (2017)
20. Sharp, T., et al.: Accurate, robust, and flexible real-time hand tracking. In: Proceedings of the 33rd Annual ACM Conference on Human Factors in Computing Systems, pp. 3633–3642. ACM (2015)
21. Simon, T., Joo, H., Matthews, I., Sheikh, Y.: Hand keypoint detection in single images using multiview bootstrapping. In: The IEEE Conference on Computer Vision and Pattern Recognition (CVPR), vol. 2 (2017)

22. Sridhar, S., Oulasvirta, A., Theobalt, C.: Interactive markerless articulated hand motion tracking using rgb and depth data. In: Proceedings of the IEEE International Conference on Computer Vision, pp. 2456–2463 (2013)

23. Sun, X., Wei, Y., Liang, S., Tang, X., Sun, J.: Cascaded hand pose regression. In: Proceedings of the IEEE Conference on Computer Vision and Pattern Recognition, pp. 824–832 (2015)

24. Supancic, J.S., Rogez, G., Yang, Y., Shotton, J., Ramanan, D.: Depth-based hand pose estimation: data, methods, and challenges. In: IEEE International Conference on Computer Vision, pp. 1868–1876 (2015)

25. Tagliasacchi, A., Schröder, M., Tkach, A., Bouaziz, S., Botsch, M., Pauly, M.: Robust articulated-icp for real-time hand tracking. In: Computer Graphics Forum, vol. 34, pp. 101–114. Wiley Online Library (2015)

26. Tang, D., Jin Chang, H., Tejani, A., Kim, T.K.: Latent regression forest: structured estimation of 3D articulated hand posture. In: Proceedings of the IEEE Conference on Computer Vision and Pattern Recognition, pp. 3786–3793 (2014)

27. Tompson, J., Stein, M., Lecun, Y., Perlin, K.: Real-time continuous pose recovery of human hands using convolutional networks. ACM Trans. Graph. (ToG) **33**(5), 169 (2014)

28. Wan, C., Probst, T., Van Gool, L., Yao, A.: Crossing nets: combining GANs and VAEs with a shared latent space for hand pose estimation. In: 2017 IEEE Conference on Computer Vision and Pattern Recognition (CVPR). IEEE (2017)

29. Wan, C., Probst, T., Van Gool, L., Yao, A.: Dense 3D regression for hand pose estimation. arXiv preprint arXiv:1711.08996 (2017)

30. Wan, C., Yao, A., Van Gool, L.: Hand pose estimation from local surface normals. In: Leibe, B., Matas, J., Sebe, N., Welling, M. (eds.) ECCV 2016. LNCS, vol. 9907, pp. 554–569. Springer, Cham (2016). https://doi.org/10.1007/978-3-319-46487-9_34

31. Wang, G., Chen, X., Guo, H., Zhang, C.: Region ensemble network: towards good practices for deep 3D hand pose estimation. J. Vis. Commun. Image Represent. (2018)

32. Xu, C., Govindarajan, L.N., Zhang, Y., Cheng, L.: Lie-x: depth image based articulated object pose estimation, tracking, and action recognition on lie groups. Int. J. Comput. Vis. **123**, 454–478 (2017)

33. Ye, Q., Yuan, S., Kim, T.-K.: Spatial attention deep net with partial PSO for hierarchical hybrid hand pose estimation. In: Leibe, B., Matas, J., Sebe, N., Welling, M. (eds.) ECCV 2016. LNCS, vol. 9912, pp. 346–361. Springer, Cham (2016). https://doi.org/10.1007/978-3-319-46484-8_21

34. Yuan, S., et al.: Depth-based 3D hand pose estimation: from current achievements to future goals. In: IEEE CVPR (2018)

35. Zhou, X., Wan, Q., Zhang, W., Xue, X., Wei, Y.: Model-based deep hand pose estimation. In: IJCAI (2016)

36. Zimmermann, C., Brox, T.: Learning to estimate 3D hand pose from single RGB images. In: International Conference on Computer Vision (2017)

Universal Web-Based Tracking
for Augmented Reality Applications

Yannic Bonenberger, Jason Rambach$^{(\boxtimes)}$, Alain Pagani, and Didier Stricker

German Research Center for Artificial Intelligence (DFKI), Kaiserslautern, Germany
`Jason.Rambach@dfki.de`

Abstract. Augmented Reality (AR) is a growing technology which begins to reach its maturity and address a broad spectrum of areas. However, current augmented reality applications still tend to be confined to a single use case or a single set of devices. In this paper, we explore web-based augmented reality systems using a single cross-platform binary to address a wide range of devices, which can dramatically decrease the developmental effort to create applications and therefore help to satisfy the growing demand for them. To this extent, we discuss the implementation of a feature tracking system using WebAssembly and evaluate its real-time capabilities on a wide range of devices and operating systems. Additionally, we also demonstrate a simple AR application making use of our tracker.

Keywords: Augmented Reality · Web-based · 6DoF Pose Tracking

1 Introduction

Augmented Reality (AR) is an emerging technology combining virtual scenes with the real world [5]. With the progress in mobile computing devices like smartphones or tablets in recent years, there is a growing demand in AR applications in various consumer-oriented fields like entertainment or education, and also in other areas like industrial construction and maintenance or medicine and rehabilitation [8,10,11,26].

The main enabling technology for an AR system is a 6 Degree of Freedom (6DoF) pose estimation and tracking system. Knowledge of the camera pose allows for correct placement of virtual augmentations in the real world [23]. Model-based tracking approaches use a predefined target model for localization [25] while Simultaneous Localization and Mapping (SLAM)-based approaches operate without prior knowledge of the environment meaning that it also needs to be uncovered in parallel to the localization [20]. An advantage of model-based systems is the reduced complexity and the ability to create AR content that is specific to the tracked model, while SLAM systems can provide localization out-of-the-box without any user involvement.

There is a large number of devices like smartphones or tablets with at least one camera and sufficient computing power which are capable of running AR

© Springer Nature Switzerland AG 2018
P. Bourdot et al. (Eds.): EuroVR 2018, LNCS 11162, pp. 18–27, 2018.
https://doi.org/10.1007/978-3-030-01790-3_2

Fig. 1. Our application running on a smartphone.

software. These devices have one major issue: They run many different operating systems and therefore have their own ecosystem, most of them not compatible with other ones. An example thereof is ARKit [9] which is developed by Apple and only supports the latest generation of iOS devices. Users with older devices will not be able to run applications using these features, even though lots of these devices have sufficient computation power to run them. Smartphones and tablets from other brands are also excluded from running these applications. For users with Android devices, there is ARCore [13] which only supports the latest generations of Android smartphones from vendors like Samsung or Google. It is even more complicated if developers want to bring their applications to the desktop. There is, however, one ecosystem that all of the mentioned devices support: And this is the WorldWideWeb. The WorldWideWeb was developed by Berners-Lee and Cailliau at CERN in 1990 [6,7] and grew from a platform to access static HTML files to a platform with support for large applications which can do most of what native applications can [14].

A significant milestone was the recent addition of WebAssembly, "a binary instruction format for a stack-based virtual machine" [3,17] which aims to execute at native speed on a wide range of platforms. It is available in all major browsers including Google Chrome, Microsoft Edge, Mozilla Firefox and Apple Safari [4]. With these technologies, it is possible to write fully functional AR applications which can replace native applications on the desktop and mobile devices. This has the potential of reducing the amount of work and therefore the costs to develop an augmented reality application, which is eventually necessary to satisfy the growing demand.

In this paper, we investigated whether it is possible to develop augmented reality applications using only technologies provided by the modern web platform without additional plugins or usage of particular browsers with built-in support for AR [15,16,22]. To demonstrate this, we developed a simple model based AR application using traditional web languages like HTML5 and ECMAScript as well as compiled languages like C, which could traditionally only be used to create native applications, and compile them to WebAssembly using Emscripten (Fig. 1). To evaluate whether the performance of such applications is sufficient for use in AR, we compared the performance of our implementation if we compile to a native binary to the performance of our implementation if we compile to a WebAssembly binary.

2   Related Work

Building AR systems using web technologies has traditionally been very challenging because browsers did not provide sufficient speed to run these computationally heavy applications. To our knowledge, this is the first paper presenting a purely web-based approach running in standard browsers without additional plugins. However, some approaches for applications using a browser to display their interface have been presented. In [31], a prototype of an AR system with a web-based client was presented. To use this application, users use the front-end to capture images of the scene which are then uploaded to a server, processed, and the augmented result is sent back to the client. While this approach can provide high-quality augmentations, it has the disadvantage that only images can be processed and, due to possibly slow network connections, real-time processing is impossible.

Previous research also investigated whether it is possible to use browser plugins like Flash which have more computational power than ECMAScript for AR systems [21,29]. While this approach is similar to ours, it has the disadvantage that it is not available in all browsers across all platforms and that users must install plugins before they can use the application.

Another highly interesting concept are browsers with built-in support for AR [15,16,22]. However, these approaches require that users install dedicated applications on their devices to be able to use such systems. To our knowledge, none of these applications are available for download and must be compiled from source which makes them unusable for arbitrary users. It is also very likely that these dedicated browsers will be abandoned once browsers add native support for AR [19].

Other research in the field of AR and the web investigated how web-based systems can be utilized to create content for native augmented reality applications [12,30] or whether it is possible to embed web technologies into native AR systems to create interactive augmentations [18]. Researchers have also investigated how web-based AR systems can protect the privacy of their users [24].

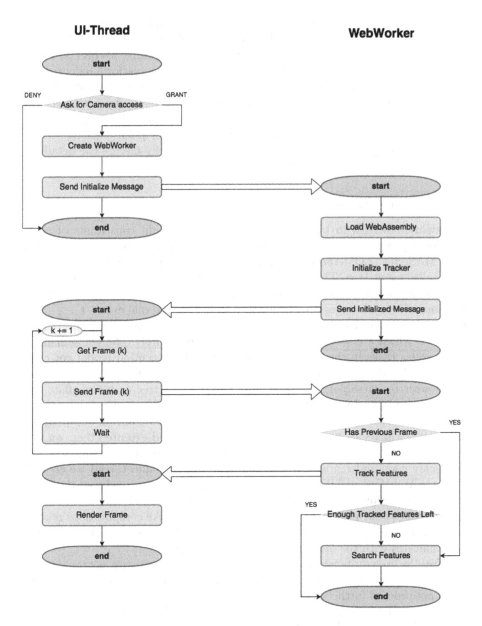

Fig. 2. Architecture of our system, split into UI-thread (left) and Web-Worker (right).

3   Implementation

In this section, we will discuss the architecture and implementation of our application and the difficulties we encountered. For our implementation we used a combination of well-established web technologies like HTML5 or ECMAScript and technologies more recently added to the web platform like WebRTC, which provides access to the camera, or WebAssembly, which is a platform independent binary instruction format that aims to achieve native-like execution speed.

The content of this section is divided into these three parts: First, we will present the overall architecture of our system and discuss the challenges of building AR systems in the browser. Then, we will present the point tracking system we used in our application, and in the end, we will briefly discuss the details of our simple web-based AR system.

3.1   System Architecture

The main challenges to building web-based AR are tight constraints of computational power available in the browser and the unique concurrency model of ECMAScript. ECMAScript's concurrency is based on a queue-based model often called event-loop. This means that the runtime "contains a message queue which stores a list of messages to be processed and their associated callback functions. These messages are queued in response to external events (. . .) given a callback function has been provided" [27]. With the more recent addition of Promises, which are so-called microtasks and have entirely different semantics than regular tasks in the event-loop, ECMAScript's execution model got even more convoluted. To complicate things further, the main thread is also used by the browser to parse pages from HTML into a DOM tree or to calculate the layout of a website. In order to be able to implement AR systems on a platform using this concurrency model, we split our application into multiple independent subsystems which can run completely independently and executed them on two different threads: A UI-thread, which is also the default thread browsers use to execute code and render the page on, and a background thread we created using the WebWorker API [2]. As it can be seen in Fig. 2, we reduced the number of computations on the UI-thread to a minimum and only executed what is directly related to the user-interface of our application. All computations related to tracking objects between frames are executed in a dedicated WebWorker which communicates with the other thread asynchronously.

After the browser finished downloading the initial website, we ask the user for their permission to use their camera. Since this is mandatory for our application, we do not proceed further if this permission is denied. When our application has the permission to use the camera, a dedicated WebWorker is created and the browser downloads and executes our separate worker script. Additionally, we immediately send an initialization message to the newly created worker which then downloads the external WebAssembly module. When the worker is fully initialized, it sends a message back to the UI-thread to indicate that it is ready to receive frames. When this message is received by the UI-thread, we start capturing frames from the camera and send them to the worker thread for processing. For convenience, we use a fixed frame rate, augment the message to the worker with the current timestamp and drop the frame in the worker if it is older than a predefined amount of time. All other frames are used to track features and then send back to the UI-thread. If too many features are lost, or if there was no previous frame, the current frame is also used to search for new features. Every time the UI-thread receives a processed frame, the user interface is updated and the image is shown to the user. With this architecture, we were able to achieve sufficient computational power and have an interface which is responsive to interactions with the user.

3.2   Tracking

We decided to use the well known Kanade-Lucas-Tomasi (KLT) algorithm [28] for our tracker. We use KLT tracking to follow image patches between consecutive frames by performing a local search to minimize the photometric error between the patch in the previous image and its match in the current one (see Fig. 3). Initial evaluations revealed that processing a single image is sufficiently fast and we do not need to split the algorithm into independent parts which can be executed asynchronously to use KLT in our applications. However, existing implementations such as the one from OpenCV could not be ported easily, thus we decided to make our own implementation. To be able to perform a fair evaluation of the performance of our system, we ensured that the implementation of our tracker does not make any assumptions about the architecture it is executed on.

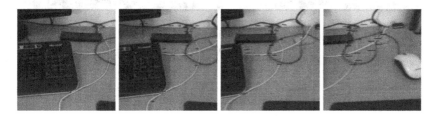

Fig. 3. KLT feature tracker, from the first frame on the left to the last frame on the right.

3.3   Application

The architecture of our application is based on the tracker architecture presented in Fig. 2. As a marker for pose estimation, a 2D image rich in texture is used. Thus, the estimated pose is given with respect to a coordinate system defined by this marker. The use of an image with natural features allows to have a registration step where a user can select his own image to be used for tracking. The tracking application follows the principles of other systems such as [25]. A set of Oriented FAST and rotated BRIEF (ORB) features are stored along with their 3D positions in order to register the tracking target. To start the application, we initialize the camera and ask the user for their permission. If the user grants us permission to use the camera, we periodically capture a frame, extract features from this frame and match them to registered ORB features of our marker. Once the number of matches is above a certain threshold, we compute a homography between the marker and the picture, project the boundaries of the marker into the frame, and filter outliers which are outside this projection, as it can be seen in Fig. 4. Having estimated an initial pose once enough inliers are found, we use KLT to track them from frame to frame which ensures a fast update of the pose. The tracked pose can be used to render virtual augmentations on the marker. As an example, we draw a virtual cube over the marker as can be seen in Fig. 4.

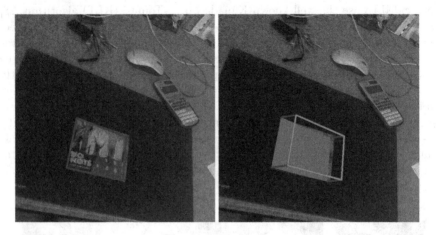

Fig. 4. On the left, projection of the boundaries of the marker into the scene and an example of a virtual cube rendered on top of our marker on the right.

4   Evaluation

In this section, we present and discuss the results of our runtime evaluation of the proposed KLT tracker. To get a comprehensive overview of the performance of our application, we executed our tests on various common devices and operating systems and across all popular browsers available on these platforms. Primarily, we used a MacBook Pro (Mid 2015) with an Intel Core i7 processor at 2.8 GHz and 16 GB RAM, running macOS 10.13, a desktop PC with an Intel Xeon E5 processor at 2.6 GHz running Windows 10 respectively Ubuntu 16.04, an iPhone X running iOS 11 and a Samsung Galaxy S8 running Android 7 to run the tests. We also tested our application on various other devices, including low-end mobile devices, which showed results comparable to the results we observed during our runtime evaluation.

Table 1. Runtime performance across different browsers and operating systems.

	Native	Chrome 66	Edge 17	Firefox 60	Safari 11.1	Node.JS 10
macOS	7.2 ms	13.6 ms	N/A	9.6 ms	10.1 ms	10.9 ms
Windows	9.5 ms	17.6 ms	14.1 ms	13.9 ms	N/A	15.8 ms
Ubuntu	8.0 ms	13.2 ms	N/A	13.1 ms	N/A	11.4 ms
iOS	N/A	12.4 ms	12.4 ms	12.3 ms	12.5 ms	N/A
Android	N/A	15.2 ms	N/A	14.9 ms	N/A	N/A

The runtime performance was evaluated using a single test binary, once compiled to a native binary and once to a WebAssembly module. Both binaries were produced using the highest optimization level available. To account for differences in the architectures of the underlying platforms, we used a fixed set of test images which were inlined into the binary.

Analysis of the raw data we collected during our tests revealed that the time required to track features in the first frame is roughly double the time required to track features in all subsequent frames. Investigations revealed that this is caused by the fact that we compute the gradient image for both pictures for the first image, and only for one picture in all other images. Due to this, we decided to exclude the first image from our analysis.

In Table 1, we present the average time in ms to perform the computations to track points from one image to another, which is the central part of our application. We observe that the runtime of the native binary is 36.9% lower than the runtime in browsers. However, the average time of 13.4 ms required for the tracking in the browser indicates that a frame rate of 74 fps can be achieved. This high frame rate leaves sufficient time for the rendering of quality augmentations and other application content.

Further investigations revealed that roughly 80% of the time we need to process a frame is spent computing the gradient image for the KLT. Given that we currently run these computations on the CPU, we expect that the frame rate will further increase when we can use OffscreenCanvas [1] to accelerate this on a GPU. It is also worth mentioning that getting precise timestamps in browsers requires several switches in the execution context and the operation is therefore slightly more expensive than its native equivalent. To mitigate the effects of the recently published processor exploits spectre and meltdown, browser vendors also reduced the maximum precision of timestamps in the browser. However, investigations of the impact of these changes revealed that we were still able to compute time differences with sub-millisecond precision. Given that our measurements showed a runtime that was a lot higher than that, we think that these changes did not affect our evaluation.

5   Conclusion

In this paper, we investigated the possibility to develop a universal cross-device, cross-browser based AR application using only web development tools. Our proposed system is built using WebAssembly, and implements a marker based KLT tracker for AR without using common computer vision libraries that are still unavailable or partially functional for Web Assembly. A runtime evaluation performed a selection of commonly used devices for AR, based on different operating systems proved the general feasibility of the approach. Future work includes dealing with the rendering of more complex virtual models for more demanding AR applications, and the improvement of tracking and user experience by further optimization, addition of camera intrinsics self-calibration and usage of 3D objects as tracking targets instead of 2D marker images.

Acknowledgments. This work has been partially funded by the Federal Ministry of Education and Research of the Federal Republic of Germany as part of the research projects PROWILAN and BeGreifen (Grant numbers 16KIS0243K and 16SV7525K).

References

1. OffscreenCanvas   (2018).   https://developer.mozilla.org/en/docs/Web/API/ OffscreenCanvas
2. Web worker API (2018). https://developer.mozilla.org/en/docs/Web/API/Web_ Workers_API
3. WebAssembly (2018). https://webassembly.org
4. WebAssembly (2018). https://developer.mozilla.org/en/docs/WebAssembly
5. Barfield, W.: Fundamentals of Wearable Computers and Augmented Reality. CRC Press, Boca Raton (2015)
6. Berners-Lee, T., Cailliau, R.: WorldWideWeb: Proposal for a Hypertext Project, November 1990. https://www.w3.org/Proposal.html
7. Berners-Lee, T., Fischetti, M.: Weaving the Web: The Original Design and Ultimate Destiny of the World Wide Web by Its Inventor. DIANE Publishing Company, Collingdale (2001)
8. Billinghurst, M., Clark, A., Lee, G.: A survey of augmented reality. Found. Trends Hum.-Comput. Interact. **8**(2–3), 73–272 (2015)
9. Buerli, M., Misslinger, S.: Introducing ARKit-augmented reality for iOS. In: Apple Worldwide Developers Conference (WWDC 2017), pp. 1–187 (2017)
10. Chen, L., Day, T., Tang, W., John, N.: Recent developments and future challenges in medical mixed reality. In: IEEE International Symposium on Mixed and Augmented Reality (ISMAR), pp. 123–135. IEEE (2017)
11. Dunleavy, M., Dede, C.: Augmented reality teaching and learning. In: Spector, J., Merrill, M., Elen, J., Bishop, M. (eds.) Handbook of Research on Educational Communications and Technology, pp. 735–745. Springer, New York (2014). https://doi. org/10.1007/978-1-4614-3185-5_59
12. Feuerstack, S., de Oliveira, Á., dos Santos Anjo, M., Araujo, R.B., Pizzolato, E.B.: Model-based design of multimodal interaction for augmented reality web applications. In: Proceedings of the 20th International Conference on 3D Web Technology, pp. 259–267. ACM (2015)

13. Google: ARCore Overview (2017). https://developers.google.com/ar/discover
14. Google: Web Fundamentals (2018). https://developers.google.com/web/fundamentals
15. Google: WebARonARcore (2018). https://github.com/google-ar/WebARonARCore
16. Google: WebARonARKit (2018). https://github.com/google-ar/WebARonARKit
17. Haas, A., et al.: Bringing the web up to speed with WebAssembly. In: Proceedings of the 38th ACM SIGPLAN Conference on Programming Language Design and Implementation, pp. 185–200. ACM (2017)
18. Hill, A., MacIntyre, B., Gandy, M., Davidson, B., Rouzati, H.: KHARMA: an open KML/HTML architecture for mobile augmented reality applications. In: 9th IEEE International Symposium on Mixed and Augmented Reality (ISMAR), pp. 233–234. IEEE (2010)
19. Jones, B., Waliczek, N.: WebXR device API (2018). https://immersive-web.github.io/webxr
20. Klein, G., Murray, D.: Parallel tracking and mapping for small AR workspaces. In: 6th IEEE and ACM International Symposium on Mixed and Augmented Reality, ISMAR, pp. 225–234. IEEE (2007)
21. Leppänen, T., Heikkinen, A., Karhu, A., Harjula, E., Riekki, J., Koskela, T.: Augmented reality web applications with mobile agents in the Internet of Things. In: Eighth International Conference on Next Generation Mobile Apps, Services and Technologies (NGMAST), pp. 54–59. IEEE (2014)
22. MacIntyre, B., Hill, A., Rouzati, H., Gandy, M., Davidson, B.: The Argon AR Web Browser and standards-based AR application environment. In: 2011 10th IEEE International Symposium on Mixed and Augmented Reality (ISMAR), pp. 65–74. IEEE (2011)
23. Marchand, E., Uchiyama, H., Spindler, F.: Pose estimation for augmented reality: a hands-on survey. IEEE Trans. Vis. Comput. Graph. **22**, 2633–2651 (2015)
24. Molnar, D., et al.: Protecting privacy in web-based immersive augmented reality, 13 June 2017. US Patent 9,679,144
25. Rambach, J., Pagani, A., Stricker, D.: [POSTER] augmented things: enhancing AR applications leveraging the Internet of Things and universal 3D object tracking. In: 2017 IEEE International Symposium on Mixed and Augmented Reality (ISMAR-Adjunct), pp. 103–108. IEEE (2017)
26. Schneider, M., Rambach, J., Stricker, D.: Augmented Reality based on edge computing using the example of remote live support. In: IEEE International Conference on Industrial Technology (ICIT) (2017)
27. Swenson-Healey, E.: The Javascript Event Loop: Explained (2013). https://blog.carbonfive.com/2013/10/27/the-javascript-event-loop-explained
28. Tomasi, C., Kanade, T.: Detection and tracking of point features (1991)
29. Vert, S., Dragulescu, B., Vasiu, R.: LOD4AR: exploring linked open data with a mobile augmented reality web application. In: International Semantic Web Conference (Posters & Demos), pp. 185–188. Citeseer (2014)
30. Walczak, K., Wiza, W., Wojciechowski, R., Wójtowicz, A., Rumiński, D., Cellary, W.: Building augmented reality presentations with Web 2.0 tools. In: Herrero, Á., Baruque, B., Sedano, J., Quintián, H., Corchado, E. (eds.) CISIS 2015. AISC, vol. 369, pp. 595–605. Springer, Cham (2015). https://doi.org/10.1007/978-3-319-19713-5_52
31. Wang, C., et al.: ARShop: a cloud-based augmented reality system for shopping. Proc. VLDB Endow. **10**(12), 1845–1848 (2017)

Fully Automatic Multi-person Human Motion Capture for VR Applications

Ahmed Elhayek[1,2(✉)], Onorina Kovalenko[1(✉)], Pramod Murthy[1,2(✉)],
Jameel Malik[1,2(✉)], and Didier Stricker[1,2(✉)]

[1] German Research Centre for Artificial Intelligence (DFKI), Kaiserslautern,
Germany
{ahmed.elhayek,onorina.kovalenko,pramod.murthy,jameel.malik,
didier.stricker}@dfki.de
[2] University of Kaiserslautern, Kaiserslautern, Germany

Abstract. Fully automatic tracking of articulated motion in real-time
with monocular RGB camera is a challenging problem which is essential
for many virtual reality (VR) applications. In this paper, we propose a
novel temporally stable solution for this problem which can be directly
employed in VR practical applications. Our algorithm automatically estimates the number of persons in the scene, generates their corresponding
person specific 3D skeletons, and estimates their initial 3D locations. For
every frame, it fits each 3D skeleton to the corresponding 2D body-parts
locations which are estimated with one of the existing CNN-based 2D
pose estimation methods. The 3D pose of every person is estimated by
maximizing an objective function that combines a skeleton fitting term
with motion and pose priors. Our algorithm detects persons who enter
or leave the scene, and dynamically generates or deletes their 3D skeletons. This makes our algorithm the first monocular RGB method usable
in real-time applications such as dynamically including multiple persons
in a virtual environment using the camera of the VR-headset. We show
that our algorithm is applicable for tracking multiple persons in outdoor
scenes, community videos and low quality videos captured with mobile-
phone cameras.

Keywords: Human motion capture · Convolutional neural network
Anthropometric data

1 Introduction

Human motion capture has applications in many fields such as VR, augmented
reality (AR), 3D character animation (i.e. for movies and games), human-
computer interaction, and sports. The last decade have witnessed significant
progress in marker-less human motion capture approaches which work directly
on real-world video streams [38,43,48]. Although, many marker-less algorithms
have achieved high accuracy under challenging conditions, most commercial VR

P. Bourdot et al. (Eds.): EuroVR 2018, LNCS 11162, pp. 28–47, 2018.
https://doi.org/10.1007/978-3-030-01790-3_3

systems still use marker-based algorithms that require to place markers on the human body. One of the main reasons is that marker-less algorithms require several manual initialization steps (e.g. 3D human model generation and initial pose estimation) which are cumbersome, require a lot of experience and time consuming.

Monocular RGB cameras are very common in many VR-headsets, laptops, and smartphones. Thus, developing a fully automatic real-time multi-person marker-less human motion capture algorithm that works with such monocular cameras is essential for many VR applications. An example of these applications is to include and animate multiple 3D characters in a VR environment using the camera of a VR-headset. Furthermore, this algorithm allows to interface PCs, laptops, or smartphones with their cameras (e.g. play games). However, developing such algorithm is challenging and requires (1) automatic estimation of number of persons in the scene (2) automatic generation of their 3D skeletons (3) automatic estimation of their initial 3D location (4) dynamical generation or deletion of 3D skeletons for persons entering or leaving the scene; respectively (5) real-time multi-person fitting energy function.

Fig. 1. Our algorithm recovers 3D skeletons poses in real-time. It captures complex motions of 8 persons in a community video (left), 3 persons in a video from the Marconi [19] datasets (middle) and 3 persons in a video captured with our mobile-phone RGB camera (right). Top row shows overlaid 2D skeletons and bottom row shows 3D visualizations of the captured skeletons.

Most of marker-less approaches estimate the articulated joint angles of moving subjects from multi-view video recordings [19–21,50]. These algorithms require manual estimation of persons number, their 3D models, and their initial poses. Moreover, they fail to reliably track articulated motion in general scenes with single RGB camera. While many recent algorithms have managed to estimate accurate human motion from monocular depth cameras [5,16,56], only few algorithms work accurately with monocular RGB cameras [36,37,57]. Although some of these algorithms achieve better accuracy than our algorithm, they do not succeed under our challenging multi-person tracking conditions. For instance, [37] does not succeed with multi-person and assumes an initial human pose to be given. Moreover, it's skeleton initialization requires given 2D body parts detections from several frames and height of the person. In addition to these limitations, other monocular algorithms such as [36,57] are offline and exhibits jitter over time due to per frame estimation. To the best of our knowledge, our algorithm is the first that performs automatic personalized skeleton generation and initial pose localization of varying number of persons in real-time. Moreover, it reconstructs the motion of multi-person in real-time using a single off-the-shelf RGB camera.

Our algorithm allows to overcome the limitations of RGB-D cameras which fail in general outdoor scenes due to sunlight interference. These cameras have lower resolution, limited range, higher power consumption, and are not widely available as RGB cameras. Our algorithm is able to track multiple persons moving in front of cluttered and non-static backgrounds with moving low quality camera which suffers from high distortion. It also succeeds in case of strong illumination changes. It works with any mobile-phone cameras, webcams, and community videos (e.g. YouTube videos). Our novel algorithmic contributions that enable this, are:

1. Real-time, simple and automatic multi-person human 3D skeletons generation; see Sect. 4.1.
2. Automatic initial 3D location estimation of each person in the scene; see Sect. 4.2.
3. Automatic detection of the change in number of persons and generating or deleting the corresponding 3D skeletons on the fly while tracking; see Sect. 4.3.
4. Novel algorithm which tracks full articulated joint angles of multiple persons at high accuracy and temporal stability in real-time, given 2D body-part locations; see Sect. 4.3.

The estimated multi-person motions can be used in many fields such as VR, AR, motion-driven 3D game character control, and human computer interaction. Furthermore, our algorithm can be optimized for smartphones and driving assistance applications. In our experiments, we show that our algorithm can capture even complex and fast body motion of multi-person in real-time; see Fig. 1. We managed to capture complex motions of multiple persons in outdoor scenes with a moving mobile phone camera, a spherical camera in a car, and a webcam in an office.

2   Related Work

Video-based human motion capture has seen great advances in recent years. We refer the reader to the surveys [38,43,48] for an overview. We focus the discussion in this section on two categories: methods based on multi-view input and methods that rely on a monocular RGB camera.

Multi-view: Most multi-view marker-less motion capture setups employ a human 3D model whose pose parameters are computed by optimizing an overlap measure between the projected 3D model and the input images. They attain high accuracy by tracking the human model over the image sequence with offline computation [9,10,49]. In [23], the pose is estimated from silhouette and color information. The approaches presented in [7,29,32] use training data to learn a motion model or a mapping from image features to the 3D pose. Tracking without silhouette information is also possible by combining model-guided segmentation and pose estimation. Earlier methods, such as [42], attempted to capture human skeletal motion from stereo footage, but did not achieve the same accuracy as methods using dense camera setups.

Amin et al. [3] propose a multi-view pictorial structures model that incorporates evidence across multiple viewpoints to allow robust 3D pose estimation. Belagiannis et al. [6] extend [3] for 3D pose estimation of multiple humans. However, a common problem with these approaches is jitter due to missing temporal information at each time step. The approach by [50] introduced an analytic formulation for calculating the model-to-image similarity based on a Sums-of-Gaussians model. Other works extend multi-view motion capture approaches towards tracking with moving or unsynchronized cameras [20,21,24,47]. These methods need separate initialization (e.g. using [8,45] at the beginning of each sequence and after loss of track in local minima of their non-convex fitting functions). Robustness can be increased with a combination of generative and discriminative estimation [19,44]. An accurate manually initialized human 3D model is essential for these methods. We propose an approach for automatic multiple skeletons generation which avoids using human model projection to speed up estimation. This allows to utilize generative tracking components and ensure temporal stability.

Monocular RGB: Depth-based motion capture methods [16,56] have achieved robust real-time results. However, in this section, we focus on RGB-based methods. These methods can be divided into generative and discriminative methods. The generative motion capture problem is fundamentally under-constrained in case of monocular input. Thus, it is only successful for motion capture from short clips and when combined with strong motion priors [53]. Manual annotation and correction of frames is suitable for some applications such as actor reshaping in movies [27] and garment replacement in videos [46]. These generative algorithms preclude live applications because of manual interaction and expensive optimization.

Recently, many monocular discriminative human pose estimation methods have been introduced. Some of them discriminatively learned mapping from the image directly to human joint locations [1,26,28]. CNN based 2D and 3D human pose estimation approaches achieve state-of-the-art accuracy. For instance, [17,33,35,51] estimate human 3D pose directly from monocular image or video.

Chen et al. [15] automatically synthesize training images with ground truth pose annotations and train CNNs with these synthetic images for 3D pose estimation.

Other approaches estimate 3D human pose from 2D body parts locations in a monocular image [2,22,30,31,54]. Many of these works have been realized by assuming manually labeled 2D body part locations. Recently, many CNN-based 2D pose estimation methods were proposed [11,13,14,25,52,55]. All these methods provide 2D body parts locations which can be used for 3D human pose estimation. For example, Cao et al. [13] managed to efficiently detect the 2D poses of multiple persons in an image using a nonparametric representation, which allows to learn associations between body parts of each individual in the image. Bogo et al. [8] used 2D body parts locations detected by [41] to automatically estimate the 3D pose and shape of the human body from a single unconstrained image. However, this method is not real-time and works for single person only.

Most closely related to the present paper are approaches for real-time recovery of 3D human pose with monocular RGB camera. Only a few methods target this problem for temporally stable results which is directly usable in practical applications. The top performing single RGB 3D pose estimation methods are based on CNNs [34,36,37,40,57]. Mehta et al. [36] use a 100-layer CNN architecture to predict 2D and 3D joint positions simultaneously. However, [36] is unsuitable for real-time execution due to the additional preprocessing steps such as bounding box extraction. Mehta et al. [37] propose a 3D pose estimation approach that uses CNN to detect 2D and 3D pose jointly. Then, an optimization based skeletal fitting method is applied to estimate 3D poses in real-time. All these methods, however, work for single person only. On the other hand, we propose a multi-person 3D pose estimation approach which automatically estimates person-specific 3D skeleton and initial 3D location for each person in

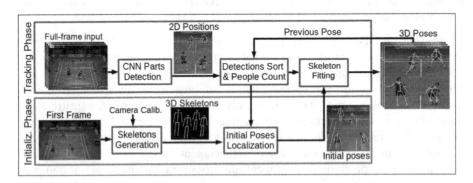

Fig. 2. Overview. We generate multiple person-specific 3D skeletons based on anthropometric data, and estimate the initial location of each person in an initialization phase (bottom, Sect. 4.1). In the tracking phase, we estimate 2D body-parts positions from the input video streams. These 2D positions are used to estimate global 3D poses by skeleton fitting (top, Sect. 4.3). The *Dynamic Scene Update* step generates or deletes 3D skeletons for persons who enter or leave the scene.

the scene. Thereafter, the pose of every person is estimated by means of optimizing an energy function for multi-person skeleton fitting.

3   Overview

Input to our approach can be either the live stream of a monocular RGB camera (e.g. webcam or VR-headset), YouTube video, or video captured with a mobile-phone camera. Any of these inputs yield a single frame I_i at discrete points in time $i = \{1, 2, 3, ...\}$. For frame I_i, the final output is $\mathbf{X} = \{X_1, ..., X_{prsn}\}$ where $prsn$ is the number of persons in the scene . X_j is the 3D skeletal pose parameters of the person with index j. This output is temporally consistent and in global 3D space which makes it perfect for applications such as virtual reality and character control. Our algorithm works with any camera (i.e. moving, static, webcam, or spherical camera with strong distortion) and general scenes (i.e. indoors or outdoors with strong illumination changes).

An outline of the processing pipeline is given in Fig. 2. Many human motion capture algorithms such as [19,20,50] assume given person-specific 3D skeletons and initial pose parameters X_{init}. This number of skeletons is fixed over the whole sequence. In contrast to these algorithms, we automatically estimate the number of persons in the scene. Then, we automatically generate person-specific 3D skeletons and estimate the initial location of each person in the scene. All these automatic steps are done in real-time at the beginning of each sequence which we refer to as **initialization phase**. The basic idea of our automatic skeleton generation approach is to adapt a default human skeleton to the length of each bone of each person. To this end, anthropometric data tables are used to define the length of each bone as a function of the height of each person; see Sect. 4.2 for details.

Given the person-specific 3D skeletons, it is still not possible to start the tracking process without defining the initial pose of each person. Existing human motion capture algorithms either estimate the initial pose manually or use computationally expensive methods such as [8]. In this paper, we automatically estimate the 3D root location of each person in the scene which resolves this limitation; see Sect. 4.2 for details.

In the tracking phase, we start with a CNN-based approach [11,13] to estimate the 2D locations of the body-parts for each person in the scene. The output of this step is the matrix $\mathbf{J} = [J_1, ..., J_{prsn}]$ where J_i contains body-parts locations of person i. However, the order and number of the persons in $\mathbf{J}$ may vary from frame to frame. Therefore, we use Eq. 4 to find the 2D body-parts positions J_i corresponding to specific 3D skeleton. Thereafter, we dynamically generate 3D skeletons for persons who enter the scene and delete the skeletons of those who left; see Sect. 4.3 for details.

The pose parameters $\mathbf{X} = \{X_1, ..., X_{prsn}\}$ are optimized given the 2D body-parts positions with the following energy function at each time frame I_i:

$$E(\mathbf{X}, \mathbf{J}) = E_{FIT}(\mathbf{X}, \mathbf{J}) - w_L E_L(\mathbf{X}) - w_A E_A(\mathbf{X}) \tag{1}$$

where $E_{FIT}(\mathbf{X}, \mathbf{J})$ is the skeletons fitting term (Sect. 4.3). $E_L(\mathbf{X})$ enforces joint limits, and $E_A(\mathbf{X})$ is a smoothness term penalizing strong accelerations; see [50] for details. The weights $w_l = 0.1$ and $w_a = 0.05$ were found experimentally and are kept constant in all experiments. This energy function is smooth and analytically differentiable. Thus, it can be optimized efficiently using standard gradient ascent initialized with the initial pose estimated in Sect. 4.2.

4   Real-Time Multi-person 3D Human Pose Estimation

In this section, we describe in detail the components of our fully automatic algorithm which captures articulated skeleton motion of several subjects in general scenes from monocular RGB input. The initialization phase is discussed in Sects. 4.1 and 4.2, while the tracking phase is explained in Sect. 4.3.

4.1   Automatic 3D Skeletons Generation

Human motion capture algorithms require human 3D model with properly personalized skeleton and/or body shape and appearance to successfully track a single person. Many algorithms consider model personalization as a different problem and use manual or semi-automatic model generation approach, which greatly reduces their applicability. In this section, we propose a novel automatic approach that generates a skeleton specific to each person.

In [45], an automatic algorithm that jointly creates skeleton and body model of a single person is presented. However, this algorithm requires many RGB cameras to estimate the body model. In [19,20], the skeleton and the body model of each person is generated in a semi-automatic way from a set of calibration poses prior to motion recording. Nonetheless, in case of no control over the footage and person motion, their method fails. Therefore, developing a simple, efficient, and automatic human 3D skeleton estimation approach is very important as it enables our solution to be adopted in more practical applications where the manual model generation is not feasible. We propose the first skeleton generation approach to automatically estimate skeletons for many persons in real-time.

In our approach, we generate a default skeleton for every person. The initial number of persons is automatically estimated given the 2D detections of the first frame. Then, we adapt the bone length of each skeleton to match the corresponding person. Our default skeleton consists of 25 bones and 26 joints. Each joint is defined by an offset to its parent joint and a rotation represented in axis-angle form. In total, the model consists of 73 parameters (70 rotational and 3 translational); see [19] for details. The anthropomorphic data tables [12] allow to define the length of each bone in the skeleton as a function of the height of the person. Figure 3 shows part of the anthropomorphic data table which defines the relation between the length of the upper arm bone and the height of the person. With these tables, the skeleton generation task is simplified to the estimation of a single parameter (i.e. the height of the person). Inspired by [17,39], the height of each person can be estimated from monocular RGB camera by back-projecting 2D features of an object into the 3D scene space. The output of this step is a person-specific human 3D skeleton for every person in the scene.

4.2   Multi-person Skeleton Localization

Given the personalized skeleton, the motion capture process can not start without initial 3D pose of each person. This essential initialization is, unfortunately, neglected by many methods and solved with manual initialization step, or with a different computationally expensive approach such as [8]. As our algorithm is stable even with inaccurate initial poses, we simplify the initial pose estimation problem to the estimation of the initial root position (i.e. 3D point between hips) of each person. To this end, we use the heights H_i^{3D} of each person i, their 2D body-part detections in the first frame J_i , and the monocular camera focal length f. The individual heights H_i^{3D} can be estimated as in Sect. 4.1, while the 2D body-parts detections J_i are estimated using the CNN-based algorithm; see Sect. 4.3 for details. As the upper body is usually more visible than the lower body, we use the height of the torso $H_{trs,i}^{3D} \approx 0.3 * H_i^{3D}$ for estimating the root depth. The 2D height of the torso $H_{trs,i}^{2D}$ is the distance between the neck $j_{nck,j}$ and the root $j_{rt,i} = (j_{lhip,i} + j_{rhip,i})/2$. With this, the depth of the root is calculated by:

$$z_i^{3D} = \frac{H_{trs,i}^{3D} * f}{H_{trs,i}^{2D}}. \qquad (2)$$

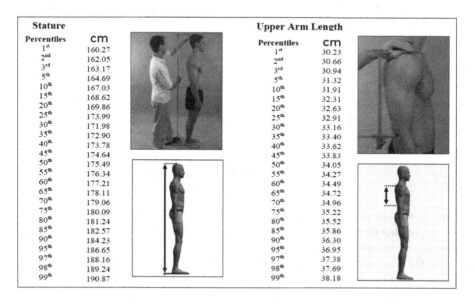

Stature			Upper Arm Length		
Percentiles	**cm**		**Percentiles**	**cm**	
1st	160.27		1st	30.23	
2nd	162.05		2nd	30.66	
3rd	163.17		3rd	30.94	
5th	164.69		5th	31.32	
10th	167.03		10th	31.91	
15th	168.62		15th	32.31	
20th	169.86		20th	32.63	
25th	173.99		25th	32.91	
30th	171.98		30th	33.16	
35th	172.90		35th	33.40	
40th	173.78		40th	33.62	
45th	174.64		45th	33.83	
50th	175.49		50th	34.05	
55th	176.34		55th	34.27	
60th	177.21		60th	34.49	
65th	178.11		65th	34.72	
70th	179.06		70th	34.96	
75th	180.09		75th	35.22	
80th	181.24		80th	35.52	
85th	182.57		85th	35.86	
90th	184.23		90th	36.30	
95th	186.65		95th	36.95	
97th	188.16		97th	37.38	
98th	189.24		98th	37.69	
99th	190.87		99th	38.18	

Fig. 3. Part of the anthropometric data tables which is used for person-specific 3D human skeletons generation: height data table (left), the corresponding table of upper arm length [12] (right).

Then, the 3D root position is calculated by:

$$\{x_i^{3D}, y_i^{3D}, z_i^{3D}\} = \mathbf{\Phi}^{-1}(j_{rt,i}^x * z_i^{3D}, j_{rt,i}^y * z_i^{3D}, z_i^{3D}) \tag{3}$$

where $\mathbf{\Phi}$ is the projection operator. Thereafter, each skeleton is automatically moved such that its root position matches the root location of the corresponding person in 3D space.

4.3   Skeleton Fitting for Dynamic Number of Persons

In the initialization phase, personalized skeletons and their initial 3D locations are estimated in real-time once at the beginning of the tracking process. On the other hand, the tracking phase is repeated for every frame. The first step of the tracking phase is the estimation of the 2D body-parts positions. Recently, many CNN based methods managed to accurately estimate these 2D body-parts positions [11,13,25]. Although, any of these methods can be used in our framework, we used both [13] and [11] in our experiments. As [13] achieves state-of-the art accuracy with multi-person, the majority of our results are based on this algorithm. Therefore, in this section, we assume, without loss of generality, that 2D body-part positions are estimated with [13].

The 2D body-part detection algorithm does not have any temporal relation between consecutive frames. Thus, the order of the resulting 2D body-part detections in $\mathbf{J} = [J_1, ..., J_{prsn}]$ for one frame can be different the previous frame. This means that the body-parts positions J_m may correspond to a different person in each frame. For this reason, the next step in our tracking phase is to associate each existing 3D skeleton with the corresponding 2D detections J_m in each frame. To this end, we define a similarity measure between the skeleton defined by pose parameters X_k and $J_m = [j_{m,1}, ... j_{m,prt}]$ where prt is the number of 2D body part detections of one person. This is done by first projecting the 3D joint positions defined by X_k into the 2D image plane using the projection operator $\mathbf{\Phi}$. Thereafter, the distance between each projected 3D joint and the corresponding 2D detection is calculated. The final similarity between skeleton with index k and detections in J_m is defined as follows:

$$SIM_{k,m} = \sum_{l=1}^{n_{prt}} \|\mathbf{\Phi}(\mathbf{f}_{k,l}(X_k)) - j_{m,l}\| \tag{4}$$

where $\mathbf{f}_{k,l}$ is the 3D joint position corresponding to the 2D body part $j_{m,l}$. At the end of this step, each skeleton with index k will be associated with the 2D detection J_i where $i = \arg\min_x SIM_{k,x}$.

For tracking varying number of persons, we need to generate a new 3D skeleton for each person who enters the scene and remove the skeleton of those who leave the scene. After associating each 3D skeleton with the corresponding 2D detections J_i, some items of $\mathbf{J}$ may be left without a corresponding 3D skeleton. These items correspond to either persons who just entered the scene or false positive detection of a human. To distinguish between these two cases, we use the confidence of each body part detection in J_i which is an additional output of the CNN-based approach. This confidence allows to compute a score for each J_i which corresponds to probability of a new person entering the scene. For each new J_i with score above the threshold $\alpha = 0.5$, we generate 3D skeleton for the corresponding person and estimate the respective initial 3D location. On the other hand, in case of a person leaving the scene or largely occluded, J_i corresponding to an existing skeleton will either have very low score or disappear from $\mathbf{J}$. In both cases, we remove that skeleton.

Our multi-person skeleton fitting term measures the similarities between a given skeleton pose X_n corresponding to one of the persons and 2D body-parts positions J_n of that person. Similar to Eq. 4, we project each 3D joint position and calculate the distance to the corresponding 2D detection $j_{n,l}$. The final fitting term is defined as:

$$
E_{FIT}(X, J) =
$$
$$
\sum_{n=1}^{n_{prsn}} \sum_{l=1}^{n_{prt}} w(j_{n,l}) \exp \left(-\frac{\|\mathbf{\Phi}(\mathbf{f}_{n,l}(X_n)) - j_{n,l}\|^2}{\sigma^2} \right) \tag{5}
$$

where $w(j_{n,l})$ is the confidence of the 2D body-parts detection $j_{n,l}$. This confidence is estimated by the CNN body-parts estimation method.

Applying per-frame pose estimation techniques on a video does not ensure temporal consistency of motion. Thus, small pose inaccuracies lead to temporal jitter. Therefore, we combine our multi-person skeletons fitting energy with temporal filtering and smoothing in a joint optimization framework to obtain an accurate, temporally stable and robust result; see Eq. 1.

5   Experiments and Results

We demonstrate the effectiveness of our algorithm through experimental evaluations of more than 20 challenging real world sequences. Some of these sequences were acquired from community videos including varying number of persons performing complex and fast motions. We also captured many outdoor and indoor sequences with mobile-phone and spherical camera. One of the outdoor sequences was recorded in car with spherical camera to illustrate the usefulness of our algorithm for applications such as driving assistance system. We performed live tracking of multiple persons at around 23 Hz with low quality webcam. In addition to that, we used many sequences from the Human3.6M [26] and the Marconi [19] datasets. These sequences vary in numbers and identities of persons, complexity and speed of the motion, the lighting conditions, cameras types (e.g. mobile-phone, GoPro, spherical cameras, and webcams), the frame resolutions, and the frame rates. Our algorithm is the first multi-person monocular human motion capture method which does not require any manual work for 3D human model and initial pose adaptation. It automatically generates 3D skeletons and estimates initial poses for multiple person. It operates with input images without the need of bounding box cropping. As a result of

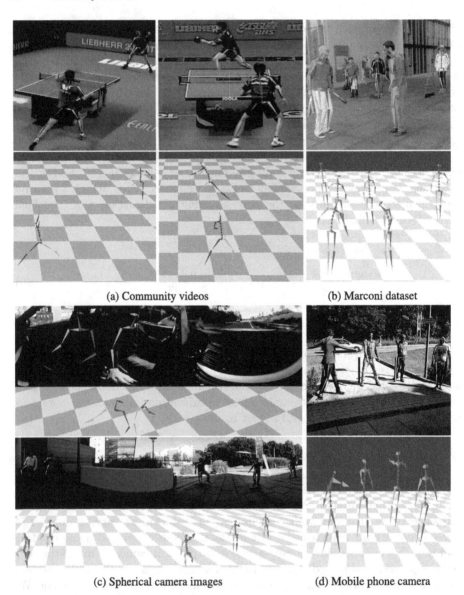

(a) Community videos

(b) Marconi dataset

(c) Spherical camera images

(d) Mobile phone camera

Fig. 4. Sample results with overlaid 2D skeletons estimated with **Implementation 1** (top) and respective 3D reconstructions (bottom) which show successful multi-person tracking in challenging scenarios. (a) shows multi-person pose results over YouTube videos playing table tennis and fencing sports. (b) shows results over selected difficult sequences from Marconi dataset. (c) shows pose estimation results inside a car and outdoor scene recorded using a spherical RGB camera. (d) shows tracking results with strong illumination changes in outdoor scene captured using mobile phone camera

this, our experimental setup is very simple. Given the input images and the focal length of a single RGB camera, we produce high quality reconstruction results. Qualitative results can be viewed in accompanying supplementary video. The run-time of our algorithm depends on the number of persons in the scene, the complexity of the motion and the resolution of the input frames. Our computations are performed on a 8-core Xeon CPU and a GeForce GTX 1080 GPU. Although our algorithm's implementation is not yet well optimized for improved run-time performance, average processing time of a single frame from a single person sequence (e.g. the Greeting sequence from the Human3.6M dataset [26]) is 44 ms. The 2D body parts detection [13] takes 32 ms while the 3D skeleton fitting takes 12 ms. Given the body parts detections of the first frame and the height of each person, the initialization phase takes around 0.01 ms.

Our algorithm is not restricted to use a particular 2D body-parts detection method. Hence, we show results of our algorithm with two different body parts detection methods. The first implementation **Implementation 1** uses [13] for 2D body-parts detections. This implementation is discussed in details in Sect. 4. Notably, in contrast to other 2D body part detection methods, [13] does not require cropping to track multi-person sequences. On the other hand, our second implementation **Implementation 2**, which is based on [11], requires cropping of every person. However, our algorithm can perform cropping automatically

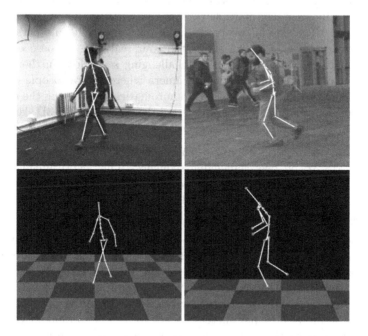

Fig. 5. Sample images from the H3.6M dataset (left column) and the Marconi dataset (right column) with overlaid 2D Skeleton along-with respective 3D pose recovery using **Implementation 2** .

and without significant change to our original pipeline in Fig. 2. To this end, the rough pose of each person is estimated by extrapolating his pose from the previous frame. The bounding box of each person is estimated by projecting each 3D skeleton to the camera view. This allows to crop and scale each person. With this additional automatic step, [11] can be used instead of [13] in our pipeline for 2D body part detections.

Qualitative Results: We used our first implementation **Implementation 1** to track mroe than 15 sequences. Sample frames from the tracked sequences are shown in Figs. 1 and 4. Please, see the supplementary video for more detailed tracking results. Our algorithm successfully estimated the pose parameters of multiple persons in challenging outdoor and indoor sequences with monocular RGB camera. This shows the ability of our algorithm to successfully track sequences with many (i.e. up to eight) persons performing complex and fast motions under strong lighting variations and strong distortion. Previous monocular methods such as [36,37,57] fail to track these sequences in real-time. We also tracked a sequence captured in car and several sequences captured with mobilephone. This shows that our approach is suitable for practical applications in different fields including VR. In Fig. 5, we show the 3D pose reconstruction results based on our second implementation **Implementation 2**. Two sequences from the public datasets the Human3.6M and the Marconi are successfully tracked.

To demonstrate the usefulness of our algorithm for real-time applications (e.g. dynamically including multiple persons in a virtual environment using the camera of the VR-headset), we tracked the motion of multiple persons from live stream of webcam. Figure 6 shows that our real-time 3D pose estimation provides a natural motion interface in challenging scenarios. Furthermore, we capture sequence with a mobile-phone camera where several people enter and leave the scene. Our algorithm succeed in automatically detecting the change in number of persons and generating or deleting the corresponding 3D skeletons on the fly while tracking; see the supplementary video.

Comparison: In Fig. 7, we compare the accuracy of our algorithm with the accuracy of [18,37] on two challenging sequences. Our algorithm managed to accurately track all the persons in two sequences; see the supplementary video for more detailed tracking results. While [18] work only offline, [37] achieved lower tracking accuracy for only one of the two persons in the scene.

System Components Evaluation: We quantitatively evaluate the importance of the components of our algorithm by creating different alternatives of it. The first alternative is constructed by removing the skeleton generation step. This means that the default skeleton is used without adaptation to the tracked person. The second alternative is constructed by removing the initial pose localization step where the initial pose parameters are set to zero or to random values. We evaluated these alternatives by tracking the *Walking* sequence from Human3.6M dataset [26] which captures Subject $S9$. The Mean Per Joint Position Error (MPJPE) with our complete algorithm is 90 mm while it is 460 mm without the first alternative. The second alternative fails completely because the energy

Fig. 6. The real-time 3D pose estimation with **Implementation 1** (Top) and **Implementation 2** (Bottom). Our algorithm provides a natural motion interface on images from live webcam video.

Fig. 7. Side-by-side comparison of our method against the monocular single-person human pose estimation methods of Mehta et al. [37] (top right) and the offline method of Elhayek et al. [18] (bottom right) which tracks two persons with three cameras. Our approach succeeds in accurately tracking all persons in the scene (left column).

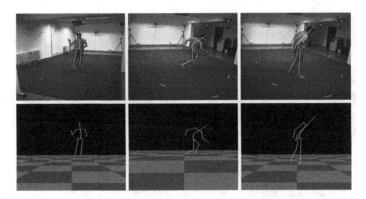

Fig. 8. Sample images from H3.6M sequences used for quantitative evaluations. Top row shows overlaid 2D Skeletons and bottom row shows 3D visualizations of the captured skeletons. From left to right, we show tracking results of *Directions*, *Posing* and *Waiting* sequences for Subject *S*9 whose Mean Per Joint Position Error is 153 mm, 158 mm and 167 mm respectively.

function is non-convex which leads to stuck in a local maxima; see Fig. 9 and the supplementary video.

Quantitative Evaluation: We quantitatively evaluate our algorithm using the *Directions*, *Posing* and *Waiting* sequences from Human3.6M dataset [26] which capture Subject S9. Figure 8 shows sample images with overlaid 2D skeletons and respective 3D reconstructions from these sequences. The average error of all frames of these three sequences is 159.33 mm. [37] achieves lower error with monocular RGB camera. However, the CNN body-parts detector of [37] is trained on images from the test dataset (i.e. the Human3.6M dataset [26]). On the other hand, the CNN body-parts detectors which we use, are trained on different datasets such as the MPII Human Pose dataset [4].

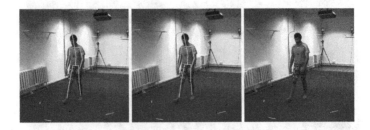

Fig. 9. Importance of algorithmic components. Left: tracking result of our algorithm; MPJPE 90 mm. Middle: an alternative of our algorithm constructed by removing the skeleton generation step (i.e. using the default skeleton); MPJPE 460 mm. Right: second alternative constructed by removing initial pose localization step which fails completely.

Discussion: Our approach is subject to a few limitations. Currently, the depth estimation of our algorithm is not very accurate, especially in case of occlusion of wrists and ankles. This causes relatively higher 3D joint position errors in comparison to other methods. However, this is also a common problem with approaches relying on a monocular camera setup as depth estimation is severely ill posed. Thus, a slight inaccuracy in the 2D body-parts estimation leads to big error in the depth estimation. Unlike other methods, our approach is still able to recover from the tracking failures, even after long occlusion of many body-parts; see the supplementary video. Our tracking results of many sequences show that our algorithm succeeds in challenging multi-person scenarios where all other human motion tracking methods based on single RGB camera fail. Moreover, we achieve high temporal stability and reasonable accuracy. This accuracy can also be improved by using 2D body part detector which is more stable to occlusions.

6   Conclusion and Future Work

We have presented the first fully automatic method to estimate 3D kinematic poses of multiple persons in temporally stable manner directly from a single RGB camera. Our approach automatically detects the number of persons in the scene and generates corresponding person-specific 3D skeletons based on anthropometric data tables. It also automatically estimates the initial 3D location of each person which allows to define their coarse initial poses. In the tracking phase, it fits each 3D skeleton to the corresponding 2D body-parts detections. These detections can be estimated using any 2D body-part estimation method which allows to easily upgrade our algorithm with any progress in 2D pose estimation. Our algorithm dynamically generates 3D skeletons for persons who enter the scene and delete the skeletons of those who leave. In contrast to previous works, our fully automatic algorithm can operate with multiple persons in real-time without the need of bounding boxes. This makes our algorithm optimal for VR application. We have demonstrated the effectiveness of our system by tracking many sequences with strong distortion in videos, strong illumination changes, and multiple persons performing complex motions. Moreover, we have shown results in real-time scenarios, including live streaming from a webcam. As future work, we are going to investigate the problem of depth estimation uncertainty which could be reduced with domain specific knowledge. Furthermore, in order to improve the run-time of our algorithm, we intend to employ more advanced optimization algorithms.

Acknowledgements. This work has been partially funded by the Federal Ministry of Education and Research of the Federal Republic of Germany as part of the research projects DYNAMICS (Grant number 01IW15003) and VIDETE (Grant number 01IW18002).

References

1. Agarwal, A., Triggs, B.: Recovering 3D human pose from monocular images. IEEE Trans. Pattern Anal. Mach. Intell. **28**(1), 44–58 (2006)
2. Akhter, I., Black, M.J.: Pose-conditioned joint angle limits for 3D human pose reconstruction. In: Proceedings of the IEEE Conference on Computer Vision and Pattern Recognition, pp. 1446–1455 (2015)
3. Amin, S., Andriluka, M., Rohrbach, M., Schiele, B.: Multi-view pictorial structures for 3D human pose estimation. In: BMVC (2013)
4. Andriluka, M., Pishchulin, L., Gehler, P., Schiele, B.: 2D human pose estimation: new benchmark and state of the art analysis. In: IEEE Conference on Computer Vision and Pattern Recognition (CVPR), June 2014
5. Baak, A., Müller, M., Bharaj, G., Seidel, H.P., Theobalt, C.: A data-driven approach for real-time full body pose reconstruction from a depth camera. In: Proceedings of ICCV, pp. 1092–1099 (2011)
6. Belagiannis, V., Amin, S., Andriluka, M., Schiele, B., Navab, N., Ilic, S.: 3D pictorial structures for multiple human pose estimation. In: CVPR. IEEE, June 2014
7. Bo, L., Sminchisescu, C.: Twin Gaussian processes for structured prediction. IJCV **87**, 28–52 (2010)
8. Bogo, F., Kanazawa, A., Lassner, C., Gehler, P., Romero, J., Black, M.J.: Keep it SMPL: automatic estimation of 3D human pose and shape from a single image. In: ECCV, pp. 561–578 (2016)
9. Bogo, F., Romero, J., Loper, M., Black, M.J.: FAUST: dataset and evaluation for 3D mesh registration. In: CVPR (2014)
10. Bregler, C., Malik, J.: Tracking people with twists and exponential maps. In: CVPR, pp. 8–15 (1998)
11. Bulat, A., Tzimiropoulos, G.: Human pose estimation via convolutional part heatmap regression. In: Leibe, B., Matas, J., Sebe, N., Welling, M. (eds.) ECCV 2016. LNCS, vol. 9911, pp. 717–732. Springer, Cham (2016). https://doi.org/10.1007/978-3-319-46478-7_44
12. Gordon, C., Blackwell, C., Mucher, M., Kristensen, S.: 2012 anthropometric survey of u.s. army personnel: methods and summary statistics (Natick/TR-15/007) (2014)
13. Cao, Z., Simon, T., Wei, S.E., Sheikh, Y.: Realtime multi-person 2D pose estimation using part affinity fields. In: CVPR (2017)
14. Charles, J., Pfister, T., Magee, D.R., Hogg, D.C., Zisserman, A.: Personalizing human video pose estimation. CoRR abs/1511.06676 (2015). http://arxiv.org/abs/1511.06676
15. Chen, W., et al.: Synthesizing training images for boosting human 3D pose estimation. In: 3D Vision (3DV) (2016)
16. Dou, M., et al.: Fusion4D: real-time performance capture of challenging scenes. ACM Trans. Graph. (TOG) **35**(4), 114 (2016)
17. Du, Y.: Marker-less 3D human motion capture with monocular image sequence and height-maps. In: Leibe, B., Matas, J., Sebe, N., Welling, M. (eds.) ECCV 2016. LNCS, vol. 9908, pp. 20–36. Springer, Cham (2016). https://doi.org/10.1007/978-3-319-46493-0_2
18. Elhayek, A., et al.: Marconi: convnet-based marker-less motion capture in outdoor and indoor scenes. IEEE Trans. Pattern Anal. Mach. Intell. **39**(3), 501–514 (2017). https://doi.org/10.1109/TPAMI.2016.2557779

19. Elhayek, A., et al.: Efficient convnet-based marker-less motion capture in general scenes with a low number of cameras. In: IEEE Conference on Computer Vision and Pattern Recognition (CVPR), June 2015

20. Elhayek, A., Stoll, C., Hasler, N., Kim, K.I., Seidel, H.P., Theobaltl, C.: Spatio-temporal motion tracking with unsynchronized cameras. In: Proceedings of CVPR (2012)

21. Elhayek, A., Stoll, C., Hasler, N., Kim, K.I., Theobaltl, C.: Outdoor human motion capture by simultaneous optimization of pose and camera parameters. In: Proceedings of CGF (2014)

22. Fan, X., Zheng, K., Zhou, Y., Wang, S.: Pose locality constrained representation for 3D human pose reconstruction. In: Fleet, D., Pajdla, T., Schiele, B., Tuytelaars, T. (eds.) ECCV 2014. LNCS, vol. 8689, pp. 174–188. Springer, Cham (2014). https://doi.org/10.1007/978-3-319-10590-1_12

23. Gall, J., Rosenhahn, B., Brox, T., Seidel, H.P.: Optimization and filtering for human motion capture - a multi-layer framework. IJCV **87**, 75–92 (2010)

24. Hasler, N., Rosenhahn, B., Thormählen, T., Wand, M., Gall, J., Seidel, H.P.: Markerless motion capture with unsynchronized moving cameras. In: CVPR (2009)

25. Insafutdinov, E., Pishchulin, L., Andres, B., Andriluka, M., Schiele, B.: DeeperCut: a deeper, stronger, and faster multi-person pose estimation model. In: Leibe, B., Matas, J., Sebe, N., Welling, M. (eds.) ECCV 2016. LNCS, vol. 9910, pp. 34–50. Springer, Cham (2016). https://doi.org/10.1007/978-3-319-46466-4_3. http://arxiv.org/abs/1605.03170

26. Ionescu, C., Papava, D., Olaru, V., Sminchisescu, C.: Human3.6m: large scale datasets and predictive methods for 3D human sensing in natural environments. IEEE Trans. Pattern Anal. Mach. Intell. **36**(7), 1325–1339 (2014)

27. Jain, A., Thormählen, T., Seidel, H.P., Theobalt, C.: Moviereshape: tracking and reshaping of humans in videos. ACM Trans. Graph. **29**(5) (2010). (Proceedings of SIGGRAPH Asia 2010)

28. Kostrikov, I., Gall, J.: Depth sweep regression forests for estimating 3D human pose from images. In: BMVC, vol. 1, p. 5 (2014)

29. Lee, C.S., Elgammal, A.: Coupled visual and kinematic manifold models for tracking. IJCV **87**, 118–139 (2010)

30. Lee, H.J., Chen, Z.: Determination of 3D human body postures from a single view. Comput. Vis. Graph. Image Process. **30**(2), 148–168 (1985)

31. Leonardos, S., Zhou, X., Daniilidis, K.: Articulated motion estimation from a monocular image sequence using spherical tangent bundles. In: 2016 IEEE International Conference on Robotics and Automation (ICRA), pp. 587–593. IEEE (2016)

32. Li, R., Tian, T.P., Sclaroff, S., Yang, M.H.: 3D human motion tracking with a coordinated mixture of factor analyzers. IJCV **87**, 170–190 (2010)

33. Li, S., Chan, A.B.: 3D human pose estimation from monocular images with deep convolutional neural network. In: Cremers, D., Reid, I., Saito, H., Yang, M.-H. (eds.) ACCV 2014. LNCS, vol. 9004, pp. 332–347. Springer, Cham (2015). https://doi.org/10.1007/978-3-319-16808-1_23

34. Li, S., Liu, Z.Q., Chan, A.B.: Heterogeneous multi-task learning for human pose estimation with deep convolutional neural network. In: The IEEE Conference on Computer Vision and Pattern Recognition (CVPR) Workshops, June 2014

35. Li, S., Zhang, W., Chan, A.B.: Maximum-margin structured learning with deep networks for 3D human pose estimation. In: Proceedings of the IEEE International Conference on Computer Vision, pp. 2848–2856 (2015)

36. Mehta, D., Rhodin, H., Casas, D., Sotnychenko, O., Xu, W., Theobalt, C.: Monocular 3D human pose estimation using transfer learning and improved CNN supervision. arXiv preprint arXiv:1611.09813 (2016)

37. Mehta, D., et al.: VNect: real-time 3D human pose estimation with a single RGB camera. ACM Trans. Graph. **36** (2017)

38. Moeslund, T., Hilton, A., Krüger, V.: A survey of advances in vision-based human motion capture and analysis. CVIU **104**(2), 90–126 (2006)

39. Park, S.-W., Kim, T.-E., Choi, J.-S.: Robust estimation of heights of moving people using a single camera. In: Kim, K.J., Ahn, S.J. (eds.) Proceedings of the International Conference on IT Convergence and Security 2011. LNEE, vol. 120, pp. 389–405. Springer, Dordrecht (2012). https://doi.org/10.1007/978-94-007-2911-7_36

40. Pavlakos, G., Zhou, X., Derpanis, K.G., Daniilidis, K.: Coarse-to-fine volumetric prediction for single-image 3D human pose. CoRR abs/1611.07828 (2016). http://arxiv.org/abs/1611.07828

41. Pishchulin, L., et al.: Deepcut: joint subset partition and labeling for multi person pose estimation. In: Proceedings of the IEEE Conference on Computer Vision and Pattern Recognition, pp. 4929–4937 (2016)

42. Plankers, R., Fua, P.: Tracking and modeling people in video sequences. CVIU **88**, 285–302 (2001)

43. Poppe, R.: Vision-based human motion analysis: an overview. CVIU **108**(1–2), 4–18 (2007)

44. Rhodin, H., et al.: Egocap: egocentric marker-less motion capture with two fisheye cameras. ACM Trans. Graph. **35**(6), 162:1–162:11 (2016). https://doi.org/10.1145/2980179.2980235

45. Rhodin, H., Robertini, N., Casas, D., Richardt, C., Seidel, H.-P., Theobalt, C.: General automatic human shape and motion capture using volumetric contour cues. In: Leibe, B., Matas, J., Sebe, N., Welling, M. (eds.) ECCV 2016. LNCS, vol. 9909, pp. 509–526. Springer, Cham (2016). https://doi.org/10.1007/978-3-319-46454-1_31

46. Rogge, L., Klose, F., Stengel, M., Eisemann, M., Magnor, M.: Garment replacement in monocular video sequences. ACM Trans. Graph. **34**(1), 6:1–6:10 (2014)

47. Shiratori, T., Park, H.S., Sigal, L., Sheikh, Y., Hodgins, J.K.: Motion capture from body-mounted cameras. ACM Trans. Graph. **30**(4), 31:1–31:10 (2011)

48. Sigal, L., Balan, A., Black, M.: Humaneva: synchronized video and motion capture dataset and baseline algorithm for evaluation of articulated human motion. IJCV **87**, 4–27 (2010)

49. Starck, J., Hilton, A.: Model-based multiple view reconstruction of people. In: ICCV, pp. 915–922 (2003)

50. Stoll, C., Hasler, N., Gall, J., Seidel, H.P., Theobalt, C.: Fast articulated motion tracking using a sums of Gaussians body model. In: ICCV (2011)

51. Tekin, B., Rozantsev, A., Lepetit, V., Fua, P.: Direct prediction of 3D body poses from motion compensated sequences. In: Proceedings of the IEEE Conference on Computer Vision and Pattern Recognition, pp. 991–1000 (2016)

52. Toshev, A., Szegedy, C.: Deeppose: human pose estimation via deep neural networks. In: Proceedings of the IEEE Conference on Computer Vision and Pattern Recognition, pp. 1653–1660 (2014)

53. Urtasun, R., Fleet, D.J., Fua, P.: Temporal motion models for monocular and multiview 3d human body tracking. Comput. Vis. Image Underst. **104**(2), 157–177 (2006). https://doi.org/10.1016/j.cviu.2006.08.006

54. Valmadre, J., Lucey, S.: Deterministic 3D human pose estimation using rigid structure. In: Daniilidis, K., Maragos, P., Paragios, N. (eds.) ECCV 2010. LNCS, vol. 6313, pp. 467–480. Springer, Heidelberg (2010). https://doi.org/10.1007/978-3-642-15558-1_34

55. Wei, S.E., Ramakrishna, V., Kanade, T., Sheikh, Y.: Convolutional pose machines. In: Proceedings of the IEEE Conference on Computer Vision and Pattern Recognition, pp. 4724–4732 (2016)

56. Ye, M., Shen, Y., Du, C., Pan, Z., Yang, R.: Real-time simultaneous pose and shape estimation for articulated objects using a single depth camera. IEEE Trans. Pattern Anal. Mach. Intell. **38**(8), 1517–1532 (2016). https://doi.org/10.1109/TPAMI.2016.2557783

57. Zhou, X., Zhu, M., Pavlakos, G., Leonardos, S., Derpanis, K.G., Daniilidis, K.: Monocap: monocular human motion capture using a CNN coupled with a geometric prior. CoRR abs/1701.02354 (2017). http://arxiv.org/abs/1701.02354

3D Acquisition and 3D Reconstruction

HDM-Net: Monocular Non-rigid 3D Reconstruction with Learned Deformation Model

Vladislav Golyanik[1,2](✉), Soshi Shimada[1,2], Kiran Varanasi[1], and Didier Stricker[1,2]

[1] Augmented Vision, DFKI, Kaiserslautern, Germany
vladislav.golyanik@dfki.de
[2] University of Kaiserslautern, Kaiserslautern, Germany
https://av.dfki.de

Abstract. Monocular dense 3D reconstruction of deformable objects is a hard ill-posed problem in computer vision. Current techniques either require dense correspondences and rely on motion and deformation cues, or assume a highly accurate reconstruction (referred to as a template) of at least a single frame given in advance and operate in the manner of non-rigid tracking. Accurate computation of dense point tracks often requires multiple frames and might be computationally expensive. Availability of a template is a very strong prior which restricts system operation to a pre-defined environment and scenarios. In this work, we propose a new hybrid approach for monocular non-rigid reconstruction which we call *Hybrid Deformation Model Network* (HDM-Net). In our approach, a deformation model is learned by a deep neural network, with a combination of domain-specific loss functions. We train the network with multiple states of a non-rigidly deforming structure with a known shape at rest. HDM-Net learns different reconstruction cues including texture-dependent surface deformations, shading and contours. We show generalisability of HDM-Net to states not presented in the training dataset, with unseen textures and under new illumination conditions. Experiments with noisy data and a comparison with other methods demonstrate the robustness and accuracy of the proposed approach and suggest possible application scenarios of the new technique in interventional diagnostics and augmented reality.

Keywords: Monocular non-rigid reconstruction
Hybrid deformation model · Deep neural network

1 Introduction

The objective of monocular non-rigid 3D reconstruction (MNR) is the recovery of a time-varying geometry observed by a single moving camera. In the general case, none of the states is observed from multiple views, and at the same time, both

© Springer Nature Switzerland AG 2018
P. Bourdot et al. (Eds.): EuroVR 2018, LNCS 11162, pp. 51–72, 2018.
https://doi.org/10.1007/978-3-030-01790-3_4

the object and the camera move rigidly. This problem is highly ill-posed in the sense of Hadamard since multiple states can cause similar 2D observations. To obtain a reasonable solution, multiple additional priors about the scene, types of motions and deformations as well as camera trajectory are required. Application domains of MNR are numerous and include robotics, medical applications and visual communication systems. MNR also has a long history in augmented reality (AR), and multiple applications have been proposed over the last twenty years ranging from medical systems to communication and entertainment [15,38].

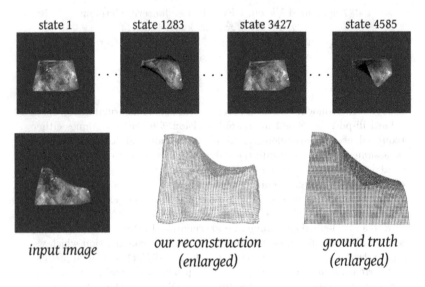

Fig. 1. Reconstruction of an endoscopically textured surface with the proposed HDM-Net. The network is trained on a textured synthetic image sequence with ground truth geometry and accurately reconstructs unseen views in a small fraction of a second (∼5 ms). Our architecture is potentially suitable for real-time augmented reality applications.

All approaches to MNR can be divided into two main model-based classes—non-rigid structure from motion (NRSfM) and template-based reconstruction (TBR). NRSfM relies on motion and deformation cues and requires dense point correspondences over multiple frames [26,31]. Most accurate methods for dense correspondences operate on multiple frames and are prohibitively slow for real-time applications [66]. Moreover, their accuracy is volatile and influenced by changing illumination and shading effects in the scene. TBR, per definition, assumes a known template of the scene or an object, *i.e.*, a highly accurate reconstruction for at least one frame of the scene [55,80]. Sometimes, the template also needs to be accurately positioned, with a minimal initial reprojection error to the reference frame. In this context, TBR can also be comprehended as non-rigid tracking [62]. Obtaining a template is beyond the scope of TBR, though joint solutions were demonstrated in the literature. In some cases, a template is obtained under the rigidity assumption, which might not always be fulfiled in practical applications [80].

Apart from the main classes, methods for monocular scene flow (MSF) and hybrid NRSfM can be named. MSF jointly reconstructs non-rigid geometry and 3D displacement fields [48]. In some cases, it relies on a known camera trajectory or proxy geometry (an initial coarse geometry estimate) [7]. In hybrid NRSfM, a scene-specific shape prior is obtained on-the-fly under non-rigidity, and the input is a sequence of point tracks [31]. Geometry estimation is then conditioned upon the shape prior.

MNR has only recently entered the realm of dense reconstructions [7,58,80]. The dense setting brings additional challenges for augmented reality applications such as scalability with the number of points and increased computational and memory complexity.

1.1   Contributions

The scope of this paper is general-purpose MNR, *i.e.*, the reconstruction scenarios are not known in advance. We propose deep neural network (DNN) based deformation model for MNR. We train DNN with a new synthetically generated dataset covering the variety of smooth and isometric deformations occurring in the real world (*e.g.*, clothes deformations, waving flags, bending paper and, to some extent, biological soft tissues). The proposed DNN architecture combines supervised learning with domain-specific loss functions. Our approach with a learned deformation model—Hybrid Deformation Model Network (HDM-Net)— surpasses performances of the evaluated state-of-the-art NRSfM and template-based methods by a considerable margin. We do not require dense point tracks or a well-positioned template. Our initialisation-free solution supports large deformations and copes well with several textures and illuminations. At the same time, it is robust to self-occlusions and noise. In contrast to existing DNN architectures for 3D, we directly regress 3D point clouds (surfaces) and depart from depth maps or volumetric representations.

In the context of MNR methods, our solution can be seen as a TBR with considerably relaxed initial conditions and a broader applicability range per single learned deformation model. Thus, it constitutes a new class of methods— instead of a template, we rather work with a weak shape prior and a shape at rest for a known scenario class.

We generate a new dataset which fills a gap for training DNNs for non-rigid scenes[1] and perform series of extensive tests and comparisons with state-of-the-art MNR methods. Figure 1 provides an overview of the proposed approach— after training the network, we accurately infer 3D geometry of a deforming surface. Figure 2 provides a high-level overview of the proposed architecture.

The rest of the paper is partitioned in Related Work (Sect. 2), Architecture of HDM-Net (Sect. 3), Geometry Regression and Comparisons (Sect. 5) and Concluding Remarks (Sect. 6) Sections.

---

[1] The dataset is available upon request.

2   Related Work

In this section, we review several algorithm classes and position the proposed HDM-Net among them.

2.1   Non-rigid Structure from Motion

NRSfM requires coordinates of tracked points throughout an image sequence. The seminal work of Bregler *et al.* [10] marks the origin of batch NRSfM. It constrained surfaces to lie in a linear subspace of several unknown basis shapes. This idea was pursued by several successor methods [9,51,73]. Since the basis shapes, as well as their number, are unknown, this subclass is sensitive to noise and parameter choice. Furthermore, an optimal number of basis shapes allowing to express all observed deformation modes does not necessarily always exist [73]. Along with that, multiple further priors were proposed for NRSfM including temporal smoothness [34,82], basis [79], inextensibility [13,22,75] and shape prior [12,31,67], among others. The inextensibility constraint penalises deviations from configurations increasing the total surface area. In other words, non-dilatable states are preferred. Several methods investigate a dual trajectory basis and considerably reduce the number of unknowns [5], whereas the other ones explicitly model deformations using physical laws [4]. Multiple general-purpose unsupervised learning techniques were successfully applied to NRSfM including non-linear dimensionality reduction [67] (diffusion maps), [34,37] (kernel trick) and expectation-maximisation [3,43]. A milestone in NRSfM was accompanied by a further decrease in the number of unknowns and required prior knowledge for reconstruction. Thus, some of the methods perform a low-rank approximation of a stacked shape matrix [18,26]. A further milestone is associated with the ability to perform dense reconstructions [3,6,26,31,33].

Several methods allow sequential processing [1,52,82]. Starting from an initial estimate obtained on several first frames of a sequence, they perform reconstructions upon arrival of every new frame in an incremental manner. The accuracy of sequential methods is consistently lower than those of the batch counterparts. While still relying on point tracks, they can enable lowest latencies in real-time and interactive applications. Several methods learn and update an elastic model of the observed scene on-the-fly [2] (similarly to the sequential methods, point tracks over the complete sequence are not required). Solving the underlying equations might be slow, and the solution was demonstrated only for sparse settings.

2.2   Template-Based Reconstruction

Approaches of this class assume a known template, *i.e.*, an accurate reconstruction of at least one frame of the sequence. Most methods operate on a short window of frames or single frames. Some TBR methods are known as non-rigid trackers [62]. Early physics-based techniques formalised 3D reconstruction with elastic models and modal analysis [15,47]. They assumed that some material

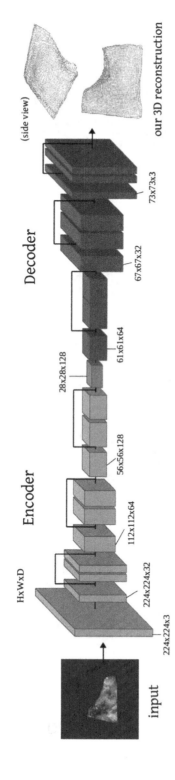

Fig. 2. An overview of the architecture of the proposed HDM-Net with encoder and decoder. The input of HDM-Net is an image of dimensions 224×224 with three channels, and the output is a dense reconstructed 3D surface of dimensions $73 \times 73 \times 3$ (a point cloud with 73^2 points).

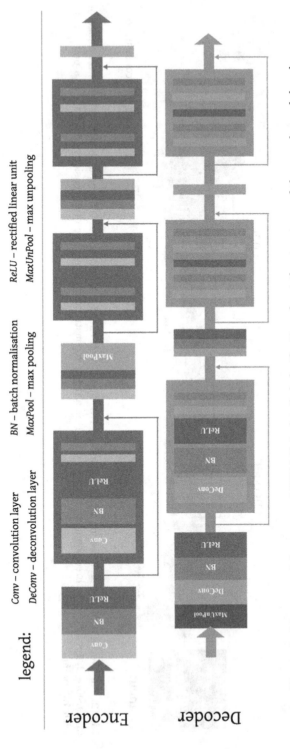

Fig. 3. Architecture of the proposed HDM-Net: detailed clarification about the structures of the encoder and decoder.

properties (such as the elastic modulus) of the surface are known and could handle small non-linear deformations.

Multiple priors developed for NRSfM proved their effectiveness for TBR including isometry [11,49,55,60], statistical priors [59], temporal smoothness [61,80], inextensibility priors [11,55] and mechanical priors in an improved form [38,46]. Moreover, modelling image formation process by decomposing observed intensities into lighting, shading and albedo components was also shown to improve tracking accuracy [24,25,45,49,77].

2.3 Monocular Scene Flow

A somewhat exotic class of approaches developed in parallel to NRSfM and TBR is monocular scene flow (MSF). Birkbeck *etal.*'s approach can handle non-rigid scenes relying on a known constant camera motion [7]. While camera trajectory can be sometimes available in AR systems, there is no guarantee of its linearity. In [48], a variational solution to rigid multi-body scenes was proposed. Recently, Xiao *et al.* proposed an energy-based method for rigid MSF in the context of automotive scenarios. Their approach is based on a temporal velocity constancy constraint [78].

In general, MSF methods are restricted in the handling of non-rigid surfaces. One exception—NRSfM-Flow of Golyanik *et al.* [32]—takes advantage of known 2D-3D correspondences and relies on batch NRSfM techniques for an accurate scene flow estimation of non-rigid scenes. It inherits the properties of NRSfM and does not assume a known camera trajectory or proxy geometry.

2.4 Specialised Models for Faces and Bodies

For completeness, we provide a concise overview of specialised approaches. Compared to TBR, they are dedicated to the reconstruction of single object classes like human faces [8,28,63,65] or human bodies [35,76]. They do not use a single prior state (a template), but a whole space of states with feasible deformations and variations. The models et al. are learned from extensive data collections showing a wide variety of forms, expressions (poses) and textures. In almost all cases, reconstruction with these methods means projection into the space of known shapes. To obtain accurate results, post-processing steps are required (*e.g.*, for transferring subtle details to the initial coarse estimates). In many applications, solutions with predefined models might be a right choice, and their accuracy and speed may be sufficient.

2.5 DNN-Based 3D Reconstruction

In the recent three years, several promising approaches for inferring 2.5D and 3D geometry have been developed. Most of them regress depth maps [20,27,30,44,68] or use volumetric representations [14,57] akin to sign distance fields [17]. Currently, the balance of DNN-based methods for 3D reconstruction is perhaps in favour of face regressors [19,40,63,69]. The alternatives to sparse NRSfM of Tome *et al.* and Zhou *et al.* work exclusively for human poses [72,81]. The 3D-R2N2 network generates 3D reconstructions from single and multiple views and requires large data collections for training [14]. In contrast to several other methods, it does not require image annotations. Point set generation network of Fan *et al.* [21] is trained for a single view reconstruction of rigid objects and directly outputs point sets. More and more methods combine supervised learning and model-based losses thus imposing additional problem-specific constraints [21,27,69]. Also, this has often the side effect of decreasing the volume requirements on the datasets [30,69]. The work of Pumarola *et al.* [56] is most closely related to ours. The architecture is separated into three sub-networks which have different roles—creating heat-map of 2D images, depth estimation and 3D geometry inference. Those sub-networks are jointly trained. Our architecture is relatively simple. Encoder and decoder are employed and the output is penalized with three kinds of losses which have different geometrical properties— 3D geometry, smooth surface and contour information after projection onto a 2D plane.

2.6   Attributes of HDM-Net

In this section, we position the proposed approach among the vast body of the literature on MNR. HDM-Net bears a resemblance to DNN-based regressors which use encoder-decoder architecture [69]. In contrast to many DNN-based 3D regressors [14,21,69], our network does not include fully connected layers as they impede generalisability (lead to overfitting) as applied to MNR. As most 3D reconstruction approaches, it contains a 3D loss.

In many cases, isometry is an effective and realistic constraint for TBR, as shown in [13,55]. In HDM-Net, isometry is imposed through training data. The network learns the notion of isometry from the opposite, *i.e.*, by not observing other deformation modes. Another strong constraint in TBR is contour information which, however, has not found wide use in MSR, with only a few exceptions [36,74]. In HDM-Net, we explicitly impose contour constraints by comparing projections of the learned and ground truth surfaces.

Under isometry, the solution space for a given contour is much better constrained compared to the extensible cases. The combined isometry and contour cues enable efficient occlusion handling in HDM-Net. Moreover, contours enable texture invariance up to a certain degree, as a contour remains unchanged irrespective of the texture. Next, through variation of light source positions, we train the network for the notion of shading. Since for every light source configuration, the underlying geometry is the same, HDM-Net acquires awareness of varying illumination. Besides, contours and shading in combination enable reconstruction of texture-less surfaces. To summarise, our framework has unique properties among MSR methods which are rarely found in other MNR techniques, especially when combined.

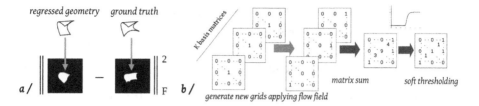

Fig. 4. Our contour loss penalises deviations between reprojections of the regressed geometry and reprojections of the ground truth.

3   Architecture of HDM-Net

We propose a DNN architecture with encoder and decoder depicted in Fig. 2 (a general overview). The network takes as an input an image of dimensions 224×224 with three channels. Initially, the encoder extracts contour, shading and texture deformation cues and generates a compact latent space representation of dimensions $28 \times 28 \times 128$. Next, the decoder applies a series of deconvolutions and outputs a 3D surface of dimensions $73 \times 73 \times 3$ (a point cloud). It lifts the dimensionality of the latent space until the dimensionality of activation becomes identical to the dimensionality of ground truth. The transition from the implicit representation into 3D occurs on the later stage of decoder through a deconvolution. Figure 3 provides a detailed clarification about the structures of encoder and decoder.

As can be seen in Figs. 2 and 3, we skip some connections in HDM-Net to avoid vanishing gradients, similar to *resnet* [39]. Due to the nature of convolutions, our deep network might potentially lose some important information in the forward path which might be advantageous in the deeper layers. Thus, connection skipping compensates for this side effect—for each convolution layer—which results in the increased performance. Moreover, in the backward path, shortcut connections help to overcome the vanishing gradient problem, *i.e.*, a series of numerically unstable gradient multiplications leading to vanishing gradients. Thus, the gradients are successfully passed to the shallow layers.

Fully connected (FC) layers are often used in classification tasks [42]. They have more parameters than convolution layers and are known as a frequent cause of overfitting. We have tried FC layers in HDM-Net and observed overfitting on the training dataset. Thus, FC layers reduce generalisation ability of our network. Furthermore, spatial information is destroyed as the data in the decoder is concatenated before being passed to the FC layer. In our task, needless to say, spatial cues are essential for 3D regression. In the end, we omit FC layers and successfully show generalisation ability of 3D reconstruction on the test data.

3.1   Loss Functions

Let $\mathbf{S} = \{\mathbf{S}_f\}$, $f \in \{1, \dots, F\}$ denote predicted 3D states, and $\mathbf{S}^{GT} = \{\mathbf{S}_f^{GT}\}$ is the ground truth geometry; F is the total number of frames and N is the number of points in the 3D surface. In HDM-Net, contour similarity and the isometry constraint are the key innovations and we apply three types of loss functions summarised into the loss energy:

$$\mathbf{E}(\mathbf{S}, \mathbf{S}^{GT}) = \mathbf{E}_{3D}(\mathbf{S}, \mathbf{S}^{GT}) + \mathbf{E}_{iso}(\mathbf{S}) + \mathbf{E}_{cont.}(\mathbf{S}, \mathbf{S}^{GT}). \tag{1}$$

3D Error: The 3D loss is the main loss in 3D regression. It penalises the differences between predicted and ground truth 3D states and is common in training for 3D data:

$$\mathbf{E}_{3D}(\mathbf{S}, \mathbf{S}^{GT}) = \frac{1}{F} \sum_{f=1}^{F} \|\mathbf{S}_f^{GT} - \mathbf{S}_f\|_{\mathscr{F}}^2, \tag{2}$$

where $\|\cdot\|_{\mathscr{F}}$ denotes the Frobenius norm. Note that we take an average of the squared Frobenius norms of the differences between the learned and ground truth geometries.

Isometry Prior: To additionally constrain the regression space, we embed isometry loss which enforces the neighbouring vertices to be located close to each other. Several versions of inextensibility and isometry constraints can be found in MSR—a common one is based on differences between Euclidean and geodesic distances. For our DNN architecture, we choose a differentiable loss which performs Gaussian smoothing of $\mathbf{S}_f$ and penalises the difference between the unembellished and smoothed version $\hat{\mathbf{S}}_i$:

$$\mathbf{E}_{iso}(\mathbf{S}) = \frac{1}{F} \sum_{f=1}^{F} \|\hat{\mathbf{S}}_f - \mathbf{S}_f\|_{\mathscr{F}}, \tag{3}$$

with

$$\hat{\mathbf{S}}_f = \frac{1}{2\pi\sigma^2} \exp\left(-\frac{x^2 + y^2}{2\sigma^2}\right) * \mathbf{S}_f, \tag{4}$$

where $*$ denotes a convolution operator and σ^2 is the variance of Gaussian.

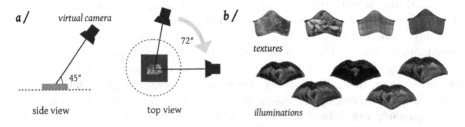

Fig. 5. Camera poses used for the dataset generation (a); different textures applied to the dataset: *endoscopy, graffiti, clothes* and *carpet* (b-top) and different illuminations (b-bottom).

Contour Loss: If the output of the network and the ground truth coordinates are similar, the contour shapes after projection onto a 2D plane have to be similar as well. The main idea of the reprojection loss is visualised in Fig. 4-(a). After the inference of the 3D coordinates by the network, we project them onto the 2D plane and compute the difference between the two projected contours. If focal lengths f_x, f_y as well as the principal point (c_x, c_y) of the camera are known (the $\mathbf{K}$ used for the dataset generation is provided in Sect. 4), observed 3D points $\mathbf{p} = (p_x, p_y, p_z)$ are projected to the image plane by the projection operator $\pi : \mathbb{R}^3 \rightarrow \mathbb{R}^2$:

$$\mathbf{p}'(u, v) = \pi(\mathbf{p}) = \left(f_x \frac{p_x}{p_z} + c_x, f_y \frac{p_y}{p_z} + c_y \right)^{\mathsf{T}}, \tag{5}$$

where $\mathbf{p}'$ is the 2D projection of $\mathbf{p}$ with 2D coordinates u and v. Otherwise, we apply an orthographic camera model.

A naïve shadow casting of a 3D point cloud onto a 2D plane is not differentiable, *i.e.*, the network cannot backpropagate gradients to update the network parameters. The reason is twofold. In particular, the cause for indifferentiability is the transition from point intensities to binary shadow indicators with an ordinary step function (the numerical reason) using point coordinates as indexes on the image grid (the framework-related reason).

Figure 4-(b) shows how we circumvent this problem. The first step of the procedure is the projection of 3D coordinates onto a 2D plane using either a perspective or an orthographic projection. As a result of this step, we obtain a set of 2D points. We generate $K = 73^2$ translation matrices $\mathbf{T}_j = \left(\begin{smallmatrix} 1 & 0 & u \\ 0 & 1 & v \end{smallmatrix} \right)$ using 2D points and a flow field tensor of dimension $K \times 99 \times 99 \times 2$ (the size of each binary image is 99×99). Next, we apply bilinear interpolation [41] with generated flow fields on the replicated basis matrix $\mathbf{B}$ K times and obtain K translation indicators. $\mathbf{B}_{99 \times 99}$ is a sparse matrix with only a single central non-zero element which equals to 1. Finally, we sum up all translation indicators and softly threshold positive values in the sums to ≈ 1, *i.e.*, our shadow indicator. Note that to avoid indifferentiability in the last step, the thresholding is performed by a combination of a rectified linear unit (ReLU) and tanh function (see Fig. 4-(b)):

$$\tau(\mathscr{I}(\mathbf{s}_f(n))) = \max(\tanh(2\,\mathbf{S}_f(n)), 0), \tag{6}$$

where $n \in \{1, \dots, N\}$ denotes the point index, $\mathbf{s}_f(n)$ denotes a reprojected point $\mathbf{S}_f(n)$ in frame f, and $\mathscr{I}(\cdot)$ fetches intensity of a given point. We denote the differentiable projection operator and differentiable soft thresholding operator by the symbols $\pi^{\dagger}(\cdot)$ and $\tau(\cdot)$ respectively. Finally, the contour loss reads

$$\mathbf{E}_{cont.}(\mathbf{S}, \mathbf{S}^{GT}) = \frac{1}{F} \sum_{f=1}^{F} \| \tau(\pi^{\dagger}(\mathbf{S}_f)) - \tau(\pi^{\dagger}(\mathbf{S}_f^{GT})) \|_{\mathscr{F}}^2. \tag{7}$$

Note that object contours correspond to 0–1 transitions.

4 Dataset and Training

For our study, we generated a dataset with a non-rigidly deforming object using *Blender* [23]. In total, there are 4648 different temporally smooth 3D deformation states with structure bendings, smooth foldings and wavings, rendered under Cook-Torrance illumination model [16] (see Fig. 1 for the exemplary frames from our dataset). We have applied five different camera poses, five different light source positions and four different textures corresponding to the scenarios we are interested in—*endoscopy*, *graffiti* (it resembles a waving flag) *clothes* and *carpet* (an example of an arbitrary texture). The endoscopic texture is taken from [29]. Illuminations are generated based on the scheme in Fig. 5-(a), the textures and illuminations are shown in Fig. 5-(b). We project the generated 3D scene by a virtual camera onto a 2D plane upon Eq. (5), with $\mathbf{K} = \left(\begin{smallmatrix} 280 & 0 & 128 \\ 0 & 497.7 & 128 \\ 0 & 0 & 1 \end{smallmatrix} \right)$. The background in every image is of the same opaque colour. We split the data into training and test subsets in a repetitive manner, see Fig. 6 for the pattern. We train HDM-Net jointly on several textures and illuminations, with the purpose of illumination-invariant and texture-invariant regression. One illumination and one texture are reserved for the test dataset exclusively. Our images are of the dimensions 256×256. They reside in 15.2 Gb of memory, and the ground truth geometry requires 1.2 Gb (in total, 16.4 Gb). The hardware configuration consists of two six-core processors Intel(R) Xeon(R) CPU E5-1650 v4 running at 3.60 GHz, 16 GB RAM and a GEFORCE GTX 1080Ti GPU with 11 GB of global memory. In total, we train for 95 epochs, and the training takes two days in *pytorch* [53,54]. The evolution of the loss energy is visualised in Fig. 11-(a). The inference of one state takes ca. 5 ms.

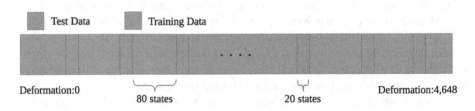

Fig. 6. The pattern of the training and test datasets.

5 Geometry Regression and Comparisons

We compare our method with the template-based reconstruction of Yu *et al.* [80], variational NRSfM approach (VA) of Garg *et al.* [26] and NRSfM method of Golyanik *et al.* [33]—Accelerated Metric Projections (AMP). We use an optimised heterogeneous CPU-GPU version of VA written in C++ and CUDA C [50]. AMP is a C++ CPU version which relies on an efficient solution of a semidefinite programming problem and is currently one of the fastest batch NRSfM methods. For VA and AMP, we compute required dense point tracks. Following the standard praxis in NRSfM, we project the ground truth shapes onto a virtual image plane by a slowly moving virtual camera. Camera rotations are parametrised by Euler angles around the x-, y- and z-axes. We rotate for up to

$20°$ around each axis, with five degrees per frame. This variety in motion yields minimal depth changes required for an accurate initialisation in NRSfM. We report runtimes, 3D error

$$e_{3D} = \frac{1}{F} \sum_{f=1}^{F} \frac{\|\mathbf{S}_f^{GT} - \mathbf{S}_f\|_{\mathscr{F}}}{\|\mathbf{S}_f^{GT}\|_{\mathscr{F}}} \qquad (8)$$

and standard deviation σ of e_{3D}. Before computing e_{3D}, we align $\mathbf{S}_f$ and the corresponding $\mathbf{S}_f^{GT}$ with Procrustes analysis.

Runtimes, e_{3D} and σ for all three methods are summarised in Table 1. AMP achieves around 30 *fps* and can execute only for 100 frames per batch at a time. However, this estimate does not include often prohibitive computation time of dense correspondences with multi-frame optical flow methods such as [66]. Note that runtime of batch NRSfM depends on the batch size, and the batch size influences the accuracy and ability to reconstruct. VA takes advantage of a GPU and executes with 2.5 *fps*. Yu *et al.* [80] achieves around 0.3 *fps*. In contrast, HDM-Net processes one frame in only 5 ms. This is by far faster than the compared methods. Thus, HDM-Net can compete in runtime with rigid structure from motion [71]. The runtime of the latter method is still considered as the lower runtime bound for NRSfM[2].

At the same time, the accuracy of HDM-Net is the highest among all tested methods. Selected results with complex deformations are shown in Fig. 7. We see that Yu *et al.* [80] copes well with rather small deformations, and our approach accurately resolves even challenging cases not exposed during the training. In the case of Yu *et al.* [80], the high e_{3D} is explained by a weak handling of self-occlusions and large deformations. In the case of NRSfM methods, the reason for the high e_{3D} is an inaccurate initialisation. Moreover, VA does not handle foldings and large deformations well.

Table 3 summarises e_{3D} for our method under different illumination conditions. We notice that our network copes well with all generated illuminations—the difference in e_{3D} is under 3%. Table 2 shows e_{3D} comparison for different textures. Here, the accuracy of HDM-Net drops on the previously unseen texture by the factor of three, which still corresponds to reasonable reconstructions with the captured main deformation mode. Another quantitative comparison is shown in Fig. 9. In this example, all methods execute on the first 100 frames of the sequence. AMP [33] captures the main deformation mode with $e_{3D} = 0.1564$ but struggles to perform a fine-grained distinction (in Table 1, e_{3D} is reported over the sequence of 400 frames, hence the differing metrics). VA suffers under an inaccurate initialisation under rigidity assumption and Yu *et al.* [80], by contrast, does not recognise the variations in the structure. All in all, HDM-Net copes well with self-occlusions. Graphs of e_{3D} as functions of the state index under varying illuminations and textures can be found in Fig. 11-(b,c). Table 4 shows the

---

[2] When executed in a batch of 100 frames with 73^2 points each, a C++ version of [71] takes 1.47 ms per frame on our hardware; for 400 frames long batch, it requires 5.27 ms per frame.

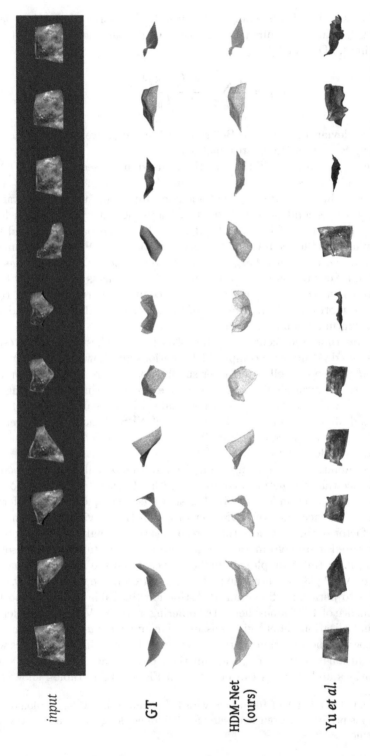

Fig. 7. Selected reconstruction results on endoscopically textured surfaces for HDM-Net (our method) and Yu *et al.* [80].

Table 1. Per-frame runtime t in *seconds*, e_{3D} and σ comparisons of Yu *et al.* [80], AMP [33] and HDM-Net (proposed method).

	Yu *et al.* [80]	AMP [33]	VA [26]	HDM-Net
t, s	3.305	0.035	0.39	**0.005**
e_{3D}	1.3258	1.6189	0.46	**0.0251**
σ	**0.0077**	1.23	0.0334	0.03

Table 2. Comparison of 3D error for different textures and the same illumination (number 1).

	endoscopy	*graffiti*	*clothes*	*carpet*
e_{3D}	**0.0485**	0.0499	0.0489	0.1442
σ	**0.01356**	0.022	0.02648	0.02694

Table 3. Comparison of 3D error for different illuminations.

	illum. 1	*illum. 2*	*illum. 3*	*illum. 4*	*illum. 5*
e_{3D}	0.07952	0.0801	0.07942	**0.07845**	0.07827
σ	**0.0525**	0.0742	0.0888	0.1009	0.1123

Table 4. Comparison of effects of loss functions.

	3D	3D + Con.	3D + Iso.	3D + Con. + Iso.
e_{3D}	0.0698	**0.0688**	0.0784	0.0773
σ	**0.0761**	0.0736	0.0784	0.0789

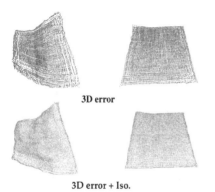

3D error

3D error + Iso.

Fig. 8. Comparison of 3D reconstruction with 3D error (top row) and 3D error + isometry prior (bottom row)

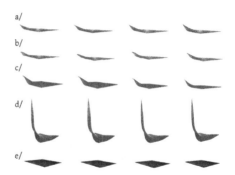

Fig. 9. Qualitative comparisons of ground truth (a), HDM-Net (proposed method) (b), AMP [33] (c), VA [26] (d) and Yu *et al.* [80] (e) on several frames of our test sequence from the first 100 frames (each column corresponds to one frame).

comparison of e_{3D} using networks trained with various combinations of loss functions. *3D + Con.* shows the lowest e_{3D} and applying *isometry prior* increases e_{3D}. Since *isometry prior* is smoothing loss, the 3D grid becomes smaller in comparison to the outputs without *isometry prior* hence higher e_{3D}. However, as shown in Fig. 8, isometry prior allows the network to generate smoother 3D geometries preserving deformation states.

Next, we evaluate the performance of HDM-Net on noisy input images. Therefore, we augment the dataset with increasing amounts of uniform

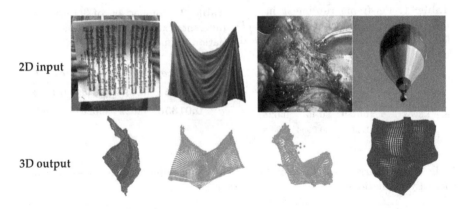

Fig. 10. Exemplary reconstructions from real images obtained by HDM-Net (music notes, a fabric, surgery and an air balloon)

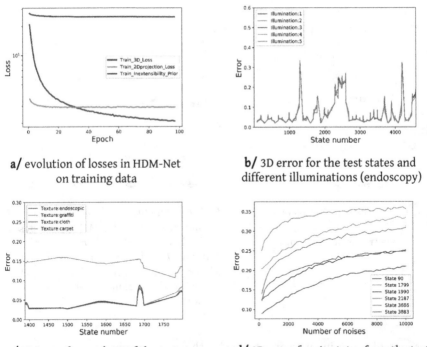

a/ evolution of losses in HDM-Net on training data

b/ 3D error for the test states and different illuminations (endoscopy)

c/ 3D error for a subset of the test states and different textures (illumination 1)

d/ 3D error for six states from the test sequence and increasing amount of noise

Fig. 11. Graphs of e_{3D} for varying illuminations (for *endoscopy* texture), varying textures (for illumination 1) as well as six states under increasing amount of noise. Note that in b/ and c/, only the errors obtained on the test data are plotted. For c/, HDM-Net was trained on a subset of training states (three main textures and one illumination).

salt-pepper noise. Figure 11-(d) shows the evolution of the e_{3D} as a function of the amount of noise, for several exemplary frames corresponding to different input difficulties for the network. We observe that HDM-Net is well-posed w.r.t noise—starting from the respective values obtained for the noiseless images, the e_{3D} increases gradually.

We tested HDM-Net on several challenging real images. Figure 10 shows the tested images and our reconstructions. We recorded a music note image for an evaluation of our network in real-world scenario. Despite different origin of the inputs (music notes, a fabric [70], an endoscopic view during a surgery [29] and an air balloon [64]), HDM-Net produces realistic and plausible results. Note how different are the regressed geometries which suggests the generalisation ability of the proposed solution.

In many real-world cases, HDM-Net produces acceptable results. However, if the observed states differ a lot from the states in the training data, HDM-Net might fail to recognise and regress the state. This can be addressed by an extension or tailoring of the data set for specific cases. Adding training data originating from motion and geometry capture of real objects might also be an option.

6   Concluding Remarks

We have presented a new monocular surface recovery method with a deformation model replaced by a DNN—HDM-Net. The new method reconstructs time-varying geometry from a single image and is robust to self-occlusions, changing illumination and varying texture. Our DNN architecture consists of an encoder, a latent space and a decoder, and is furnished with three domain-specific losses. Apart from the conventional 3D data loss, we propose isometry and reprojection losses. We train HDM-Net with a newly generated dataset with ca. four an a half thousands states, four different illuminations, five different camera poses and three different textures. Experimental results show the validity of our approach and its suitability for reconstruction of small and moderate isometric deformations under self-occlusions. Comparisons with one template-based and two template-free methods have demonstrated a higher accuracy in favour of HDM-Net. Since HDM-Net is one of the first approach of the new kind, there are multiple avenues for investigations and improvements. One apparent direction is the further augmentation of the test dataset with different backgrounds, textures and illuminations. Next, we are going to test more advanced architectures such as generative adversarial networks and recurrent connections for the enhanced temporal smoothness. Currently, we are also investigating the relevance of HDM-Net for medical applications with augmentation of soft biological tissues.

Acknowledgement. Development of HDM-Net was supported by the project DYMANICS (01IW15003) of the German Federal Ministry of Education and Research (BMBF). The authors thank NVIDIA Corporation for the hardware donations.

References

1. Agudo, A., Agapito, L., Calvo, B., Montiel, J.M.M.: Good vibrations: a modal analysis approach for sequential non-rigid structure from motion. In: Computer Vision and Pattern Recognition (CVPR), pp. 1558–1565 (2014)
2. Agudo, A., Moreno-Noguer, F.: Force-based representation for non-rigid shape and elastic model estimation. Trans. Pattern Anal. Mach. Intell. (TPAMI) **40**(9), 2137–2150 (2018)
3. Agudo, A., Moreno-Noguer, F.: A scalable, efficient, and accurate solution to non-rigid structure from motion. Comput. Vis. Image Underst. (CVIU), **167**, 121–133 (2018)
4. Agudo, A., Moreno-Noguer, F., Calvo, B., Montiel, J.M.M.: Sequential non-rigid structure from motion using physical priors. Trans. Pattern Anal. Mach. Intell. (TPAMI) **38**, 979–994 (2016)
5. Akhter, I., Sheikh, Y., Khan, S., Kanade, T.: Trajectory space: a dual representation for nonrigid structure from motion. Trans. Pattern Anal. Mach. Intell. (TPAMI) **33**(7), 1442–1456 (2011)
6. Ansari, M., Golyanik, V., Stricker, D.: Scalable dense monocular surface reconstruction. In: International Conference on 3D Vision (3DV) (2017)
7. Birkbeck, N., Cobza, D., Jägersand, M.: Basis constrained 3D scene flow on a dynamic proxy. In: International Conference on Computer Vision (ICCV), pp. 1967–1974 (2011)
8. Blanz, V., Vetter, T.: A morphable model for the synthesis of 3D faces. ACM Trans. Graph. (TOG) 187–194 (1999)
9. Brand, M.: A direct method for 3D factorization of nonrigid motion observed in 2D. In: Computer Vision and Pattern Recognition (CVPR), vol. 2, pp. 122–128 (2005)
10. Bregler, C., Hertzmann, A., Biermann, H.: Recovering non-rigid 3D shape from image streams. In: Computer Vision and Pattern Recognition (CVPR), pp. 690–696 (2000)
11. Brunet, F., Hartley, R., Bartoli, A., Navab, N., Malgouyres, R.: Monocular template-based reconstruction of smooth and inextensible surfaces. In: Kimmel, R., Klette, R., Sugimoto, A. (eds.) ACCV 2010. LNCS, vol. 6494, pp. 52–66. Springer, Heidelberg (2011). https://doi.org/10.1007/978-3-642-19318-7_5
12. Del Bue, A.: A factorization approach to structure from motion with shape priors. In: Computer Vision and Pattern Recognition (CVPR) (2008)
13. Chhatkuli, A., Pizarro, D., Collins, T., Bartoli, A.: Inextensible non-rigid structure-from-motion by second-order cone programming. Trans. Pattern Anal. Mach. Intell. (TPAMI) **40**(1), 2428–2441 (2018)
14. Choy, C.B., Xu, D., Gwak, J.Y., Chen, K., Savarese, S.: 3D-R2N2: a unified approach for single and multi-view 3D object reconstruction. In: Leibe, B., Matas, J., Sebe, N., Welling, M. (eds.) ECCV 2016. LNCS, vol. 9912, pp. 628–644. Springer, Cham (2016). https://doi.org/10.1007/978-3-319-46484-8_38
15. Cohen, L.D., Cohen, I.: Deformable models for 3-D medical images using finite elements and balloons. In: Computer Vision and Pattern Recognition (CVPR), pp. 592–598 (1992)
16. Cook, R.L., Torrance, K.E.: A reflectance model for computer graphics. ACM Trans. Graph. (TOG) **1**(1), 7–24 (1982)
17. Curless, B., Levoy, M.: A volumetric method for building complex models from range images. ACM Trans. Graph. (TOG) 303–312 (1996)

18. Dai, Y., Li, H., He, M.: A simple prior-free method for non-rigid structure-from-motion factorization. Int. J. Comput. Vis. **107**(2), 101–122 (2014)
19. Dou, P., Shah, S.K., Kakadiaris, I.A.: End-to-end 3D face reconstruction with deep neural networks. In: Computer Vision and Pattern Recognition (CVPR) (2017)
20. Eigen, D., Puhrsch, C., Fergus, R.: Depth map prediction from a single image using a multi-scale deep network. In: Advances in Neural Information Processing Systems (NIPS), pp. 2366–2374 (2014)
21. Fan, H., Su, H., Guibas, L.J.: A point set generation network for 3D object reconstruction from a single image. In: Computer Vision and Pattern Recognition (CVPR) (2017)
22. Fayad, J., Agapito, L., Del Bue, A.: Piecewise quadratic reconstruction of non-rigid surfaces from monocular sequences. In: Daniilidis, K., Maragos, P., Paragios, N. (eds.) ECCV 2010. LNCS, vol. 6314, pp. 297–310. Springer, Heidelberg (2010). https://doi.org/10.1007/978-3-642-15561-1_22
23. Blender Foundation: blender, v. 2.79a. open source 3d creation (2018). https://www.blender.org/
24. Gallardo, M., Collins, T., Bartoli, A.: Using shading and a 3D template to reconstruct complex surface deformations. In: British Machine Vision Conference (BMVC) (2016)
25. Gallardo, M., Collins, T., Bartoli, A.: Dense non-rigid structure-from-motion and shading with unknown albedos. In: International Conference on Computer Vision (ICCV) (2017)
26. Garg, R., Roussos, A., Agapito, L.: Dense variational reconstruction of non-rigid surfaces from monocular video. In: Computer Vision and Pattern Recognition (CVPR), pp. 1272–1279 (2013)
27. Garg, R., Kumar, V.B.G., Carneiro, G., Reid, I.: Unsupervised CNN for single view depth estimation: geometry to the rescue. In: Leibe, B., Matas, J., Sebe, N., Welling, M. (eds.) ECCV 2016. LNCS, vol. 9912, pp. 740–756. Springer, Cham (2016). https://doi.org/10.1007/978-3-319-46484-8_45
28. Garrido, P., et al.: Reconstruction of personalized 3D face rigs from monocular video **35**(3), 28:1–28:15 (2016)
29. Giannarou, S., Visentini-Scarzanella, M., Yang, G.Z.: Probabilistic tracking of affine-invariant anisotropic regions. Trans. Pattern Anal. Mach. Intell. (TPAMI) **35**(1), 130–143 (2013)
30. Godard, C., Mac Aodha, O., Brostow, G.J.: Unsupervised monocular depth estimation with left-right consistency. In: Computer Vision and Pattern Recognition (CVPR) (2017)
31. Golyanik, V., Fetzer, T., Stricker, D.: Accurate 3D reconstruction of dynamic scenes from monocular image sequences with severe occlusions. In: Winter Conference on Applications of Computer Vision (WACV) (2017)
32. Golyanik, V., Mathur, A.S., Stricker, D.: NRSFM-flow: recovering non-rigid scene flow from monocular image sequences. In: British Machine Vision Conference (BMVC) (2016)
33. Golyanik, V., Stricker, D.: Dense batch non-rigid structure from motion in a second. In: Winter Conference on Applications of Computer Vision (WACV), pp. 254–263 (2017)
34. Gotardo, P.F.U., Martinez, A.M.: Non-rigid structure from motion with complementary rank-3 spaces. In: Computer Vision and Pattern Recognition (CVPR), pp. 3065–3072 (2011)

35. Guan, P., Weiss, A., Blan, A.O., Black, M.J.: Estimating human shape and pose from a single image. In: International Conference on Computer Vision (ICCV), pp. 1381–1388 (2009)
36. Gumerov, N., Zandifar, A., Duraiswami, R., Davis, L.S.: Structure of applicable surfaces from single views. In: Pajdla, T., Matas, J. (eds.) ECCV 2004. LNCS, vol. 3023, pp. 482–496. Springer, Heidelberg (2004). https://doi.org/10.1007/978-3-540-24672-5_38
37. Hamsici, O.C., Gotardo, P.F.U., Martinez, A.M.: Learning spatially-smooth mappings in non-rigid structure from motion. In: Fitzgibbon, A., Lazebnik, S., Perona, P., Sato, Y., Schmid, C. (eds.) ECCV 2012. LNCS, vol. 7575, pp. 260–273. Springer, Heidelberg (2012). https://doi.org/10.1007/978-3-642-33765-9_19
38. Haouchine, N., Dequidt, J., Berger, M.O., Cotin, S.: Single view augmentation of 3D elastic objects. In: International Symposium on Mixed and Augmented Reality (ISMAR), pp. 229–236 (2014)
39. He, K., Zhang, X., Ren, S., Sun, J.: Deep residual learning for image recognition. In: Computer Vision and Pattern Recognition (CVPR) (2016)
40. Jackson, A.S., Bulat, A., Argyriou, V., Tzimiropoulos, G.: Large pose 3D face reconstruction from a single image via direct volumetric CNN regression. In: International Conference on Computer Vision (ICCV) (2017)
41. Jaderberg, M., Simonyan, K., Zisserman, A., Kavukcuoglu, K.: Spatial transformer networks. In: Advances in Neural Information Processing Systems (NIPS), pp. 2017–2025 (2015)
42. Krizhevsky, A., Sutskever, I., Hinton, G.E.: Imagenet classification with deep convolutional neural networks. In: Advances in Neural Information Processing Systems (NIPS), pp. 1097–1105 (2012)
43. Lee, M., Cho, J., Oh, S.: Procrustean normal distribution for non-rigid structure from motion. Trans. Pattern Anal. Mach. Intell. (TPAMI) **39**(7), 1388–1400 (2017)
44. Liu, F., Shen, C., Lin, G.: Deep convolutional neural fields for depth estimation from a single image. In: Computer Vision and Pattern Recognition (CVPR) (2015)
45. Liu-Yin, Q., Yu, R., Agapito, L., Fitzgibbon, A., Russell, C.: Better together: joint reasoning for non-rigid 3D reconstruction with specularities and shading. In: British Machine Vision Conference (BMVC) (2016)
46. Malti, A., Hartley, R., Bartoli, A., Kim, J.H.: Monocular template-based 3D reconstruction of extensible surfaces with local linear elasticity. In: Computer Vision and Pattern Recognition (CVPR), pp. 1522–1529 (2013)
47. McInerney, T., Terzopoulos, D.: A finite element model for 3D shape reconstruction and nonrigid motion tracking. In: International Conference on Computer Vision (ICCV), pp. 518–523 (1993)
48. Mitiche, A., Mathlouthi, Y., Ben Ayed, I.: Monocular concurrent recovery of structure and motion scene flow. Front. ICT **2**, 16 (2015)
49. Moreno-Noguer, F., Porta, J.M., Fua, P.: Exploring ambiguities for monocular nonrigid shape estimation. In: Daniilidis, K., Maragos, P., Paragios, N. (eds.) ECCV 2010. LNCS, vol. 6313, pp. 370–383. Springer, Heidelberg (2010). https://doi.org/10.1007/978-3-642-15558-1_27
50. NVIDIA Corporation: NVIDIA CUDA C programming guide (2018). Version 9.0
51. Paladini, M., Del Bue, A., Xavier, J., Agapito, L., Stosić, M., Dodig, M.: Optimal metric projections for deformable and articulated structure-from-motion. Int. J. Comput. Vis. (IJCV) **96**(2), 252–276 (2012)

52. Paladini, M., Bartoli, A., Agapito, L.: Sequential non-rigid structure-from-motion with the 3D-implicit low-rank shape model. In: Daniilidis, K., Maragos, P., Paragios, N. (eds.) ECCV 2010. LNCS, vol. 6312, pp. 15–28. Springer, Heidelberg (2010). https://doi.org/10.1007/978-3-642-15552-9_2

53. Paszke, A., et al.: Automatic differentiation in pytorch. In: Advances in Neural Information Processing Systems Workshops (NIPS-W) (2017)

54. Paszke, A., Gross, S., Massa, F., Chintala, S.: pytorch (2018). https://github.com/pytorch

55. Perriollat, M., Hartley, R., Bartoli, A.: Monocular template-based reconstruction of inextensible surfaces. Int. J. Comput. Vis. (IJCV) **95**(2), 124–137 (2011)

56. Pumarola, A., Agudo, A., Porzi, L., Sanfeliu, A., Lepetit, V., Moreno-Noguer, F.: Geometry-aware network for non-rigid shape prediction from a single view. In: Computer Vision and Pattern Recognition (CVPR), pp. 4681–4690 (2018)

57. Riegler, G., Ulusoy, A.O., Bischof, H., Geiger, A.: OctNetFusion: learning depth fusion from data. In: International Conference on 3D Vision (3DV) (2017)

58. Russell, C., Fayad, J., Agapito, L.: Dense non-rigid structure from motion. In: International Conference on 3D Imaging, Modeling, Processing, Visualization and Transmission (3DIMPVT), pp. 509–516 (2012)

59. Salzmann, M., Fua, P.: Reconstructing sharply folding surfaces: a convex formulation. In: Computer Vision and Pattern Recognition (CVPR), pp. 1054–1061 (2009)

60. Salzmann, M., Fua, P.: Linear local models for monocular reconstruction of deformable surfaces. Trans. Pattern Anal. Mach. Intell. (TPAMI) **33**(5), 931–944 (2011)

61. Salzmann, M., Hartley, R., Fua, P.: Convex optimization for deformable surface 3-D tracking. In: International Conference on Computer Vision (ICCV) (2007)

62. Salzmann, M., Lepetit, V., Fua, P.: Deformable surface tracking ambiguities. In: Computer Vision and Pattern Recognition (CVPR) (2007)

63. Sela, M., Richardson, E., Kimmel, R.: Unrestricted facial geometry reconstruction using image-to-image translation. In: International Conference on Computer Vision (ICCV) (2017)

64. Stay & Play Rotorua Ltd: A hot balloon. http://stayandplaynz.com/rotorua/the-real-new-zealand-experience/. Accessed 29 June 2018

65. Suwajanakorn, S., Kemelmacher-Shlizerman, I., Seitz, S.M.: Total moving face reconstruction. In: Fleet, D., Pajdla, T., Schiele, B., Tuytelaars, T. (eds.) ECCV 2014. LNCS, vol. 8692, pp. 796–812. Springer, Cham (2014). https://doi.org/10.1007/978-3-319-10593-2_52

66. Taetz, B., Bleser, G., Golyanik, V., Stricker, D.: Occlusion-aware video registration for highly non-rigid objects. In: Winter Conference on Applications of Computer Vision (WACV) (2016)

67. Tao, L., Matuszewski, B.J.: Non-rigid structure from motion with diffusion maps prior. In: Computer Vision and Pattern Recognition (CVPR), pp. 1530–1537 (2013)

68. Tateno, K., Tombari, F., Laina, I., Navab, N.: CNN-SLAM: real-time dense monocular slam with learned depth prediction. In: Computer Vision and Pattern Recognition (CVPR) (2017)

69. Tewari, A., et al.: Mofa: model-based deep convolutional face autoencoder for unsupervised monocular reconstruction. In: International Conference on Computer Vision (ICCV) (2017)

70. Textures.com: WrinklesHanging0037. https://www.textures.com/browse/hanging/112398. Accessed 29 June 2018

71. Tomasi, C., Kanade, T.: Shape and motion from image streams under orthography: a factorization method. Int. J. Comput. Vis. (IJCV) **9**, 137–154 (1992)

72. Tome, D., Russell, C., Agapito, L.: Lifting from the deep: convolutional 3D pose estimation from a single image. In: Computer Vision and Pattern Recognition (CVPR) (2017)
73. Torresani, L., Hertzmann, A., Bregler, C.: Nonrigid structure-from-motion: estimating shape and motion with hierarchical priors. Trans. Pattern Anal. Mach. Intell. (TPAMI) **30**(5), 878–892 (2008)
74. Varol, A., Shaji, A., Salzmann, M., Fua, P.: Monocular 3D reconstruction of locally textured surfaces. Trans. Pattern Anal. Mach. Intell. (TPAMI) **34**(6), 1118–1130 (2012)
75. Vicente, S., Agapito, L.: Soft inextensibility constraints for template-free non-rigid reconstruction. In: Fitzgibbon, A., Lazebnik, S., Perona, P., Sato, Y., Schmid, C. (eds.) ECCV 2012. LNCS, vol. 7574, pp. 426–440. Springer, Heidelberg (2012). https://doi.org/10.1007/978-3-642-33712-3_31
76. Wandt, B., Ackermann, H., Rosenhahn, B.: 3D reconstruction of human motion from monocular image sequences. Trans. Pattern Anal. Mach. Intell. (TPAMI) **38**(8), 1505–1516 (2016)
77. White, R., Forsyth, D.A.: Combining cues: shape from shading and texture. In: Computer Vision and Pattern Recognition (CVPR), pp. 1809–1816 (2006)
78. Xiao, D., Yang, Q., Yang, B., Wei, W.: Monocular scene flow estimation via variational method. Multimedia Tools Appl. **76**(8), 10575–10597 (2017)
79. Xiao, J., Chai, J., Kanade, T.: A closed-form solution to non-rigid shape and motion recovery. Int. J. Comput. Vis. (IJCV) **67**(2), 233–246 (2006)
80. Yu, R., Russell, C., Campbell, N.D.F., Agapito, L.: Direct, dense, and deformable: template-based non-rigid 3D reconstruction from RGB video. In: International Conference on Computer Vision (ICCV) (2015)
81. Zhou, X., Zhu, M., Pavlakos, G., Leonardos, S., Derpanis, K.G., Daniilidis, K.: Monocap: monocular human motion capture using a CNN coupled with a geometric prior. Trans. Pattern Anal. Mach. Intell. (TPAMI) (2018)
82. Zhu, S., Zhang, L., Smith, B.M.: Model evolution: an incremental approach to non-rigid structure from motion. In: Computer Vision and Pattern Recognition (CVPR), pp. 1165–1172 (2010)

HMD-Guided Image-Based Modeling and Rendering of Indoor Scenes

Daniel Andersen$^{(\boxtimes)}$ and Voicu Popescu

Purdue University, West Lafayette, IN 47907, USA
{andersed,popescu}@purdue.edu

Abstract. We present a system that enables a novice user to acquire a large indoor scene in minutes as a collection of images sufficient for five degrees-of-freedom virtual navigation by image morphing. The user walks through the scene wearing an augmented reality head-mounted display (AR HMD) enhanced with a panoramic video camera. The AR HMD shows a 2D grid of a dynamically generated floor plan, which guides the user to acquire a panorama from each grid cell. After acquisition, panoramas are preliminarily registered using the AR HMD tracking data, corresponding features are detected in pairs of neighboring panoramas, and the correspondences are used to refine panorama registration. The registered panoramas and their correspondences support rendering the scene interactively with any view direction and from any viewpoint on the acquisition plane. An HMD VR interface guides the user who optimizes visualization fidelity interactively, by aligning the viewpoint with one of the hundreds of acquisition locations evenly sampling the floor plane.

Keywords: Augmented reality · 3D acquisition
Image-based rendering

1 Introduction

Applications such as virtual tourism, real estate advertisement, or cultural heritage preservation require rendering real world scenes convincingly at interactive rates. However, efficient photorealistic acquisition of real world scenes is a challenging problem. Traditional texture mapped geometric models are difficult to acquire to a level of completeness necessary for high-fidelity rendering. The alternative approach of image-based modeling and rendering (IBMR) has been proposed over twenty years ago. The scene is captured with a database of rays, which is queried at run time to show the scene from the desired view. Assembling the output image is fast, and good results are obtained as long as the image-based model covers densely the entire viewing volume.

However, efficient image-based modeling of a large indoor space remains an open problem. Practical image-based modeling approaches acquire 2D ray databases, i.e., panoramas, which confine the user to the acquisition location. Image-based modeling that enables virtual scene navigation with more degrees

© Springer Nature Switzerland AG 2018
P. Bourdot et al. (Eds.): EuroVR 2018, LNCS 11162, pp. 73–93, 2018.
https://doi.org/10.1007/978-3-030-01790-3_5

Fig. 1. AR-guided acquisition (a), acquisition map visualization (b), guided VR visualization frame from viewpoint at acquisition location (c) at barycenter of acquisition location triplet (d), and at midpoint of acquisition path segment (e). (Color figure online)

of freedom have the disadvantages of expensive acquisition devices, of long acquisition times, and of reliance on operator expertise. Another challenge is the lack of immediate feedback during acquisition, which makes it difficult for the user to capture the scene reliably from all necessary viewpoints. Returning to the scene long after initial acquisition to acquire additional viewpoints is impractical.

After acquisition, the panoramas are processed offline with a pipeline that preregisters the panoramas using the AR HMD tracking data, triangulates acquisition locations, refines panorama registration using corresponding features in panorama through a RANSAC approach, enriches the set of correspondences using the scene geometry proxy acquired by the AR HMD, and builds panorama 3D morphing meshes by triangulating correspondences.

The resulting 3D morphing meshes supports interactive five degree of freedom (5-DOF) visualization through a virtual reality (VR) HMD, with correct depth perception. The desired image is rendered by morphing and blending the three panoramas that define the acquisition location triangle that contains the viewpoint. We do not focus on the difficult task of reconstructing a high-fidelity 6-DOF 3D mesh; instead, we recognize that most reasonable views of the scene will be on the 2D plane near head height and five degrees of freedom sufficiently describes the scene.

Like any image-based model, our model caters to the set of all possible output views with non-uniform fidelity. We allow the user to take advantage of the highest fidelity provided by our model by displaying through the VR HMD a visualization map with the current viewpoint position and the nearby panorama acquisition locations. Therefore, the VR HMD does not only show the scene to the user, but also guides the user who can optimize visualization quality interactively by easily aligning their viewpoint with the acquisition viewpoints.

The frame in Fig. 1c has a viewpoint that is near one of the acquisition locations, where the morph converges to the identity function, and artifact-free frames are rendered by resampling the acquisition panorama. The frame in Fig. 1d has a viewpoint (yellow dot at visualization map center) that is between its neighboring acquisition locations (white dots on map). Parts of the scene rich with correspondences, such as the book shelves, doors, walls, and floors, are visualized with high quality. Parts of the scene where correspondences are sparse, such as the nearby geometry in the bottom left corner of the frame and the near row of ceiling spotlights, exhibit ghosting artifacts. The visualization map can also show the acquisition path (gray line segments in Fig. 1e). When the user translates the viewpoint along a segment of the acquisition path, a high-fidelity visualization is provided by morphing between two consecutive panoramas saved with higher density along the acquisition path (green circles in Fig. 1e). Leveraging the high density of the acquisition and the visualization of the acquisition locations, the user achieves a high-quality interactive visualization of the scene, with brief transitions between acquisition locations, and with photorealistic pan-tilt sequences from viewpoints aligned with acquisition locations.

In summary, our paper contributes a complete image based modeling and rendering system, with an AR HMD interface that guides a novice user to achieve a complete inside-looking-out acquisition of a large indoor space in minutes, and with a VR HMD interface that guides the user to optimize visualization fidelity.

2   Prior Work

We first discuss prior image-based modeling and rendering techniques relevant to our approach, and then we discuss prior work on guided scene acquisition.

2.1   Image-Based Modeling and Rendering

Aliaga and Carlbom presented a plenoptic stitching method that acquired image based models of indoor environments by moving an omnidirectional camera through a room in a regular pattern [2]. Synthetic views were generated by interpolating images captured from surrounding views. However, their approach did not provide interactive guidance on how to efficiently traverse the interior of the environment, so pre-planning was required. The visualization method also required a virtual camera location to be surrounded by a closed loop of acquired images, which leads to tedious acquisition paths when the environment is cluttered. In contrast, our approach gives guidance during acquisition, and the user only needs to visit each acquisition location a single time.

Bradley et al. presented a system for virtual navigation through a real-world scene by switching the view between densely sampled panoramas along a series of corridors [3]. Zhang and Zhu similarly built virtual tours from spherical panoramas acquired at regular intervals on a tabletop [30]. The sampling was dense but lacked morphing, so the user perceives discontinuities during translation. Such acquisition was also limited to a pre-defined path planned by consulting an existing map of the scene.

Some prior work examines the question of interpolation between panoramas for image-based navigation. Chiang et al. presented a method for image-based interpolation between cylindrical panoramas, but the method required manual input for determining adjacency between neighboring images [4]. Several methods achieve panorama interpolation, but only in one dimension along the path of acquisition [14,17,31], which results in a 4-DOF visualization. Kawai et al. extended such works to support navigation in two dimensions by bilinear interpolation of panoramas, but without automatically finding correspondences between panoramas [16]. Kawai later reformulated the problem as a sparse light field supporting transitions between panoramas but at the cost of highly noticeable artifacts [15]. Xiao and Shah's tri-view morphing method allows for novel viewpoints of a scene by grouping triples of neighboring cameras; however, it only makes use of conventional images and not panoramas, and correspondences must be enriched manually [28].

Shi presented a method for interpolation of cubemap panoramas for image-based navigation [25]. However, without a method to guide the user to capture such imagery at a minimum density, there is no guarantee of coverage or of minimum quality as a user navigates through the scene. Davis et al.'s work on unstructured light fields offers some visual feedback during image-based acquisition of a target object, but their work focuses on outside-looking-in object acquisition, while we focus on inside-looking-out scene acquisition [6].

RGB-D depth maps have been used to achieve visually impressive results for scene capture and reconstruction. Hedman et al. presented a recent work for high-quality image-based modeling and rendering of indoor scenes by combining RGB color images from traditional cameras with RGB-D depth-enhanced images [11]. Dai et al. created a method for globally consistent 3D reconstruction using a hand-held depth sensor [5]. Compared to their work, our models are much farther to the image end of the geometry-image continuum, with the benefits of a simpler acquisition device and of a simpler acquisition procedure.

Recent work by Huang et al. uses panoramic video camera footage to create 6-DOF VR videos, where a user can view the captured environment with depth cues and head orientation and translation [13]. However, this work targets a single fixed viewing location with some ability to move the head within a small viewing volume, whereas we capture floor spaces of hundreds of square meters. This prior work focuses on leveraging existing video footage to build an image-based model, as opposed to our goal of guidance during acquisition to capture the best set of images.

2.2 Guided Scene Acquisition

Several prior acquisition systems attempt to guide the user to acquire imagery of scenes from as-yet-uncaptured viewpoints. Tuite et al. illustrated sparsely-sampled regions in a 3D reconstruction of a building facade as markers on a smartphone map, prompting users to take pictures from the necessary viewpoints [26,27]. However, their approach targets reconstruction of outdoor building facades, while our approach focuses on acquiring indoor environments. The indoor environments we target lack precise GPS tracking, which requires more active tracking such as in an AR HMD. Also, because many indoor environments are more likely to rapidly change appearance than outdoor buildings, the prior work's emphasis on multi-user capture over long periods of time is less suitable. Instead, we focus on providing guidance for a single user to rapidly capture an indoor environment, all in a single scanning session.

Rusinkiewicz et al. introduced an interactive method for capturing 3D models of hand-held objects while showing the in-progress model to the user [23]. Such approaches provide implicit guidance from a single viewpoint, but further manipulation of the object is required to uncover missing regions of the model. The equivalent action in our use case (acquiring large indoor environments) would be to physically traverse the environment, and so we provide additional guidance in the form of a top-down map that reduces the redundant physical traversal needed by the user. Diverdi et al. presented a method for interactively constructing an environment map; however, the output of a single environment map only provides a rough approximation of scene geometry [7]. Ahn et al. created a method to plan the placement of 3D scanning equipment in the context of digital heritage [1]. Given a top-down map and user-selected regions of interest, they automatically determined locations to place a 3D scanner to achieve a high-quality scan with sufficient coverage; however, it is not suited for casual scanning or acquisition of areas without a prior map or manual direction. Pan et al. presented an AR interface for acquiring texture imagery of a hand-held object by indicating rotations for the user to perform to reveal unscanned areas to a camera [21]. However, this particular interface is suitable only for small manipulable objects, rather than inside-out capture of a room. Pankratz and Klinker used a video pass-through AR HMD to visualize room-scale marker calibration during iterative refinement, but did not focus on capturing scenes [22].

2.3 Additional Prior Work

Recently, guided acquisition of room-sized scenes has been explored in fully-autonomous contexts, where a robot utilizes next-best-view (NBV) analysis of scene geometry to determine efficient trajectories for geometric capture [9,29]. In contrast, our work focuses on providing guidance to a human user in a casual context where robotic acquisition is infeasible, such as in cluttered environments that are difficult for robots to navigate but easy for humans to walk through.

A recent work presented a method for acquiring textured 3D models of indoor scenes using an AR HMD [8]. However, the purpose of that work was to create a

fixed-memory texture atlas during acquisition to color the AR HMD's on-board
3D geometry capture. The resulting mesh typically contains holes that cannot
be filled in after acquisition due to discarding of unused color data. Guidance is
not provided to the user during acquisition.

3   System Overview

Figure 2 gives an overview of the architecture of our system. The user acquires
scene panoramas with interactive AR guidance (Sect. 4), the panoramas are prepared offline for morphing (Sect. 5), and the panoramas are then morphed in a
guided VR interactive visualization of the scene (Sect. 6).

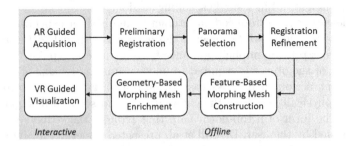

Fig. 2. System pipeline overview.

4   AR Guided Acquisition

The goal of the acquisition stage is to capture a complete and dense set of scene
images as quickly as possible, without the prerequisite of user expertise. We
achieve this goal with an acquisition device that not only captures images of the
scene, but also guides the user for efficient and reliable acquisition.

4.1   Acquisition Device

Our acquisition device consists of an AR HMD enhanced with a panoramic video
camera (Fig. 1a). The panoramic camera's pose is calibrated with respect to the
AR HMD. Our approach relies on and assumes that the AR HMD provides
inside-out tracking and some generation of rough geometric data. As the user
walks through the scene, the AR HMD tracks the user's position and orientation,
it builds a map of the scene, and it overlays onto the user's field of view the
locations from where the scene is yet to be acquired.

The AR HMD does have a built in video camera, which, in principle, could
be used to acquire the images needed to build the image-based model of the
scene. However, the AR HMD camera has a small field of view, which makes

it unsuitable for our purpose. To support free view rotation during the interactive visualization, the scene must be acquired in all view directions from each acquisition location. Covering all view directions with a small field of view camera leads to long acquisition times and blurry images from head rotation. Also, when the user pans and tilts their head to cover all view directions from a given acquisition location, it is difficult to enforce a single viewpoint constraint, which reduces the quality of the interactive visualization that has to cover the residual translation by morphing.

To improve acquisition efficiency, we capture the scene with a 360° panoramic video camera that is rigidly attached to the AR HMD. Each frame is a complete spherical pinhole panorama, which can be trivially resampled to a high-quality output image when the desired viewpoint matches an acquisition location. The resulting image-based model captures the scene with very high fidelity from the hundreds of viewpoints from where panoramas are acquired. The camera records continuously during acquisition as a panoramic video stored to the camera's flash memory. After acquisition, the panoramic video is processed offline into an image-based model of the scene as described in Sect. 5.

4.2   AR Interface

Our system relies on an AR interface to guide the user towards a fast, dense, and complete acquisition. To support 5-DOF interactive virtual navigation, i.e., two translations and three rotations, the user acquires panoramas on a horizontal plane at the user's head height, which will also be the height from where the scene is rendered during visualization. Acquisition density and coverage is controlled by partitioning the acquisition plane with a uniform 2D grid (e.g., with $0.5\,\mathrm{m} \times 0.5\,\mathrm{m}$ cells for Fig. 1b).

The 2D grid is shown as a 2D map floating in front of the user (Fig. 1b). The map rotates as the user changes direction to maintain an intuitive user perspective orientation. The map shows the parts of the grid that are yet to be discovered (empty dark cells), the parts that are inaccessible due to floor obstacles such as furniture (white), the parts that have already been traversed during acquisition (green), as well as the user's current position and orientation (yellow, at the center of the map). The floor obstacles are computed from the coarse geometric scene model acquired by the AR HMD through active depth sensing. The scene does not have to be acquired from inaccessible cells since during a typical virtual navigation, the user does not want, and is prevented from, assuming inaccessible positions (e.g., inside a book shelf or above a desk). Acquisition is complete once all accessible grid cells are traversed (Fig. 3).

As we were designing the interface, we found that relying on a first person visualization is inefficient. We initially rendered markers in the scene to illustrate target locations. This was difficult for the user to align their head with the marker, because the marker grows larger as the user approaches it. We had also tried rendering the 2D grid over the scene floor; acquisition suffered from excessive downwards head tilting needed to consult the grid visualization. In both cases, the AR HMD's low field of view meant that indicators anchored to world locations were often hidden to the user and thus could not communicate guidance. Instead we found that adding an additional perspective in the form of a virtual map was most suitable for our use case and has proven to be an efficient way of guiding the user, who can intuitively turn left and right to guide the yellow dot through the grid cells that are yet to be traversed.

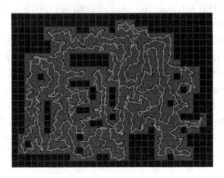

Fig. 3. Acquisition result. The acquisition path (blue line) has traversed all accessible grid cells (green). A panorama is selected for each grid cell (red dots). (Color figure online)

5   Panorama Morphing Setup

In this section, we describe our offline processing of the acquired data to transform it into a set of 3D morphing meshes suitable for interactive visualization.

5.1   Preliminary Registration

Once scanning is complete (usually about 5 to 10 min), the AR HMD has acquired (1) a video sequence of spherical panoramas along a path that intersects all empty grid cells on the floor plan, (2) a video sequence acquired by the AR HMD on-board video camera, (3) pose tracking data for the frames of the on-board video camera, and (4) a coarse geometric of the scene captured by the active depth camera built into the AR HMD. At the beginning of the scanning session we synchronize the frame sequences of the panoramic and of the on-board cameras by flashing a light. After synchronization, the pose tracking data for the on-board camera frames is transferred to the panoramic frames.

5.2   Panorama Selection

We select two sets of panoramas from the spherical panoramic video sequence to be incorporated into the image-based model of the scene: *grid cell panoramas*, for scene visualization from anywhere on the acquisition plane; and *acquisition path panoramas*, for quality visualization from anywhere on the acquisition path.

The grid cell panoramas are selected by finding the best panorama for each accessible 2D grid cell (Fig. 3). The best panorama is the one that has an acquisition location closest to the cell center, based on the tracked pose data. We exclude panoramas with high panning angular velocity since they are blurry. The angular velocity is estimated based on the tracked pose data. The acquisition viewpoints of the panoramas in the grid cell set are 2D Delaunay triangulated on the acquisition plane. This triangulation defines a *panorama triplet* for every output visualization viewpoint (Fig. 4, left). Panorama triplets may occasionally cross unvisited grid cells. This is not a problem when cells are unvisited due to containing low obstacles (desks, chairs) below head height. However, if an unvisited cell contains a wall, some morphing results could incorporate views from both sites of the wall, leading to unwanted artifacts. In practice, we cast rays against the AR HMD's coarse geometry along the triangulation edges, and discard triplets that would cross head-height obstacles.

The acquisition path panoramas are chosen from the panoramic video sequence at equal distance intervals, leveraging the tracked posed data again. The distance is smaller than the grid cell size (e.g., 0.25 m vs 0.5 m) to provide a higher quality visualization when the output viewpoint is on the acquisition path, as compared to when it is in the middle of a panorama triplet. As before, frames with high panning rotational velocity are avoided. Figure 4, right, shows in detail the triangulated grid cell panorama locations and the path panorama locations.

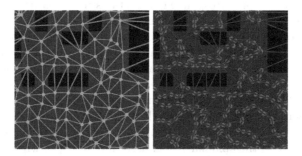

Fig. 4. Detail view of acquisition area. Left: Grid cell panoramas (red dots) triangulated in panorama triplets (red lines). Right: Acquisition path (blue line), and acquisition path panoramas (green dots). (Color figure online)

5.3   Registration Refinement

The poses provided by our AR HMD are only accurate to about 2 cm in translation and about 2° in rotation. Also, drift can accumulate in the AR HMD's pose estimation; while the HMD can internally correct itself using loop closure techniques, the raw pose data we capture during acquisition is not automatically corrected. Using estimated poses directly in the construction of our image-based model would result in reduced visualization quality from image instability along smooth visualization paths, and from ghosting when transitioning between panoramas. We refine panorama registration (1) by detecting panorama features, (2) by estimating feature correspondences between neighboring panoramas, (3) by removing outlier correspondences, and (4) by performing a global pose graph optimization of all panorama poses. Throughout our registration refinement pipeline we work with the original spherical panorama images gathered during acquisition, without resampling to a cube map.

(1) For each panorama, we compute image features using SPHORB [32], an ORB feature generalization that operates directly in the spherical domain.

(2) We define correspondences between features of panorama pairs, based on the SPHORB feature distance. Rather than computing a full pairwise set of correspondences between all panoramas, which would be computationally expensive, we only find correspondences between adjacent panoramas based on AR HMD provided poses. First, we find correspondences between panoramas that are connected by an edge of a panorama triplet (determined by the AR HMD's estimated poses). Second, we find correspondences between consecutive acquisition path panoramas. Third, we find correspondences between each acquisition path panorama p_a and the grid cell panorama p_b with the closest acquisition location to that of p_a. These additional correspondences ensure that the two sets of panoramas are correctly registered together.

(3) The resulting set of correspondences contains many outliers unsuitable for registration refinement, so we find inliers with an iterative RANSAC approach [10] on each pair of neighboring panoramas (p_1, p_2) for which correspondences were found. Each iteration selects a subset of correspondences, uses the subset to estimate the essential matrix $\mathbf{E}$ of (p_1, p_2), and computes the subset's reprojection error. Correspondences are marked as inliers or outliers by comparing reprojection error against a threshold. We work directly in the spherical domain and follow the approach of Pagani and Stricker [20] in approximating the geodesic reprojection error ϵ_p with the projected distance of a ray to the epipolar plane, according to Eq. 1, where (f_1, f_2) are a pair of corresponding features mapped onto the unit sphere that belong to two neighboring panoramas.

$$\epsilon_p = \frac{|f_2^T \mathbf{E} f_1|}{\|f_2\|\|\mathbf{E} f_1\|} \tag{1}$$

(4) The final step of panorama registration refinement performs a global nonlinear least squares optimization of panorama poses based on the inlier correspondences validated by the previous step. This optimization determines poses for all panoramas that are globally consistent. Although pairwise relative poses have been implicitly computed in the previous outlier removal step, the essential matrix determined between a pair of panoramas is sensitive to noise and to the RANSAC parameters. To ensure that relative poses

are consistent when moving between multiple panorama triplets, it is important to do a global optimization. Each panorama pose is represented with 6 parameters, i.e., 3 translations and 3 rotations. To limit the change in panorama acquisition location, we constrain translation to be within 0.1 m of the estimated translation. The rotations are unconstrained. The error targeted by the optimization is the sum of squares of correspondence pair errors. The error for a pair of corresponding features (f_1, f_2) is computed based on an approach described by Pagani et al. [19]. The essential matrix $\mathbf{E}$ of the panoramas (p_1, p_2) is computed based on current pose estimates of the two panoramas. f_1 and f_2 are mapped to 3D points on the unit sphere and the error is computed as a locally projected measure of the geodesic distance from the epipolar line. Minimizing $f_2^T \mathbf{E} f_1$, which would be appropriate for Euclidean space correspondences, would minimize the sine of the geodesic distance in our context of spherical panorama correspondences. Instead, we minimize the value d_{et} defined in Eq. 2.

$$d_{et} = \tan\left(\arcsin(f_2^T \mathbf{E} f_1)\right) = \frac{f_2^T \mathbf{E} f_1}{\sqrt{1 - (f_2^T \mathbf{E} f_1)^2}} \tag{2}$$

Both ϵ_p and d_{et} are valid approximations of the geodesic reprojection error, with ϵ_p yielding slightly better registration refinement given noisy features [20]. However, we found that optimizing over ϵ_p during registration refinement was much slower to converge, and so we favor ϵ_p during our inlier selection to ensure only high-quality matches are selected, and use d_{et} during the computationally expensive registration refinement step.

After registration refinement, we re-triangulate the grid cell panorama viewpoints to account for any shift in these viewpoints during optimization. Since the translation degrees of freedom are constrained, the viewpoints shift

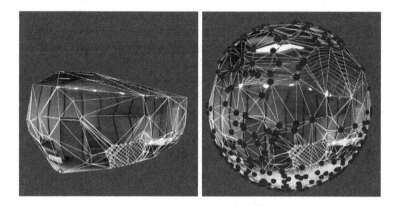

Fig. 5. Morphing mesh computed as 3D convex hull of feature point projections on unit sphere (left). Morphing mesh enriched with points (red dots) from the coarse 3D scene model acquired by the AR HMD (right). (Color figure online)

little, which preserves the uniform acquisition property of the grid cell panorama set.

5.4   Morphing Mesh Construction

When the viewpoint is located at one of the panorama acquisition locations, the scene can be visualized with high quality in any view direction by resampling the panorama to the output image. To support translations between the panorama acquisition locations, we triangulate panorama correspondences to construct a *morphing mesh*. We build morphing meshes for each grid cell panorama triplet, and for each acquisition path panorama pair.

A morphing mesh is built in three stages: (1) the mesh is triangulated from image features, (2) the mesh is enhanced using the coarse 3D geometry acquired by AR HMD's active sensors, and (3) the mesh is modified to ensure topological consistency over the panorama triplet or the panorama path segment pair.

(1) We define mesh vertices from correspondences between neighboring panoramas detected during the registration refinement stage. Given a panorama triplet (p_1, p_2, p_3), we compute the transitive closure S of correspondence pairs. A three-way correspondence (f_1, f_2, f_3) is included in S iff the two-way correspondences (f_1, f_2), (f_2, f_3), and (f_3, f_1) exist between panoramas (p_1, p_2), (p_2, p_3), and (p_3, p_1), respectively. For each three-way correspondence (f_1, f_2, f_3), we define a 3D scene feature point as the point closest to the three panorama rays through f_1, f_2, and f_3. The feature 3D points are projected on a unit sphere centered at the panorama triplet barycenter, and their projections are triangulated by computing their 3D convex hull. An example morphing mesh constructed from feature points is visualized in Fig. 5, left, on the unit sphere, and in Fig. 6, left.

(2) The feature-based morphing mesh is sparse in featureless regions (Fig. 5, left, Fig. 6, left). We increase the fidelity of the morphing mesh in a second stage by adding vertices based on the coarse geometric model acquired by the AR HMD with its built-in active depth camera (Fig. 5, right, Fig. 6, bottom). This geometric model is neither complete nor precise, so it could not be used alone. However, when combined with the panorama features, the coarse geometry increases the fidelity of the transitions between panorama viewpoints. 3D points from the coarse geometry are iteratively added to the morphing mesh only in regions where the morphing mesh is sparse. Morphing mesh triangles that are above a threshold size are subdivided by adding a vertex at the triangle center. The 3D position of the new vertex is defined by intersecting the ray from the barycenter of the panorama triplet with the coarse geometry. If the ray fails to intersect the incomplete coarse geometric model, a random point is selected inside the triangle to be subdivided. The process continues until all triangles in the morphing mesh are sufficiently small, or until no further intersections with the coarse geometry are possible.

(3) Even though we compute connectivity by computing the 3D convex hull, triangulation is performed in the 2D domain of the surface of the unit sphere.

This requires topological consistency anywhere within the panorama triplet; no mesh triangle should flip orientation as the viewpoint translates away from the barycenter. We enforce morphing mesh topological consistency with an iterative approach [31], which eliminates triangles that yield inconsistent orientation.

Fig. 6. Morphing mesh computed from features (left) and enriched with geometry points, shown as red dots (right). (Color figure online)

We have described the construction of the morphing mesh in the context of a panorama triplet. For panorama pairs defined by acquisition path segments, the process is similar and simpler. No three-way correspondences are needed during the feature-based morphing construction, and the two-way correspondences between the two panoramas are used directly. The barycenter of the panorama triplet is replaced with the midpoint of the path segment. Finally, topological consistency is achieved by checking triangle orientation at the midpoint and two endpoints of the path segment.

6 VR-Guided Interactive Visualization

Like all image-based models, our model captures the scene with non-uniform fidelity. Based on the user desired viewpoint, our model has three levels of fidelity. The first level is when the user viewpoint is inside a panorama triplet. In this case, the output image is rendered by projectively texture mapping the morphing mesh with a blend of the three triplet panoramas. The blending weights are defined by the user's viewpoint barycentric coordinates inside the triplet triangle. The user can look in any direction from within the triangle triple, leveraging the complete 360° textures and meshes. In the case where the user is not within any panorama triplet, we can either display nothing to the user or we can use the most recently visited panorama triplet at the cost of additional distortion.

The second level of fidelity is when the user viewpoint is near an acquisition path segment. In this case, we switch to a morph between the two panoramas of the segment endpoints. The segment is shorter than the triplet triangle edge, and only two panoramas are blended, so the quality of the output image is higher than in the inside the triplet case. Again, the user can look in any direction from anywhere along the acquisition path segment.

The third and highest level of fidelity of our image-based model is when the user viewpoint is near one of the panorama acquisition locations. In this case the output image is rendered by texturing the morphing mesh with a single panorama, which approaches a resampling of the panoramic frame and therefore has high fidelity in any view direction. Note that we only clamp blending weights for texture color and not for 3D viewpoint position, so that tracked HMD navigation in VR is natural and does not "stick".

We have designed a VR visualization interface that allows the user to take advantage intuitively of the highest model fidelity available in the proximity of their viewpoint. The interface shows a map of panorama acquisition locations in the bottom right corner of the frame (Fig. 1, c and d). The map shows the acquisition path segments (Fig. 1, e) and the current user location. As during acquisition, the user can easily align their visualization location with one of the panorama acquisition locations. There are hundreds of acquisition locations and so there is always one nearby. The typical navigation pattern is to translate the viewpoint to an acquisition location, to pan and tilt the viewpoint while remaining at the acquisition location to take advantage of the highest fidelity of our image-based model, and then to move to the next acquisition location, either along an acquisition path segment, or through a panorama triplet triangle.

7   Results and Discussion

Our AR acquisition device uses a Microsoft HoloLens [18] AR HMD coupled with a Samsung Gear 360 panoramic camera [24]. The camera captures $3,840 \times 1,920$ panoramic frames at 30fps. We visualize our image-based models interactively and immersively using an HTC Vive HMD [12]. Our image-based models are also suitable for visualization on conventional displays.

7.1   AR Guided Acquisition

To demonstrate our system, we acquired several indoor environments (one environment at multiple resolutions), and we conducted a user study in which ten novice participants acquired a reference environment. The acquisition cell size is $0.5\,m \times 0.5\,m$, and the path segment length is $0.25\,m$, unless otherwise specified.

Test Scenes. Table 1 gives acquisition details for our four test environments. All were acquired with hundreds of evenly distributed panoramas in 8 min or less.

We acquired the *Office* scene at multiple spatial resolutions (Table 2). As the length of the grid cell is halved, the grid cell area is quartered, so the number of grid cell panoramas will quadruple, assuming the scene is an open floor area. For floor areas with obstacles, this factor varies: from Table 2, the number of grid cell panoramas grows by a factor of 2.82 and of 3.55 as grid cell length shrinks from

0.5 m to 0.25 m to 0.125 m. Since the panoramic video camera records continuously as the user moves along the acquisition path, we expect *acquisition time* to double (not quadruple) when the grid cell's length is halved; direct movement between two locations requires the same path regardless of grid cell size. Once floor obstacles are included, this factor is affected by the user's ability to visit all accessible parts of the floor non-redundantly. From Table 2, acquisition times grow by a factor of 1.29 and 2.18, respectively.

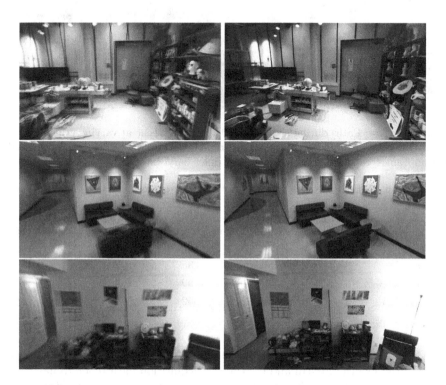

Fig. 7. Results for *Lab* (top row), *Lobby* (middle row), and *Home* (bottom row) environments, with viewpoint between acquisition locations (left), and near an acquisition location (right).

Table 1. Acquisition performance for four indoor environments.

Environment (Figures)	Floor space [m] × [m]	Path length [m]	Capture time [s]	Grid cell panoramas	Path segm. panoramas
Lab (Figs. 1(c, d) and 7 top)	10 × 13	172	307	244	688
Home (Figs. 1e and 7 btm)	7 × 10	105	284	157	420
Lobby (Fig. 7 mid)	9 × 9	131	248	215	524
Office (Fig. 8)	2.5 × 4	31	86	35	124

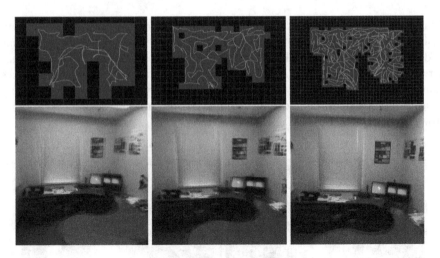

Fig. 8. Top row: Paths during acquisition of the *Office* scene at varying grid cell sizes: 0.5 m (left), 0.25 m (middle), and 0.125 m (right). Bottom row: Corresponding visualization frames, rendered from a panorama triplet barycenter.

Table 2. Acquisition performance for *Office* environment as a function of grid cell size.

Grid size [m] × [m]	Path length [m]	Time [s]	Grid cell panoramas	Path segm. panoramas
.5 × .5	31	86	35	62
.25 × .25	39	111	99	154
.125 × .125	81	242	352	648

The actual acquisition paths corresponding to Table 2 are shown in Fig. 8. For grid cell length of 0.5 m and 0.25 m, the acquisition path tends to have long straight portions, but in the case of a grid cell length of 0.125 m, the trajectory tends to be made up of small imprecise loops. Limitations in comfortable head and neck motion leads to gradual rather than sharp turns which would be needed to efficiently sample the space at such a high resolution.

Acquisition User Study. An important goal of our work is to develop an acquisition system that allows novice users to acquire a complex indoor environment in minutes. We have gathered initial evidence for reaching this goal in a user study with ten first-time users of our system who acquired the same large indoor environment (i.e., the *Lab*). The users, who had general experience with AR/VR HMDs, were asked to traverse every accessible grid cell in the room that they felt they could reasonably reach. The users were briefed in five minutes or less on how to use the acquisition system. The briefing did not include a suggested scanning strategy so as not to bias participants.

The users acquired the 10 m x 13 m scene in an average time of 7 min 5 s (min: 4 min 57 s, max: 11 min 1 s), using a grid cell size of 0.5 m × 0.5 m. On average, 268 grid cell panoramas were acquired (min: 217, max: 365). Average distance traveled was 196 m (min: 144 m, max: 232 m). Figure 9 shows the acquisition paths for the ten users. There is great variability in the acquisition paths: some users cover the floor space with large cycles around the perimeter then fill in missing interior regions, while others cover the floor space progressively with paths reminiscent of space-filling curves. Users also had different completeness criteria; because the environment was a complex scene with many floor obstacles, users differed in their willingness to move into hard-to-reach areas to achieve greater coverage. In all cases, acquisition resulted in hundreds of evenly-spaced panoramas that allow for quality interactive visualization of the environment.

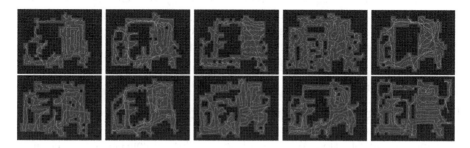

Fig. 9. Acquisition paths (blue lines) and explored grid cells (green) for first-time users of our system (grid cell of 0.5 m × 0.5 m). (Color figure online)

7.2 Panorama Morphing Setup

The acquired data is processed offline to prepare for interactive visualization. For our largest environment, i.e., the *Lab*, the entire offline processing took 227 min. Referring back to our system pipeline (Fig. 2), for the typical panorama shown in Figs. 5 and 6, the Registration Refinement stage finds 1,369 pairwise feature matches, 775 of which are inliers used during registration refinement. Registration refinement reduces the average feature reprojection error from 9.5 pixels to 1.3 pixels, which is a small error relative to the high panorama resolution of 3,840 × 1,920. For a typical panorama triplet, the Feature-Based Morphing Mesh Construction stage results in a morphing mesh with 1,126 points and 1,858 triangles, which is then refined in the Geometry-Based Morphing Mesh Enrichment stage to a final morphing mesh with 1,276 points and 2,158 triangles.

7.3 VR Guided Visualization

Our image-based models visualize the captured environments in the VR HMD at 90 fps in stereo, by rendering the current low-polygonal-count 3D morphing mesh with projective texture mapping. High fidelity is achieved near one of the hundreds of panorama acquisition locations that sample the floor space uniformly, where the visualization converges to a resampling of the high-resolution spherical panorama acquired (e.g., Figs. 1c and 7, top right). Moderately high fidelity is achieved along the acquisition path, where the two segment endpoint panoramas are merged (e.g., Fig. 1e). The lowest level of fidelity is found at the center of the panorama triplet, when undersampled geometry can lead to ghosting artifacts (e.g., ceiling lights in Fig. 1d, vertical black lines on the far wall in Fig. 7, top left, or the far end of the long hallway in Fig. 7, middle right). Using the visualization map, the user can align their viewpoint with an acquisition location or segment where visualization fidelity is highest. Movement through the visualization is orientation-preserving and non-disorienting.

Figure 8 shows visualization frames rendered from the center of panorama triplets for the three image-based models of the *Office* scene with decreasing acquisition grid cell size. As expected, the quality of the visualization increases, as a smaller grid cell size reduces the distance from the output viewpoint to the closest acquisition location, which reduces ghosting.

7.4   Limitations

The accuracy of geometry points in the morphing meshes is limited by the coarseness of the geometric model that our AR HMD acquires, and by the quality of the panorama registration. We also enforce topological consistency of the morphing mesh across the panorama triplet, which caps the maximum fidelity of the morphing mesh. Future work could explore a general, and not unit sphere-based, 3D triangulation of feature and geometry points, that allows for folds as the viewpoint translates within a panorama triplet.

Our selection of neighboring panoramas from which to find correspondences and feature points implies small baselines for optimization and triangulation. Another challenge is the registration of panoramas from adjacent rooms connected by a open door. Such panoramas do not share many common features as the panorama from room A sees only a small part of room B, and vice versa. Therefore, with the current implementation, multi room environments require assembling the overall image-based model from individual room models.

Our panoramic camera is mounted above the wearer's head, which results in a visualization that appears taller than the acquiring user's height. Since the morphing meshes are rendered in 3D, we do currently provide limited support for vertical viewpoint translation, as needed for example to cover the small range of vertical translation when walking with the VR HMD. Future prototypes could place the cameras at a lower height to better match a typical user height.

8   Conclusions and Future Work

We have presented a system for fast image-based modeling and rendering of indoor spaces, which guides the user with an AR interface towards complete and dense acquisition. A VR interface enables the user to optimize output image quality. The results of our pilot study are promising; however, we plan to conduct additional and more formal user studies to validate the effectiveness of the AR interface and the acceptability of the resulting VR visualization.

We currently only support static scenes; future work could support dynamic scenes by injecting moving geometry captured with RGB-D sensors into a captured scene. Automatic detection and removal of dynamic regions of the image-based model would also help deal with accidental intruders that interfere with acquisition, opening up the possibility of acquiring busy, in-use spaces. We are also interested in real-time use of image-based features for saliency or view-dependency during acquisition, which could allow our system to prioritize regions that would be of greater complexity or of greater interest to a viewer.

We believe our work demonstrates that image-based modeling and rendering of inside-looking-out indoor spaces can efficiently produce quality models that are ready to be integrated into applications.

Acknowledgments. We thank the ART research group at Purdue University for their feedback during development. This work was supported in part by the United States National Science Foundation under Grant DGE-1333468.

References

1. Ahn, J., Wohn, K.: Interactive scan planning for heritage recording. Multimed. Tools Appl. **75**(7), 3655–3675 (2016)
2. Aliaga, D.G., Carlbom, I.: Plenoptic stitching: a scalable method for reconstructing 3D interactive walk throughs. In: Proceedings of the 28th Annual Conference on Computer Graphics and Interactive Techniques, pp. 443–450. ACM (2001)
3. Bradley, D., Brunton, A., Fiala, M., Roth, G.: Image-based navigation in real environments using panoramas. In: IEEE International Workshop on Haptic Audio Visual Environments and their Applications, p. 3, October 2005
4. Chiang, C.C., Way, D.L., Shieh, J.W., Shen, L.S.: A new image morphing technique for smooth vista transitions in panoramic image-based virtual environment. In: Proceedings of the ACM Symposium on Virtual Reality Software and Technology, VRST 1998, pp. 81–90 (1998)
5. Dai, A., Nießner, M., Zollhöfer, M., Izadi, S., Theobalt, C.: BundleFusion: real-time globally consistent 3D reconstruction using on-the-fly surface reintegration. ACM Trans. Graph. (TOG) **36**(3), 24 (2017)
6. Davis, A., Levoy, M., Durand, F.: Unstructured light fields. In: Computer Graphics Forum. vol. 31, pp. 305–314. Wiley Online Library (2012)
7. DiVerdi, S., Wither, J., Höllerer, T.: All around the map: online spherical panorama construction. Comput. Graph. **33**(1), 73–84 (2009)
8. Dong, S., Höllerer, T.: Real-time re-textured geometry modeling using microsoft HoloLens (2018)

9. Fan, X., Zhang, L., Brown, B., Rusinkiewicz, S.: Automated view and path planning for scalable multi-object 3D scanning. ACM Trans. Graph. **35**(6), 239:1–239:13 (2016)

10. Fischler, M.A., Bolles, R.C.: Random sample consensus: a paradigm for model fitting with applications to image analysis and automated cartography. In: Readings in Computer Vision, pp. 726–740. Elsevier (1987)

11. Hedman, P., Ritschel, T., Drettakis, G., Brostow, G.: Scalable inside-out image-based rendering. ACM Trans. Graph. (TOG) **35**(6), 231 (2016)

12. HTC: VIVE (2017). www.vive.com/us

13. Huang, J., Chen, Z., Ceylan, D., Jin, H.: 6-DOF VR videos with a single 360-camera. In: 2017 IEEE Virtual Reality (VR), pp. 37–44. IEEE (2017)

14. Jung, J.-H., Kang, H.-B.: An efficient arbitrary view generation method using panoramic-based image morphing. In: Huang, D.-S., Li, K., Irwin, G.W. (eds.) ICIC 2006. LNCS, vol. 4113, pp. 1207–1212. Springer, Heidelberg (2006). https://doi.org/10.1007/11816157_150

15. Kawai, N.: A simple method for light field resampling. In: ACM SIGGRAPH 2017 Posters, SIGGRAPH 2017, pp. 15:1–15:2 (2017)

16. Kawai, N., Audras, C., Tabata, S., Matsubara, T.: Panorama image interpolation for real-time walkthrough. In: ACM SIGGRAPH Posters, pp. 33:1–33:2 (2016)

17. Kolhatkar, S., Laganaire, R.: Real-time virtual viewpoint generation on the GPU for scene navigation. In: 2010 Canadian Conference on Computer and Robot Vision, pp. 55–62, May 2010

18. Microsoft: Microsoft HoloLens (2017). www.microsoft.com/en-us/hololens

19. Pagani, A., Gava, C.C., Cui, Y., Krolla, B., Hengen, J.M., Stricker, D.: Dense 3D point cloud generation from multiple high-resolution spherical images. In: VAST, pp. 17–24 (2011)

20. Pagani, A., Stricker, D.: Structure from motion using full spherical panoramic cameras. In: 2011 IEEE International Conference on Computer Vision Workshops (ICCV Workshops), pp. 375–382. IEEE (2011)

21. Pan, Q., Reitmayr, G., Drummond, T.W.: Interactive model reconstruction with user guidance. In: 2009 8th IEEE International Symposium on Mixed and Augmented Reality, pp. 209–210, October 2009

22. Pankratz, F., Klinker, G.: [POSTER] AR4AR: using augmented reality for guidance in augmented reality systems setup. In: 2015 IEEE International Symposium on Mixed and Augmented Reality (ISMAR), pp. 140–143. IEEE (2015)

23. Rusinkiewicz, S., Hall-Holt, O., Levoy, M.: Real-time 3D model acquisition. ACM Trans. Graph. (TOG) **21**(3), 438–446 (2002)

24. Samsung: Gear 360 Camera (2017). www.samsung.com/us/explore/gear-360

25. Shi, F.: Panorama interpolation for image-based navigation. Master's thesis, University of Ottawa (2007)

26. Tuite, K., Snavely, N., Hsiao, D.Y., Smith, A.M., Popović, Z.: Reconstructing the world in 3D: bringing games with a purpose outdoors. In: Proceedings of the Fifth International Conference on the Foundations of Digital Games, pp. 232–239. ACM (2010)

27. Tuite, K., Snavely, N., Hsiao, D.Y., Tabing, N., Popovic, Z.: PhotoCity: training experts at large-scale image acquisition through a competitive game. In: Proceedings of the SIGCHI Conference on Human Factors in Computing Systems, pp. 1383–1392. ACM (2011)

28. Xiao, J., Shah, M.: Tri-view morphing. Comput. Vis. Image Underst. **96**(3), 345–366 (2004)

29. Xu, K.: 3D attention-driven depth acquisition for object identification. ACM Trans. Graph. **35**(6), 238:1–238:14 (2016)

30. Zhang, Y., Zhu, Z.: Walk-able and stereo virtual tour based on spherical panorama matrix. In: De Paolis, L.T., Bourdot, P., Mongelli, A. (eds.) AVR 2017. LNCS, vol. 10324, pp. 50–58. Springer, Cham (2017). https://doi.org/10.1007/978-3-319-60922-5_4

31. Zhao, Q., Wan, L., Feng, W., Zhang, J., Wong, T.T.: Cube2Video: navigate between cubic panoramas in real-time. IEEE Trans. Multimed. **15**(8), 1745–1754 (2013)

32. Zhao, Q., Feng, W., Wan, L., Zhang, J.: SPHORB: a fast and robust binary feature on the sphere. Int. J. Comput. Vis. **113**(2), 143–159 (2015)

Haptics and 3D Audio

KinesTouch: 3D Force-Feedback Rendering for Tactile Surfaces

Antoine Costes[1,2(✉)], Fabien Danieau[1], Ferran Argelaguet-Sanz[2],
Anatole Lécuyer[2], and Philippe Guillotel[1]

[1] Technicolor R&I, Rennes, France
antoine.costes@technicolor.com
[2] Univ. Rennes, Inria, CNRS, IRISA, Rennes, France

Abstract. In this paper, we introduce the KinesTouch, a novel approach
for tactile screen enhancement providing four types of haptic feedback
with a single force-feedback device: compliance, friction, fine roughness,
and shape. We present the design and implementation of a corresponding
set of haptic effects as well as a proof-of-concept setup. Regarding friction
in particular, we propose a novel effect based on large lateral motion that
increases or diminishes the sliding velocity between the finger and the
screen. A user study was conducted on this effect to confirm its ability
to produce distinct sliding sensations. Visual cues were confirmed to
influence sliding judgments, but further studies would help clarifying the
role of tactile cues. Finally, we showcase several use cases illustrating the
possibilities offered by the KinesTouch to enhance 2D and 3D interactions
on tactile screens in various contexts.

Keywords: Touchscreen · Surface haptics · Sliding · Force feedback

1 Introduction

Touchscreens have become ubiquitous in human-computer interaction. They
enable freehand direct interaction with 2D and 3D content and they are effectively used in numerous applications. They can be found everywhere, from public
ticket machines to mobile phones and laptops.

Despite their intrinsic qualities, as for today, touchscreens still often lack tactile sensations. Irrespective of the visual content, they feel flat, rigid, smooth and
static under the finger. Although touchscreens take advantage of finger dexterity,
they do not exploit finger sensitivity.

The haptic enhancement of touchscreens is a relatively young and active
research field known as "surface haptics" [7]. An impressive amount of work has
already been done to conceive and develop such technologies in the last decade [3,
19,23,35,36]. Most efforts have been concentrated on generating various types of
vibration that can alter the physics of the finger sliding on the screen, providing
friction and even small relief sensations [17,36]. However, such approaches do not
allow to display other haptic properties such as stiffness or large-scale shapes.

© Springer Nature Switzerland AG 2018
P. Bourdot et al. (Eds.): EuroVR 2018, LNCS 11162, pp. 97–116, 2018.
https://doi.org/10.1007/978-3-030-01790-3_6

A few solutions have proposed a touchscreen with kinesthetic feedback, i.e., able to move in space rather than vibrate, in order to involve spatial proprioception. Some approaches used parallel platforms for co-localized inclination rendering [16,20], eventually combined with variable friction [10], but they kept a focus on rendering geometric features rather than material properties like stiffness, slipperiness or roughness. Sinclair et al. have proposed a remarkable solution combining 1-DoF kinesthetic and force feedback [28,29], showcasing many interesting perceptual and interaction possibilities. Yet, besides its limitation to one axis, their device remains cumbersome and complex to spread out. The work of Takanaka et al. [30] is the only one, to our knowledge, to provide a touchscreen with lateral motion to evoke haptic properties. Interestingly, they chose to keep a non-slipping contact with the screen and simulated inertia and stiffness rather than sliding the screen against the finger to simulate friction or slipperiness. Although many innovative technologies have been developed to provide co-localized friction effects, the potential of the lateral motion of the screen under the finger has not been investigated yet.

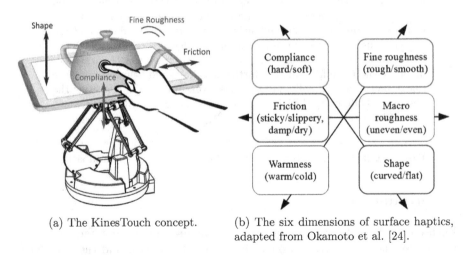

(a) The KinesTouch concept.   (b) The six dimensions of surface haptics, adapted from Okamoto et al. [24].

Fig. 1. The KinesTouch approach provides four different types of haptic feedback to a touchscreen.

In this paper, we propose to use a single force-feedback device to provide four different types of haptic feedback to a tactile tablet: Shape, Stiffness, Roughness, and Sliding (see Fig. 1). In particular, our Sliding effect alters the sliding velocity of the finger on the screen through large lateral movements, which constitute a novel approach in friction rendering.

In the remainder of this paper, we first present related work on surface haptics in the light of haptic perception of surfaces. Then, the KinesTouch concept is introduced together with our set of haptic effects. The technical feasibility of our approach is then demonstrated with a proof-of-concept prototype. The results of a user study focused on the Sliding effect are presented and discussed. Finally, several use cases of our system are exposed.

2   Related Work

2.1   Dimensionality of Surface Haptics

The dimensionality of real and artificial textures perception has been investigated in manifold studies. In a survey paper synthesizing over forty years of research, Okamoto et al. proposed five psychophysical dimensions that synthesize state of the art results: (1) compliance (hardness), (2) friction, (3) fine roughness, (4) macro roughness, and (5) warmness [24] (see Fig. 1b).

Yem and Kajimoto [39] suggested a correspondence between these five dimensions and the different types of tactile receptors in the skin. The four types of mechanoreceptors are known to be especially receptive to a specific stimuli: static pressure for SA-1, local deformation of the skin for SA-II, rapid lateral skin stretch for FA-I and high frequency vibrations for FA-II [14]. In addition, thermoreceptors are responsible for temperature gradient sensing [9]. Like Okamoto et al., they did not consider the kinesthetic sense, that is the perception of one's body movements, which is crucial to perceive large scale shapes.

The division between fine and macro roughness, was confirmed by several studies [4,11,12] many decades after it was hypothesized by Katz [15] under the famous name of "duplex theory". This theory states that fine and coarse asperities are mediated by two distinct perceptual mechanisms, the first one relying on contact vibrations and the second one involving pressure spatial distribution. It was notably found that contact vibrations are necessary to perceive asperities under 0.1 mm, indicating a perceptual shift around this scale [12]. It is noticeable that these two properties are spontaneously explored with two distinct strategies, namely lateral motion and static contact. These two "exploratory movements", identified by Lederman and Klatsky decades ago [18], are appropriate ways to elicit the most relevant stimulus, namely static pressure distribution or rubbing vibrations.

Another exploratory movement named "contour following" [18], aims at inspecting the global shape or volume of an object with large movements. In this case the kinesthesia (or proprioception) is likely to be predominant in the perceptual process. Therefore, there should be a perceptual shift from macro roughness to shape similar to the one from fine to macro roughness. The location of this shift is obviously in the vicinity of a finger width, although it would be reasonable to expect some overlap, similarly to fine and macro roughness. In the remainder of this paper, we will call this sixth dimension the "shape" dimension.

2.2   Surface Haptics Systems

Vibrators and vibrotactile feedback have been early embedded in commercial touchscreen products and can be used for fine roughness simulation. But many researchers have proposed original ways to enrich touchscreens with an additional vibrator placed either on the nail [2], between several fingers and the screen [6], on the device [5, 38, 41] or both on the device and on haptic gloves [13]. In particular, Romano and Kuchenbecker used a high-quality one-dimensional vibration to display compelling texture details through an actuated stylus, according to normal contact force and lateral speed [25].

Several variable friction devices have been developed, either using ultrasonic vibration [19, 23] or electrovibration [3, 21]. In both approaches, friction can be modulated to produce texture effects and even 3D pattern features [17, 36]. Some researchers also chose to instrument the finger, either with vibrators [2, 6] or with a lateral-force proxy [26, 27, 37]. Several solutions producing mechanical planar vibrations [33] or short-range movements [22] were also proposed. However all these approaches had no force or motion abilities in the normal direction, and thus could not provide compliance and large shapes sensations.

Parallel platforms were used for co-localized curvature feedback [16], notably the "SurfTics" [10] and the "ForceTab" [20] devices. Another approach presented in [30] consists in a touchscreen with planar force feedback and large translation and rotation abilities. These approaches were focused on shape rendering and did not address other dimensions of haptic perception.

The "TouchMover" device [28] is a touchscreen actuated and moved using force feedback in the normal direction, showcasing interesting applications notably in volumetric data manipulation. The second version [29] includes vibrators that render fine shape details at contact point. The normal force-feedback allows for stiffness or inertia simulation and shape rendering, but no lateral friction sensations. Besides its limitation to one axis and two psychophysical dimensions, the TouchMover remains rather cumbersome and complex to spread out, involving custom and expensive mechanics and electronics.

There are actually rather few systems aiming at simulating a wider range of haptic sensations. The device designed by Yem and Kajimoto [39] is able to simulate up to four psychophysical dimensions of texture perception: compliance, friction, fine and macro roughness. But this system is finger-mounted and not touchscreen-based, and it does not co-localize visual and haptic displays. Culbertson and Kuchenbecker [8] combined a pen-shaped force-feedback rendering stickiness through tangential forces with an high-quality vibrator rendering hardness through tapping transients and fine roughness through vibrations.

Table 1 provides an overview of previous contributions in surface haptics, with the type of haptic sensation they have addressed. Interestingly enough, these previous systems are able to simulate only one or two psychophysical dimensions. Temperature and macro roughness were not taken into account here, as we could not find representative examples of touchscreen enhancement involving one of them combined with another dimension.

3   The KinesTouch Approach

The KinesTouch approach enriches touchscreen interactions with a set of tactile and kinesthetic effects in both normal and lateral directions. When the user

Table 1. Main previous approaches in surface haptics. Most of them address only one or two psychophysical dimensions.

		Addressed psychophysical dimensions			
Approach	References	Compliance	Friction	Shape	Fine Roughness
Normal force feedback	[28]	Stiffness	-	Shape	-
	[29]	Inertia	-	Shape	-
Normal kinesthetic feedback	[20]	-	-	Shape	-
Lateral force feedback	[22]	-	Static & reduced friction	Smooth bumps	-
	[26]	-	-	Bumps	-
	[27]	-	-	Bumps	Increased roughness
	[30]	Lateral stiffness	-	Lateral inertia	-
Lateral force feedback + vibrations	[8]	Tapping transients	Increased friction	-	Increased roughness
Rotational kinesthetic feedback	[40]	-	-	Curvature	-
	[16]	-	-	Curvature	-
	[10]	-	-	Curvature, Edges	-
Ultrasonic friction reduction	[34]	-	-	-	Reduced roughness
	[36]	-	Reduced friction	Edges, smooth bumps	-
	[23]	-	Reduced friction	-	-
Electrostatic friction amplification	[3]	-	Increased friction	-	-
	[17]	-	-	Bumps	-
Finger-mounted vibrations	[2]	-	-	Edges, bumps	-
	[6]	-	-	Edges, bumps	-
Electrotactile	[1]	-	-	-	Increased roughness
KinesTouch: 3D force and kinesthetic feedback		Stiffness	Increased sliding, reduced sliding	Shape, bumps, edges	Increased roughness

touches an object or an image displayed on the touchscreen, the screen is given forces or motion simulating various haptic properties: it can resist more or less to pressure to render material stiffness, move up and down according to object's shape, vibrate during a stroke to evoke texture roughness, or slide laterally to change the slipperiness sensations.

In the following sections, we present our set of four co-localized haptic effects. We will focus on the case of using a 3-DOF impedance device for the control law. But the KinesTouch approach is scalable and could be used with higher end 6-DoF haptic interfaces that could allow for even more effects than what we propose hereafter.

3.1   Notations

In the remainder of this paper, vectors and matrices will be expressed in the fixed reference frame with positive z upwards. The screen is considered to be horizontal, parallel to the xy plan. Also: X_0 will refer to the 3D center position of the workspace, X_t will refer to the 3D screen position with respect to X_0,

f will refer to the 2D finger position on the screen, $\mathbf{I}_3$ will refer to the identity matrix, e_z will refer to the vertical unit vector, K_{max} will refer to a high stiffness value, depending on hardware performance, used for position control[1] (1 N/mm in our setup).

3.2   Stiffness Effect

The Stiffness effect allows the user to feel a resistance to deformation when they push an object on the screen. It simulates the elasticity of a material, and address the compliance perceptual dimension. The effect consists in a normal opposing force that increases with penalty, as shown in Fig. 2. The two other directions of the touchscreen are locked in position.

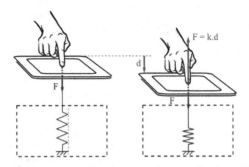

Fig. 2. Stiffness effect: the screen provides an elastic force under pressure.

Using an elastic deformation model, the control law of our Stiffness effect is:

$$\mathbf{F}_{stiffness} = \begin{bmatrix} K_{max} & 0 & 0 \\ 0 & K_{max} & 0 \\ 0 & 0 & k_{mat} \end{bmatrix} (\mathbf{X}_0 - \mathbf{X}_t) \tag{1}$$

with k_{mat} the simulated stiffness.

3.3   Shape Effect

The Shape effect allows the user to feel the 3D shape of an object. It reproduces reliefs that are larger than a finger and need active exploration to be perceived. The effect consists in a normal displacement corresponding to the change in vertical projection of the 2D finger position on the object's 3D shape, as shown in Fig. 3. The two other directions of the touchscreen are locked in position (i.e., there is no lateral motion).

---

[1] Impedance force-feedback devices provide forces to their end-effector, while measuring its position. Although they can't act directly on position, they can still be used for pseudo position control with a high stiffness force linking the measured position to the desired one.

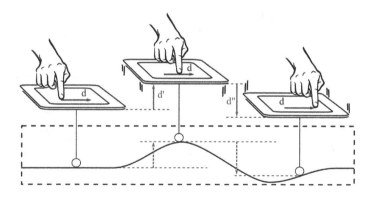

Fig. 3. Shape effect: the vertical displacement during stroke reproduces reliefs.

The control law of our Shape effect is:

$$\boldsymbol{F}_{\text{shape}} = K_{\max}\, \mathbf{I}_3\, (\boldsymbol{X}_0 + h(\boldsymbol{f})\, \boldsymbol{e}_z - \boldsymbol{X}_t) \tag{2}$$

with $h(x, y)$ the vertical projection of the finger position onto the 3D shape.

The shape is accessed "from the top": only its visible upper part, relatively to the horizontal plane, can be explored. However, a simple rotation of the shape in the virtual space allows to access its bottom part.

3.4 Roughness Effect

The Roughness effect allows the user to feel vibrations evoking a periodic grating when they stroke an object on the screen. It renders the fine roughness property, modeled by a small spatial period. The effect consists in an oscillating force taking into account both the simulated spatial period and the finger exploration velocity, as shown in Fig. 4a. The touchscreen is otherwise locked in position.

$$\boldsymbol{F}_{\text{roughness}} = \delta \sin(2\pi\lambda \|\dot{\boldsymbol{f}}\|)\, \boldsymbol{e}_z + K_{\max}\, \mathbf{I}_3\, (\boldsymbol{X}_0 - \boldsymbol{X}_t) \tag{3}$$

with δ the grating depth, λ the grating spatial period.

3.5 Sliding Effect

The Sliding effect provides various sliding sensations to the user when they stroke an object on the screen. As it modifies the sliding phenomenon between the screen and the finger, it addresses the friction perceptual dimension. It consists in a tangential movement of the screen meant to increase or diminish the relative sliding, that is the velocity difference, with the finger. We expect two different sensations corresponding to the two possible sliding directions: a "Follow effect" and a "Reverse effect" which are described hereafter. The touchscreen motion is locked here in position in the normal direction.

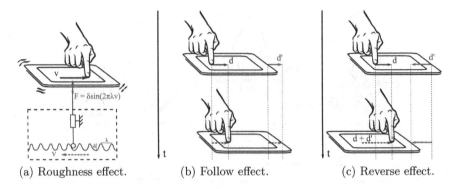

(a) Roughness effect.   (b) Follow effect.   (c) Reverse effect.

Fig. 4. Roughness effect: the screen vibrates during stroke to simulate roughness **(a)**. Sliding effect: the screen moves laterally to cancel **(b)** or increase **(c)** relative sliding.

The "Follow effect", illustrated in Fig. 4b, consists in moving the screen the same way the finger moves on the screen, so that relative sliding is decreased or even kept close to zero. In this case, while the finger moves in the reference frame, its position on the screen remains almost static.

The "Reverse effect", illustrated in Fig. 4c, consists in moving the screen in the opposite direction to finger's movement, so that relative sliding is increased.

The Sliding effect is achieved with the combination of two forces: a "moving force" proportional to finger's tangential velocity, and a damping force in the binormal direction:

$$\boldsymbol{F}_{\text{slipperiness}} = \alpha\, \dot{\boldsymbol{f}} - \nu\, \dot{\boldsymbol{f}} \wedge \boldsymbol{e}_z + K_{\max}\left(\boldsymbol{X}_0 \cdot \boldsymbol{e}_z - \boldsymbol{X}_t \cdot \boldsymbol{e}_z\right) \qquad (4)$$

with $\alpha \in [-1, 1]$ the slipperiness coefficient and ν the damping coefficient.

3.6   Idle Behavior

When the screen is not touched, it should stay still or move back to the center of the workspace, so that the force-feedback device remains close to its neutral position. This is done by applying a simple centering force instead of one of the previous effects:

$$\boldsymbol{F}_{idle} = K_{\max}\, \mathbf{I}_3 \left(\boldsymbol{X}_0 - \boldsymbol{X}_t\right) \qquad (5)$$

4   The KinesTouch Prototype

In this section, we describe the design and implementation of our prototype using a standard tablet and Novint Falcon haptic device. We designed a custom end-effector in order to be able to attach the tablet on the haptic device handle, and a prediction-correction algorithm to compensate the touch tracking latency. We also present the handling of synchronization between visual and haptic loops, and the control law for the haptic rendering.

4.1   Hardware

The Falcon is a standard 3-DoF impedance haptic device, initially designed for the gaming industry. We combined it with a Galaxy Tab SM-T810, which exhibits rather high resolution (2048×1536), comfortable size (9.7") and an acceptable weight (389g).

Assembly of Tablet and Force-Feedback Device. The Falcon's grip has several buttons and is removable, but a security mechanism deactivates the device when the grip is removed, detecting the electrical contact with the grip. This problem was overcome by unmounting the default grip and keeping only the coupling part and electronic circuit. A tablet adapter, shown in Fig. 5a, that reproduced the interlock while offering a flat shape to affix the tablet, was 3D-printed. As the precise relative positioning of the tablet was not of importance for the haptic effects presented in this paper, it was affixed to the adapter with a simple velcro grip. The Falcon was then rotated by 90 degrees and positioned sideways so that it "pushed forward" the tablet vertically, as shown in Fig. 5b.

(a) 3D printed adapter.   (b) Global setup.

Fig. 5. KinesTouch prototype.

4.2   Software

Handling Latency Issues. Besides the visual display, the tablet application is also responsible for touch tracking and filtering. In practice, the built-in touch tracking of the Galaxy Tab SM-T810 has a latency of a few dozens of ms, and the Unity application has a refresh rate of 60 Hz. This results in a delay in the position measurement up to 2 cm in usual slide movements, which is problematic for real-time haptic rendering. Furthermore, despite the high resolution of the screen, instantaneous touch velocity estimation suffers from spikes due to pixel quantization. For these reasons, touch position and velocity were computed and filtered before being sent and used in the haptic rendering loop, according to the following prediction algorithm, inspired from [31].

First, measured touch position f_{mes} is converted in real-world meter coordinates. Then, a simple linear prediction is applied to measured touched position:

$$f_{\text{pred}} = f_{\text{mes}} + k_{\text{pred}} * (f_{\text{mes}} - f_{\text{mes}}^{prev}) \tag{6}$$

where f_{mes}^{prev} is the previous measured touch position and k_{pred} the filter parameter.

Finally, an exponential smoothing filter is applied to get the corrected position:

$$f = \alpha * f_{\text{pred}}(1 - \alpha) * f_{\text{pred}}^{prev} \tag{7}$$

where f_{pred}^{prev} is the previous predicted position and α the filter parameter.

The parameters were set after testings to: $k_{\text{pred}} = 8$ and $\alpha = 0.15$.

Instantaneous touch velocity is smoothed with an exponential smoothing filter with $\alpha = 0.45$.

Visual and Haptic Loops Synchronization. The haptic rendering is computed by a dedicated application running on a laptop and using the CHAI3D framework[2]. On the tablet, a Unity application is used for the visual rendering and the touch tracking. The two applications communicate with each other using the Open Sound Control (OSC) protocol[3]. As applications run at different rates, this communication is asynchronous. On both sides, incoming messages are treated in a specific thread and update global variable values which are then used in the main thread. A network connection is emulated through the USB cable connecting the tablet and the laptop, so that OSC communication latency is kept under 1ms.

The haptic rendering is mostly located in a haptic thread running at about 1000 Hz inside the CHAI3D application. An additional 60 Hz thread is meant to send the Falcon position to the tablet application. The synchronization of the two loops is illustrated in Fig. 6. In the Unity application, a main loop updates touch information, sends them to the CHAI3D application, and updates the visual display. This visual display compensates the Falcon movements so that when the tablet is moving, displayed objects remain immobile in the user's reference frame.

Transparency. In the previous descriptions of our haptic effects, the system is supposed to be perfectly transparent, with no inertia. However the weight of the touchscreen and effector are not negligible compared to the other involved forces, and have to be compensated by adding a constant opposite force in the control law.

---

[2] http://chai3d.org/download/license.
[3] http://opensoundcontrol.org/introduction-osc.

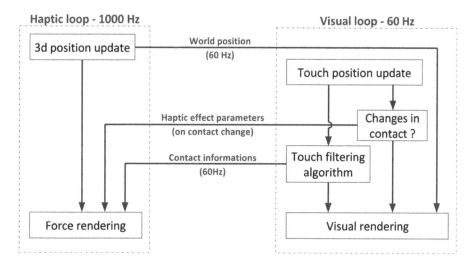

Fig. 6. Software architecture

4.3 Control Law

The final haptic rendering was obtained using a single control law that merged all our haptic effects:

$$\boldsymbol{F}_{\text{total}} = (mg + \delta\sin(2\pi\lambda||\dot{\boldsymbol{f}}||))\boldsymbol{e}_z + \alpha\dot{\boldsymbol{f}} - \nu\dot{\boldsymbol{f}} \wedge \boldsymbol{e}_z \\ + \mathbf{K}\,(\boldsymbol{X}_0 + h\boldsymbol{e}_z - \boldsymbol{X}_t) \tag{8}$$

with $\mathbf{K}$ the stabilization matrix, given in Table 2.

Table 2. Stabilization matrix values for the different effects.

Effect	Idle, shape, roughness	Stiffness	Sliding
K	$K_{\max}\,\mathbf{I}_3$	$\begin{bmatrix} K_{\max} & 0 & 0 \\ 0 & K_{\max} & 0 \\ 0 & 0 & k_{\text{mat}} \end{bmatrix}$	$\begin{bmatrix} 0 & 0 & 0 \\ 0 & 0 & 0 \\ 0 & 0 & K_{\max} \end{bmatrix}$

The Falcon was found to produce forces proportional, but not equal, to the forces requested through the CHAI3D API. This problem was overcome by applying a gain factor that was empirically found to of about 4.5 on two different Falcon devices to get the right forces. This is consistent with another study, although they found the gain to be equal to 3 [32]. This difference of value might be explained by the difference of CHAI3D version.

5   User Study

5.1   Introduction

We conducted a user study to evaluate the sensations produced by the KinesTouch prototype. Due to the large variety of our haptic effects, we have focused on our most innovative effect: the Sliding effect. Our choice was motivated by the fact that equivalents of Stiffness, Shape and Roughness effects have already been largely studied in the haptic literature. In contrast, the Sliding effect had never been explored in the literature and there are no clear assumptions on what the user's perception will be. Thus, we conducted a user study to answer the following question: are users able to consistently and efficiently discriminate different Sliding effects?

We compared three sliding sensations: the Reverse effect (REVERSE, see Fig. 4), the Follow effect (FOLLOW, see Fig. 4), and a control stimulus in which the tablet stays static (STATIC). Three hypotheses were tested:

- **H1**: different stimuli would produce different sensations.
- **H2**: seeing the moving screen contributes to distinguish between stimuli, i.e., visual cues increase the discrimination accuracy.
- **H3**: the smoothness of the screen diminishes the sensations produced, i.e., a tactile cues increase the discrimination accuracy.

5.2   Materials and Methods

Procedure. 18 volunteer unpaid subjects (16 male, age 31.2 ± 12.1) took part in the experiment which consisted in two sessions of about 45mn on different days. All of them were right-handed or ambidextrous.

After reading and signing a consent form, subjects were asked to seat with the right arm resting besides the tablet screen. For each trial, a narrow white area was displayed on the screen, and the subject was invited to slide their finger inside this area.

Each trial was composed of the active exploration of two stimuli, followed by a forced-choice question to designate on which one the subject felt the more sliding. Each stimuli lasted 3.5 s from the moment the screen was touched, then the screen turned to black and waited for the touch release to pass to the second stimulus or the question. The subject provided the answer to the question directly on the screen.

At the beginning of each session, two practice trials were first performed to ensure that subject understood the procedure. During these introductory trials, a moving target was displayed to suggest a back and forth movement at 0.5 Hz. Subjects were informed that the stimuli would be optimally felt within this range of velocities but were left free in their inspection otherwise.

Experimental Design. The experiment had three independent variables: the stimulus, the visual cues (i.e., seeing the tablet moving) and the tactile cues (i.e., screen roughness). Three pairwise comparisons were considered: REVERSE vs. FOLLOW, REVERSE vs. STATIC and FOLLOW vs. STATIC. To avoid order effects, the inverse comparisons were also considered.

In order to evaluate the importance of visual cues, half of the trials were performed with the whole mechanism being visible (V1, see Fig. 7a), and half with a black cover hiding the mechanism and its movements (V0, see Fig. 7b). In order to evaluate the importance of tactile cues, half of the trials were performed with a window privacy film applied on the screen (F1) and half without (F0). This transparent and electro-statically adhesive film had small but clearly perceptible reliefs that produced quite strong vibrations under the finger when being stroked. Affixed to the screen, there was no decrease in brightness but a tiny pixel diffraction on each relief. Trials were split in four condition blocks corresponding to the visual and tactile crossed conditions: V0F0, V0F1, V1F0, V1F1. In order to avoid order effects, the order of the blocks was given by the Latin-square method. In each of the two sessions, two condition blocks of 60 trials (10 repetitions for each of the 6 pairwise combinations) were performed.

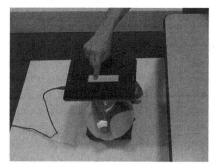
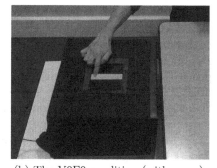

(a) The V1F0 condition (without cover).   (b) The V0F0 condition (with cover).

Fig. 7. General setup without and with cover.

Collected Data and Scoring. For each trial, the answer as well as the response time were recorded. In addition, a discrimination score for each subject was computed for each combination and factor (3 comparisons x 2 visual conditions x 2 tactile conditions). The discrimination score was computed as follows. First, each trial was counted as +1 or −1 according to stimulus chosen as the "more sliding" (the pair order being taken into account). For example, in a REVERSE vs. STATIC comparison, +1 will mean that REVERSE is considered to be more sliding that STATIC and vice-versa. Second, the data for each combination was normalized between [−1,1], showing the preference between the two stimuli. Finally, as we observed that subjects had different interpretations of the question, but were consistent in the stimulus they chose as "more sliding", we considered the absolute value of the discrimination score $[0,1]$.

Thus, as indicated in Table 3, a discrimination score of 0 indicated that the subject had no preference between the two stimuli and answered randomly (with a 50% accuracy), whereas a discrimination score of 1 indicated that the subject consistently chose one stimulus over the other (with a 100% accuracy).

Table 3. Correspondence between preference rate and discrimination score.

Preference rate	50%	60%	75%	80%	90%	95%	100%
Discrimination score	0	0.2	0.5	0.6	0.8	0.9	1

5.3   Results

Figure 8 show the distributions of the discrimination scores grouped according to the independent variables. On each figure, the red dot indicates the mean value, in addition to the median value and quartiles indicated by the box. An Anderson Darling normality test revealed that the data distribution were not normal, so we performed an aligned rank transform in order to enable a full factorial analysis using ANOVA. The three-way ANOVA comparison, visual and tactile cues vs. the discrimination score revealed a significant main effect on the visual condition ($F_{1,17} = 9.56$, p < 0.01). Post-hoc tests showed that this effect was significant (p < 0.05), V1 had a higher discrimination score ($M = 0.71$; $SD = 0.3$) compared with V0 ($M = 0.59$; $SD = 0.33$). These results support **H2**. In contrast, no main effect was found on the tactile condition ($F_{1,17} = 3.64$, p $= 0.073$). Yet, the results seems to suggest that there is an impact of the screen roughness: F0 ($M = 0.61$; $SD = 0.34$) compared to F1 ($M = 0.69$; $SD = 0.30$). Nevertheless the results do not support **H3**. Regarding the different comparisons, the ANOVA did not show a significant effect ($F_{2,17} = 3.00$, p $= 0.063$). Again, the results are close to the significance threshold. Post-hoc tests seems to suggest that subjects were less accurate for the REVERSE vs. STATIC comparison (p $= 0.053$). Finally, the ANOVA did not show any interaction effect.

Figure 8a shows the score distributions according the visual condition. Scores were significantly higher in the V1 condition, that is with the mechanism visible, than in the V0 condition, that is with a cover hiding it. Scores were also higher, but not significantly, in the F1 condition than in the F0 condition, i.e., with the textured film on the tablet rather than without. The distributions of the crossed visuo-tactile conditions are consistent with the results of the non-crossed conditions (Fig. 8a): scores were significantly higher with the mechanism visible, and not significantly higher with the textured film on the tablet rather than without. The highest average score is achieved, as expected, in the V1F1 condition, with half of the subjects having a score above 0.9.

Figure 8b shows that the scores were different regarding which stimuli were compared. When the Reverse and the Follow effects were compared, the scores

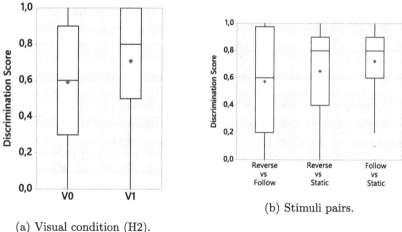

(a) Visual condition (H2).

(b) Stimuli pairs.

Fig. 8. Score distributions across visuo-tactile conditions and stimuli pairs. (Color figure online)

are distributed quite uniformly between 0 and 1. In contrast, for the comparison between the Follow effect and the control condition, half of the subjects have a discrimination score above 0.8 and a few have a score close to zero.

5.4   Discussion

Our results suggest that our Sliding effect is well and consistently discriminated by a great majority of subjects. Indeed, even in the least favorable condition, V0F0, half of the subjects had a score above 0.6, which means they were consistent in at least 80% of their answers. In the most favorable condition, V1F1, half of the subjects had a score of 0.9 or higher, indicating 95% of their answers were consistent. It is noticeable that in most conditions, score distributions were very large, ranging from 0 to 1, meaning that some subjects answered randomly and some subjects answered with a perfect consistency. The mean values, however, are above 0.5 in all conditions, which means that in average, whatever the condition, the subjects were consistent in their classification on at least 75% of the trials. Moreover, in almost all conditions this mean value is slightly lower than the median value, which indicates that it is worn down by a few values close to 0.

These results demonstrate that the subjects' ability to discriminate between the three stimuli were generally well above the random threshold with or without visual and/or tactile cues. As expected, visual cues had significant positive impact on discrimination. More surprisingly, the rough textured film on the screen had only a minor effect. We were expecting it to make the difference between stimuli very clear, as it produces strong vibrations according to sliding speed, in contrast with the very smooth screen that does not provide much sliding sensations.

However, an unexpected side effect was that the textured film was much less sticky than the screen, so that although the tactile sensations were stronger, it was much easier to stroke it fast. We think that this could have biased the answer about the "sliding" sensation, and could explain why subjects had different strategies to rank the stimuli. During the experiment, we noticed that most users had a clear ranking for a given visuo-tactile condition, but it was not necessary the same when the visual or tactile condition changed.

While the subjects were clearly able to discriminate the three stimuli, their ranking in terms of sliding was different among subjects and conditions. This might simply reflect the polysemy of the "sliding" term, and the very blurred vocabulary we have when it comes to describe tactile experiences. Further studies could disambiguate the sensations produced by the lateral sliding of the screen during stroke. For instance, asking the subjects about both roughness and sliding sensation could help to identify the dependence or independence of these two parameters. Also, a comparison with real material samples rather than between haptic effects might help avoiding misinterpretations and keep a low inter-subject variability.

6   Use Cases

The KinesTouch approach allows for various haptic effects based on force feedback and movements of the touchscreen in the 3D space. In this section we provide several illustrative use cases, illustrated Fig. 9 and in the accompany video, that we have been developed in order to show the potential of our approach.

Interacting with 3D Objects: In our first use case, the user can explore and interact with virtual 3D objects. This use case relies mainly on the Shape effect. In our implementation, the user can feel the shape of several objects such as a vase or rocks.

Perceiving the Texture of 2D Images and Pictures: In our second use case, KinesTouch is used to interact with a 2D image in order to feel its texture. This use case relies mainly on the Stiffness, Sliding, and Roughness effects. Thanks to these effects, the user can feel the changes in: local elasticity, friction, and relief in the picture. In our implementation, a picture of a plant landscape is used, associated with several "haptic maps", similarly to the normal maps used for textures in 3D engines (here: "stiffness map", "friction map" and "roughness map").

Augmenting Graphical User Interface and Haptic Widgets: In our third use case, KinesTouch is used to enhance interaction with a Graphical User Interface made of several buttons. This simple use case relies on the Stiffness effect. In our implementation, the buttons need to be pushed at a certain depth, but have different levels of stiffness, which makes them easy or hard to validate.

Exploring Interactive Maps: In our fourth use case, the user can explore the interactive map of a building. This use case relies on the Shape, Sliding,

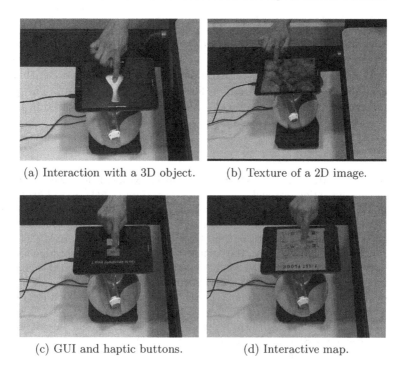

(a) Interaction with a 3D object.   (b) Texture of a 2D image.

(c) GUI and haptic buttons.   (d) Interactive map.

Fig. 9. Illustrations of our four use cases

and Roughness effects. In our implementation, the 2D map (in top-view) of a big mall with three floors is used. The user can explore the layout of the shops using the finger. When stroking over stairs the user can move up or down to a different floor. The user can be attracted or repulsed from specific points/areas of interest. A vibration can also be added in presence of a targeted item.

7   Conclusion and Future Work

In this paper we have presented KinesTouch: a novel approach to enhance touch-screen interactions using kinesthetic and force feedback. With a single device, the KinesTouch provides four different types of haptics sensations: compliance, shape, fine roughness and friction. Moreover, we address a novel way of dealing with friction rendering: lateral kinesthetic feedback. We designed a proof-of-concept prototype based on the combination of a standard tablet and a consumer-grade impedance haptic device, in order to illustrate several use cases including: interacting with 3D objects or haptic widgets, exploring an interactive map, or perceiving the texture of a 2D image. We also conducted a user study on the Sliding effect to confirm that it could well induce different sliding sensations.

Creating rich haptic effects that combine the different psychophysical dimensions is probably the most promising, but also challenging following of this work.

Except for vibrations that can be easily "added" to a force or kinesthetic rendering without much interferences, the compliance, shape, and friction dimensions are not trivial to associate, at least with a Falcon device that is limited in terms of dynamics and workspace. Beyond the device technical limitations, there are also conceptual limitations to combine force and position control. The proper algorithms and hardware able to tackle this issue should be explored in future.

References

1. Altinsoy, M.E., Merchel, S.: Electrotactile feedback for handheld devices with touch screen and simulation of roughness. IEEE Trans. Haptics **5**(1), 6–13 (2012)
2. Ando, H., Kusachi, E., Watanabe, J.: Nail-mounted tactile display for boundary/texture augmentation. In: Proceedings of the International Conference on Advances in Computer Entertainment Technology, pp. 292–293. ACM (2007)
3. Bau, O., Poupyrev, I., Israr, A., Harrison, C.: Teslatouch: electrovibration for touch surfaces. In: Proceedings of the 23nd Annual ACM Symposium on User Interface Software and Technology, pp. 283–292 (2010)
4. Bensmaïa, S., Hollins, M.: Pacinian representations of fine surface texture. Percept. Psychophys. **67**(5), 842–854 (2005)
5. Brewster, S., Chohan, F., Brown, L.: Tactile feedback for mobile interactions. In: Proceedings of the SIGCHI Conference on Human Factors in Computing Systems, pp. 159–162. ACM (2007)
6. Burch, D., Pawluk, D.: Using multiple contacts with texture-enhanced graphics. In: World Haptics Conference (WHC), pp. 287–292. IEEE (2011)
7. Chubb, E.C., Colgate, J.E., Peshkin, M.A.: Shiverpad: a glass haptic surface that produces shear force on a bare finger. IEEE Trans. Haptics **3**(3), 189–198 (2010)
8. Culbertson, H., Kuchenbecker, K.J.: Importance of matching physical friction, hardness, and texture in creating realistic haptic virtual surfaces. IEEE Trans. Haptics **10**(1), 63–74 (2017)
9. Darian-Smith, I., Johnson, K.O.: Thermal sensibility and thermoreceptors. J. Invest. Dermatol. **69**(1), 146–153 (1977)
10. Hausberger, T., Terzer, M., Enneking, F., Jonas, Z., Kim, Y.: SurfTics—kinesthetic and tactile feedback on a touchscreen device. In: 2017 IEEE World Haptics Conference (WHC), pp. 472–477. IEEE (2017)
11. Hollins, M., Bensmaïa, S., Risner, R.: The duplex theory of tactile texture perception. In: Proceedings of the 14th Annual Meeting of the International Society for Psychophysics, pp. 115–121 (1998)
12. Hollins, M., Risner, S.R.: Evidence for the duplex theory of tactile texture perception. Attention Percept. Psychophys. **62**(4), 695–705 (2000)
13. Israr, A., et al.: Po2: augmented haptics for interactive gameplay. In: ACM SIGGRAPH 2015 Emerging Technologies, p. 21 (2015)
14. Johnson, K.O.: The roles and functions of cutaneous mechanoreceptors. Curr. Opin. Neurobiol. **11**, 455–461 (2001)
15. Katz, D.: The World of Touch (le krueger, trans.). Rrlbaum, Mahwah (1925/1989). (Original work published 1925)
16. Kim, S.C., Han, B.K., Seo, J., Kwon, D.S.: Haptic interaction with virtual geometry on robotic touch surface. In: SIGGRAPH Asia 2014 Emerging Technologies, p. 8. ACM (2014)

17. Kim, S.C., Israr, A., Poupyrev, I.: Tactile rendering of 3D features on touch surfaces. In: Proceedings of the 26th Annual ACM Symposium on User Interface Software and Technology, pp. 531–538. ACM (2013)
18. Lederman, S.J., Klatzky, R.L.: Hand movements: a window into haptic object recognition. Cogn. Psychol. **19**(3), 342–368 (1987)
19. Levesque, V., et al.: Enhancing physicality in touch interaction with programmable friction. In: Proceedings of the SIGCHI Conference on Human Factors in Computing Systems, pp. 2481–2490. ACM (2011)
20. Maiero, J., Kruijff, E., Hinkenjann, A., Ghinea, G.: Forcetab: visuo-haptic interaction with a force-sensitive actuated tablet. In: 2017 IEEE International Conference on Multimedia and Expo (ICME), pp. 169–174. IEEE (2017)
21. Makinen, V., Linjama, J., Gulzar, Z.: Tactile stimulation apparatus having a composite section comprising a semiconducting material 12 May 2011. http://www.google.ch/patents/US20110109588. US Patent App. 12/900,305
22. Mullenbach, J., Johnson, D., Colgate, J.E., Peshkin, M.A.: Activepad surface haptic device. In: Haptics Symposium (HAPTICS), pp. 407–414. IEEE (2012)
23. Mullenbach, J., Shultz, C., Piper, A.M., Peshkin, M., Colgate, J.E.: Tpad fire: surface haptic tablet. In: Proceedings of HAID (2013)
24. Okamoto, S., Nagano, H., Yamada, Y.: Psychophysical dimensions of tactile perception of textures. IEEE Trans. Haptics **6**(1), 81–93 (2013)
25. Romano, J.M., Kuchenbecker, K.J.: Creating realistic virtual textures from contact acceleration data. IEEE Trans. Haptics **5**(2), 109–119 (2012)
26. Saga, S., Deguchi, K.: Lateral-force-based 2.5-dimensional tactile display for touch screen. In: Haptics Symposium (HAPTICS), pp. 15–22. IEEE (2012)
27. Saga, S., Raskar, R.: Simultaneous geometry and texture display based on lateral force for touchscreen. In: World Haptics Conference (WHC), pp. 437–442. IEEE (2013)
28. Sinclair, M., Pahud, M., Benko, H.: Touchmover: actuated 3D touchscreen with haptic feedback. In: Proceedings of the 2013 ACM International Conference on Interactive Tabletops and Surfaces, pp. 287–296 (2013)
29. Sinclair, M., Pahud, M., Benko, H.: Touchmover 2.0-3D touchscreen with force feedback and haptic texture. In: Haptics Symposium (HAPTICS), pp. 1–6. IEEE (2014)
30. Takanaka, S., Yano, H., Iwata, H.: Multitouch haptic interface with movable touch screen. In: SIGGRAPH Asia 2015 Haptic Media and Contents Design, p. 13. ACM (2015)
31. Ushirobira, R., Efimov, D., Casiez, G., Roussel, N., Perruquetti, W.: A forecasting algorithm for latency compensation in indirect human-computer interactions. In: 2016 European Control Conference (ECC), pp. 1081–1086, June 2016. https://doi.org/10.1109/ECC.2016.7810433
32. Vanacken, L., De Boeck, J., Coninx, K.: The phantom versus the falcon: force feedback magnitude effects on user's performance during target acquisition. In: Nordahl, R., Serafin, S., Fontana, F., Brewster, S. (eds.) HAID 2010. LNCS, vol. 6306, pp. 179–188. Springer, Heidelberg (2010). https://doi.org/10.1007/978-3-642-15841-4_19
33. Wang, D., Tuer, K., Rossi, M., Shu, J.: Haptic overlay device for flat panel touch displays. In: Proceedings of 12th International Symposium on Haptic Interfaces for Virtual Environment and Teleoperator Systems, HAPTICS 2004, p. 290. IEEE (2004)

34. Watanabe, T., Fukui, S.: A method for controlling tactile sensation of surface roughness using ultrasonic vibration. In: Proceedings of 1995 IEEE International Conference on Robotics and Automation, vol. 1, pp. 1134–1139, May 1995. https://doi.org/10.1109/ROBOT.1995.525433

35. Wiertlewski, M., Leonardis, D., Meyer, D.J., Peshkin, M.A., Colgate, J.E.: A high-fidelity surface-haptic device for texture rendering on bare finger. In: Auvray, M., Duriez, C. (eds.) EUROHAPTICS 2014. LNCS, vol. 8619, pp. 241–248. Springer, Heidelberg (2014). https://doi.org/10.1007/978-3-662-44196-1_30

36. Winfield, L., Glassmire, J., Colgate, J.E., Peshkin, M.: T-PaD: tactile pattern display through variable friction reduction. In: Second Joint EuroHaptics Conference, 2007 and Symposium on Haptic Interfaces for Virtual Environment and Teleoperator Systems. World Haptics 2007, pp. 421–426. IEEE (2007)

37. Yang, Y., Zhang, Y., Hou, Z., Chen, Z., Lemaire-Semail, B.: Fingviewer: a new multi-touch force feedback touch screen. In: 2011 IEEE International Conference on Consumer Electronics (ICCE), pp. 837–838. IEEE (2011)

38. Yannier, N., Israr, A., Lehman, J.F., Klatzky, R.L.: Feelsleeve: haptic feedback to enhance early reading. In: Proceedings of the 33rd Annual ACM Conference on Human Factors in Computing Systems, pp. 1015–1024. ACM (2015)

39. Yem, V., Kajimoto, H.: Wearable tactile device using mechanical and electrical stimulation for fingertip interaction with virtual world. In: Proceedings of VR, pp. 99–104. IEEE (2017)

40. Zeng, T., Lemaire-Semail, B., Giraud, F., Messaoudi, M., Bouscayrol, A.: Position control of a 3 DOF platform for haptic shape rendering. In: Power Electronics and Motion Control Conference (EPE/PEMC), p. LS6c-2. IEEE (2012)

41. Zhao, S., Israr, A., Klatzky, R.: Intermanual apparent tactile motion on handheld tablets. In: World Haptics Conference (WHC), pp. 241–247 (2015)

Wearable Tactile Interfaces Using SMA Wires

Nicola Esposito[1], Rosanna Maria Viglialoro[1(✉)],
and Vincenzo Ferrari[1,2]

[1] Department of Translational Research and New Technologies in Medicine and
Surgery, EndoCAS Center, University of Pisa, Pisa, Italy
nicola.esp19@gmail.com,
rosanna.viglialoro@endocas.org,
vincenzo.ferrari@unipi.it
[2] Information Engineering Department, University of Pisa, Pisa, Italy

Abstract. This paper describes the use of SMA (Shape Memory Alloys) wires
to develop wearable tactile interfaces. In this early work, the wearable interface
consists of a nylon glove with thin SMA wires stitched on it. The SMA wires
provide a tunable pressure sensation when they are electrically actuated
appropriately. Each wire is anchored to the fingernail-shaped support via screw
clamps to ensure both the electrical continuity of the connections and to efficiently transmit the contraction force on the fingertip. A suitable actuation
system of SMA wires has been designed and implemented on an Arduino Uno
microcontroller to prevent their overheating. The knowledge of SMA wires
mechanical, thermal and electrical properties allowed the implementation of a
proper actuation strategy. The interface was characterized in terms of response
time and force felt on the fingertip. Ten subjects have positively evaluated the
interface in terms of wearability, comfort and tactile sensations. This work paves
the way for the development of highly wearable tactile interfaces to be integrated in Virtual Reality (VR) and Augmented Reality (AR) environments.

Keywords: Tactile interfaces · Shape Memory Alloy · Haptics
Augmented Reality

1 Introduction

Haptic interfaces are computer-controlled electro-mechanical devices to allow the user
to manually interact with remote or virtual environments. When applied to virtual
environments, they allow manual exploration and manipulation of virtual objects
making the scene more realistic and even more immersive [1–3].

Haptic devices can be divided in two groups: kinesthetic interfaces that provide
sensation of force to the user, and tactile interfaces that provide sensation of contact,
heat, pressure and texture. Furthermore, such devices can be also classified as grounded
or ungrounded devices. The former are fixed into the real environment and the user can
interact with the virtual objects by manipulating a pen or a mouse integrated in the
interface (PHANTOM SensAble Technologies), while the latter is worn by the user
(such as a hand-glove, a thimble, etc.). Ungrounded devices are more mobile and can
operate over larger workspaces compared to grounded devices. However, currently

© Springer Nature Switzerland AG 2018
P. Bourdot et al. (Eds.): EuroVR 2018, LNCS 11162, pp. 117–127, 2018.
https://doi.org/10.1007/978-3-030-01790-3_7

available ungrounded devices present technological drawbacks [4] as described in the following.

The sensation of contact can be recreated using various technologies. Vibro-tactile actuators are among the most widely used in this field with various commercial applications due to their low cost and reduced size [5]. CyberTouch [6] is a commercially available system to simulate vibrations (e.g. when the user's finger touches an object in VR). The system employs vibro-tactile actuators mounted on the back of the fingers of a glove. The position of the actuators is not optimal since the contact usually happens at the fingertips. Vibro-tactile actuators are used in many research studies. For instance, Sziebig et al. [7] developed a vibro-tactile glove for VR applications composed of six vibro-tactile actuators, five on the fingertips and one on the palm. While Martinez et al. [8] presented a vibrotactile glove with twelve vibro-tactile actuators for the identification of virtual 3D objects. The main drawback of vibro-tactile actuation is due to the unrealistic sensation in case of contact stimuluses. Moreover, the mechanoreceptors of the fingers that detect vibrations have a wide receptive field that does not allow an accurate localization of the stimulus. Finally, this kind of interfaces, wrapping the entire fingertip with rigid and bulky devices, can be employed only in cases of VR application.

Pressure actuators intrinsically provide a more realistic sensation of contact.

Minamizawa et al. [9] developed a wearable interface integrating two DC motors to press a belt in contact with the user's fingertip giving a sensation of pressure. Bianchi et al. [10] developed a device with a similar design but with a lifting mechanism that can independently regulate the pressure. Such kind of devices are suitable for VR application and also for AR tactile applications. In [11] the Bianchi et al. [10] device was employed to virtually reproduce arterial pulse in a surgical simulator that includes a realistic arterial replica.

Aoky et al. [12] proposed a fingertip interface using thin wires pulled by a small coil and demonstrated that the absolute threshold to feel a pressure is lower using a wire contact than using a belt contact.

Scheibe et al. [13] investigated the use of SMA (Shape Memory Alloys) wires to generate tactile sensation to the fingertips. Specifically, they developed a thimble with SMA wires looped around it that provide an impression of contact when they are electrically actuated. Their interface has successfully been used in immersive VR applications. The bulkiness of the thimble is a critical point for its application in AR environment in which it is necessary to manipulate real as well as virtual objects, and furthermore the thimble occludes the view of the real environment.

Toyoura et al. [14] proposed a tactile interface with wires of BioMetal SMA material (by Toky Corporation) integrated in a glove. Their glove does not alter the grasp and does not occlude the view but the slow response time (about 0.5 s) of BioMetal causes a perceptible lag in VR and AR applications.

The aim of this work is to evaluate if different SMA materials, actuated with a proper strategy, can be suitable for the development of glove-based tactile interfaces in terms of response time, pressure sensation, lightweight, bulkiness, comfort and freedom of movements.

2   Materials and Methods

The following sections describe the properties of Nitinol SMA materials, an early glove design, the actuation strategy for the SMA wires, the quantitative and qualitative evaluation of our interface.

2.1   Flexinol® Wire Properties

Nickel titanium (Nitinol) SMA materials assume a different crystalline structure at different temperatures. At low temperature, the Nitinol SMA material is in martensitic phase: it can be easily stretched by a minor force. When Nitinol SMA material is heated to its transition temperature it changes to austenitic phase: the material is high strength and not easily deformed and it returns to its pre-deformed shape.

We employed thin pre-trained SMA wires: the Nitinol wires FLEXINOL® (from Dynalloy, Inc.) [15]. Specifically, the FLEXINOL® wires contract when heated typically up to 2% to 5% of their length as showed in Fig. 1.

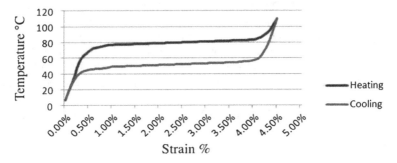

Fig. 1. Typical temperature vs. strain characteristics for the employed LT FLEXINOL® wires (70 °C).

FLEXINOL® wire is commercially available in a variety of diameters, from 0.025 up to 0.51 mm and in 2 transition temperatures: low temperature (LT) at 70 °C and high temperature (HT) at 90 °C.

We employed 0.15 mm diameter LT FLEXINOL® wires and we electrically heated them.

2.2   Design of an Early Wearable Tactile Interface

Our early interface consists of a nylon glove whit three thin SMA wires stitched on the index's fingertip. The wires are anchored to a fingernail-shaped support via screw clamps as depicted in Fig. 2. The fingernail-shaped support has a twofold function: to ensure the electrical continuity of the connections and to efficiently transmit the contraction force on the fingertip. Its shape and weight of about 1 g should ensure comfort and freedom of movements.

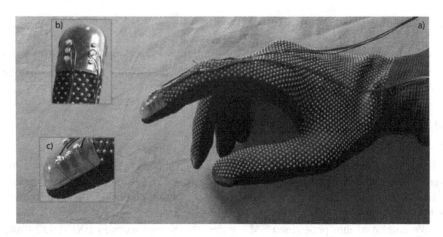

Fig. 2. (a) Early prototype of a tactile glove. (b) Detail of fingernail-shaped support with the electric wires. (c) Detail of the SMA wires stitched on the glove.

We set the length of the SMA wires to 50 mm to wrap the entire fingertip of users with large fingers. The three SMA wires are equally spaced of 4 mm; this distance is larger than two-point discrimination threshold on fingertip which is 2 mm [16]. In this way, by contracting a single wire the contact point should be discriminated.

Each SMA wire is connected to an Arduino Uno microcontroller board through a pair of electric wires. In this early design, the electric wires are positioned on the back of the hand (Fig. 2).

Specifically, we electrically heat the Nitinol wires by an appropriate current to obtain the contraction as described in the following paragraph ("Actuation strategy of SMA wires").

2.3   Actuation Strategy for the SMA Wires

An undesirable effect related to the electrical activation of Nitinol wires by a constant current is overheating, which could determine the degradation in the material shape memory effect and the discomfort up to pain for the user.

A direct measure of the temperature through temperature sensors is difficult due to the small surface of the wires. For this reason, we prevent wire overheating predicting the temperature and properly adjusting the heating current.

To this end, we employed the thermal model to predict SMA thermal behaviour proposed by Velázquez and Pissaloux [17]. Specifically, we can assume that the behaviour of SMA wire is linear and thus without hysteresis; this approximation is valid for fast wire heating. The simplified thermal model depends on both the SMA wire geometry and the material properties specified in data sheet. The following Eq. (1), describes the simplified thermal model of SMA wire:

$$\rho C V \frac{dT}{dt} = i^2 R - hS(T - Ts) \tag{1}$$

Where ρ is the density of the SMA, C is its specific heat, V is the volume of the SMA material, T is the temperature of the SMA at a time t, R is the electrical resistance of a 50 mm wire, h is the heat-exchange coefficient between the SMA and the surrounding mediums, S is the surface area of the SMA and Ts is the surrounding temperature.

Table 1 reports the physical parameters of our specific thermal model. R is calculated starting from the FLEXINOL® conductivity and the wire geometry, while Ts has been set to the typical skin temperature. The other parameters are obtained from the FLEXINOL® datasheet.

Table 1. Physical parameters of the employed SMA wires.

Property	Value	Unit
Density ρ	6450	$kg \cdot m^{-3}$
Specific heat C	320	$J \cdot kg^{-1} \cdot K^{-1}$
Volume V	$8 \cdot 10^{-10}$	m^3
Resistance R	2.75	Ω
Heat-exchange coefficient h	94.96	$W \cdot m^{-2} \cdot K^{-1}$
Surface S	$2 \cdot 10^{-5}$	m^2
Surrounding temperature Ts	36	°C

We incorporated the obtained thermal model into a simulated control system of the temperature. The simulated control system employs a proportional-integral (PI) controller in order to achieve the reference temperature with a fast response time avoiding overheating.

A classical feedback scheme has been used (Fig. 3): the estimated real-time temperature (T) is compared with the reference temperature (Tr); the error e ($T - Tr$) is the input of the PI controller. The output of the PI controller was set to a maximum value of 300 mA to prevent the degradation of material performances as suggested in the FLEXINOL® datasheet. The PI parameters were empirically set as a compromise to obtain a fast rising time and a reduced risk of overeating (Table 2).

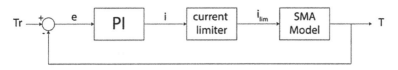

Fig. 3. Simulated feedback control system of the temperature to estimate the current actuation strategy.

Table 2. Gains of the PI controller.

Constant gains	Value
Proportional K_P	0.06
Integral K_I	0.067

Figure 4 shows the results of the simulations which were implemented in MATLAB/Simulink. The reference temperature has been set at 85 °C, this is a good temperature to achieve optimal contraction without degrading the material. The simulations highlight how, through an adequate control of the material, it is possible to obtain the desired performance.

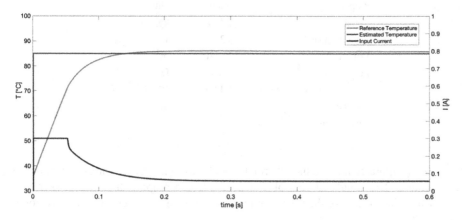

Fig. 4. Step response of close loop system.

The synthesized controller was discretized and implemented in the Arduino Uno microcontroller. The sampling time was set to 2 ms to achieve a good resolution of the transient. Since Arduino Uno microcontroller is not able to supply the required current, it was coupled with an amplification circuit based on a TIP 120 transistor. The entire system was powered by a 9 V power supply (Fig. 5).

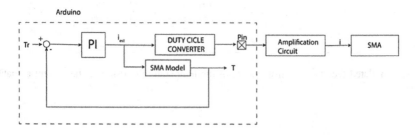

Fig. 5. Scheme of actuation system for SMA wire.

The microcontroller cyclically performs the following routines: first it estimates the temperature of the wire through the thermal model implemented; then it calculates the current required using the PI controller; finally it drives the amplification circuit in order to obtain the required current through a pulse width modulated (PWM). In this way, every time the wire actuation is required, the optimal current profile is generated starting from the estimated wire initial temperature.

2.4 Performance Evaluation

Quantitative tests were carried out to estimate three parameters: the contraction time, the relaxation time of SMA wires and the force imposed on the fingertip. The experimental setup included a simplified version of our tactile interface comprising the fingernail-shaped support with an only nitinol wire and a force sensing resistor (FSR) 400 sensor (by Interlink Electronics) as shown in Fig. 6. During the test, a volunteer has worn the simplified version of our tactile interface on the right index finger and the force sensor was placed between the user's finger and the SMA wire.

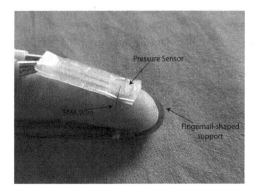

Fig. 6. Setup for the evaluation of SMA wire performances.

The SMA wire was activated and the output of the FSR sensor was measured. FSR sensor was connected to a measuring resistor RM in a voltage divider configuration, as illustrated in Fig. 7.

The contraction time was estimated as the rising time between the starting of the activation and the sensor's response up to 70% of the maximum contraction. The same for the relaxation time.

Instead, the contraction force was directly measured from the FSR sensor output using the relationships defined in [18], reported in (2) and (3), which allow an estimation of the force magnitude:

$$C_{FSR} = \left(10^6 \text{x } V_{OUT}\right) / \left((V_+ - V_{OUT}) \text{x } R_M\right) \tag{2}$$

$$F_{FSR} = \begin{cases} C_{FSR}/80 & (C_{FSR} < 1000) \\ ((C_{FSR} - 1000))/30 & (C_{FSR} > 1000) \end{cases} \tag{3}$$

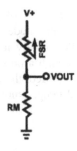

Fig. 7. Reading circuit of the FSR sensor.

where, C_{FSR} is the conductance of the sensor, V_{OUT} is the output voltage of FSR sensor, V_+ is the in voltage of 5 V, R_M is a 10 KΩ resistance and F_{FSR} is the estimation of force magnitude in Newton.

Preliminary qualitative tests were carried out to evaluate both the wearability and the ability of our tactile interface to provide tactile sensation. A total of ten subjects participated in this study. They wore the tactile interface and performed some movements to evaluate the wearability. During the tests, the tactile interface conveyed a pulse feedback on user's fingertip. The activation of the wires took place both simultaneously and individually. In the second modality, a pair of contiguous wires was activated in sequence in order to evaluate the ability to perceive distinct areas of contact. At the end of the test, each subject was asked to complete a structured questionnaire based on five-point Likert scale (1 = strongly disagree to 5 strongly agree).

3 Results

The estimated contraction time is about 50 ms which is the same time of thimble of Scheibe [13]; this result is adequate for VR and AR applications. The relaxation time is about 1 s, not acceptable in case of application requiring higher activations rate.

The measured contact force with our setup is about 1 N, that is over the absolute threshold evaluated by Aoky for the detection of the induced pressure by a wire on a finger (40 mN) [12].

The questionnaire results are illustrated in Table 3. The central tendencies of responses to a single Likert item are summarized by using median, with dispersion measured by interquartile range. Ten subjects positively evaluated the tactile interface, both in terms of wearability and in terms of the ability to generate a sensation of contact. The glove has been considered comfortable to wear and easy to adapt to the individual finger. Furthermore, the glove allows free movement of the fingers. All subjects were able to recognize the activation of the contraction and to discriminate the area of contact; moreover, this sensation was considered suitable to simulate contact with an object. The wires have been heated at 85 °C for 2 s and only a small percentage of the subjects perceived a very weak and painless temperature increasing. This is due to the low specific heat of the FLEXINOL® wires and the restricted activation time. Since the contact sensation in humans is greater in the instant of the contact and then tends to disappear, due to the adaptation behaviour of the mechanoreceptors, there are no reasons to still to be maintained the wires contracted for longer time. However, further studies need to be conducted to confirm qualitative results in a larger cohort of subjects.

Table 3. Questionnaire results. The central tendency of responses is summarized by using median with dispersion measured by IQR (25°; 75°).

Questionnaire items	Median	(IQR)
A tactile sensation is felt on the fingertip	5	(5–5)
The activation in sequence of two contiguous wires makes it possible to identify their relative position	4	(3–4)
The glove is comfortable to wear and easy to adapt to the individual finger	4	(4–5)
The glove allows free movement of the fingers and hand.	4	(4–5)
The eventual heat feel during the test is bearable.	4	(3–5)

4   Conclusions and Discussion

In this paper, we motivated and evaluated the feasibility of wearable tactile interfaces based on SMA wires to present tactile sensations on the fingertip. Our early interface consists of a nylon glove with three thin SMA wires connected through fingernail-shaped support. In addition, a suitable actuation system of SMA wires has been designed and implemented on an Arduino Uno microcontroller, to avoid their over-heating. Ten subjects positively evaluated the tactile interface, both in terms of wearability and in terms of the ability both to generate a sensation of contact and to discriminate the different contact areas. The latter can be the starting point to simulate different perceptions such as gliding by activating the wires sequentially. The greatest strength of such kind of interface is the wearability. In literature, there are tactile interfaces capable of generating even more complex and specific tactile sensations but, due to their weight and size, they are suitable for use in VR environment but not in AR environment in which it is necessary to manipulate real as well as virtual objects. Our interface instead, does not alter the grasp of the hand and does not increase the occlusion of the real environment, thus allowing a truthful interaction of the user with both real and virtual objects.

The experimental results demonstrate that the contraction time and the force exerted by the wire are adequate for our purpose. The drawback of Nitinol wires is the slow relaxation time. SMA wires can be contracted in less than 50 ms but need about 1 s to restore the initial condition.

Further studies could be carried out on glove materials to improve thermal dissipation in order to avoid any heating sensation by the user and to speed up the relaxation time. Another approach to increase the activation rate could be to add other close wires in parallel and activating them alternately.

In a more advanced version of the glove, we would like to simulate the grasp. To this end, we will need to increase the area of contact using more wires and to extend the actuation strategy up all the five fingers. In addition, the cabling could be simplified connecting together the electric wires on the same pole and encapsulating them within the glove.

In our view, this work paves for the development of highly wearable tactile interfaces to be integrated in VR and AR environments.

Acknowledgements. Work supported by the SThARS project (funded by the Italian Ministry of Health and Regione Toscana through the call "RicercaFinalizzata 2011–2012").

References

1. Pacchierotti, C., Sinclair, S., Solazzi, S.: Wearable haptic systems for the fingertip and the hand: taxonomy, review, and perspectives. IEEE Trans. Haptics **10**(4), 580–600 (2017)
2. Escobar, D., Noguez, J., Neri, L.: A review of simulators with haptic devices for medical training. J. Med. Syst. **40**(4), 104 (2016)
3. Coles, T., Meglan, D., John, N.: The role of haptics in medical training simulators: a survey of the state of the art. IEEE Trans. Haptics **4**(1), 51–66 (2011)
4. Richard, C., Cutkosky, M.: Contact force perception with an ungrounded haptic interface. In: ASME IMECE 6th Annual Symposium on Haptic Interfaces, Dallas, TX, United States (1997)
5. Alahakone, A., Senanayake, S.: Vibrotactile feedback systems: current trends in rehabilitation, sports and information display. In: 2009 Proceedings of the IEEE International Conference on Advanced Intelligent Mechatronics, Singapore, pp. 1148–1153 (2009)
6. Cyber Touch: Cyber Glove Systems. http://www.cyberglovesystems.com
7. Sziebig, G., Solvang, B.: Vibro-tactile feedback for VR systems. In: 2009 Proceedings of the Human System Interactions, Catania, Italy, pp. 406–410 (2009)
8. Martínez, J., García, A.: Identifying 3D geometric shapes with a vibrotactile glove. Comput. Graph. Appl. **36**(1), 42–51 (2014)
9. Minamizawa, K., Fukamachi, S.: Gravity grabber: wearable haptic display to present virtual mass sensation. In: ACM SIGGRAPH 2007: Emerging Technologies, San Diego, CA, United States (2007)
10. Bianchi, M., Battaglia, E.: A wearable fabric-based display for haptic multi-cue delivery. In: 2016 Proceedings of the IEEE Haptics Symposium, Philadelphia, PA, United States, pp. 277–283 (2016)
11. Condino, S., et al.: Tactile augmented reality for arteries palpation in open surgery training. In: Zheng, G., Liao, H., Jannin, P., Cattin, P., Lee, S.-L. (eds.) MIAR 2016. LNCS, vol. 9805, pp. 186–197. Springer, Cham (2016). https://doi.org/10.1007/978-3-319-43775-0_17
12. Aoky, T., Mitake, H.: Wearable haptic device to present contact sensation based on cutaneous sensation using thin wire. In: 2009 Proceedings of the International Conference on Advances in Computer Entertainment Technology, Athens, Greece, pp. 115–122 (2009)
13. Scheibe, R., Moehring, M.: Tactile feedback at the finger tips for improved direct interaction in immersive environments. In: IEEE Symposium on 3D User Interfaces 2007, Charlotte, NC, United States (2007)

14. Toyoura, M., Shono, T.: Biometal glove. In: Proceedings of the ACM Symposium on Virtual Reality Software and Technology, Hong Kong, China (2010)
15. Dynalloy: Flexinol. www.dynalloy.com
16. Dargahi, J.: Human tactile perception as a standard for artificial tactile sensing – a review. J. Med. Robot. Comput. Assist. Surg. **1**, 23–35 (2004)
17. Velázquez, R.: Modelling and temperature control of shape memory alloys with fast electrical heating. Int. J. Mech. Control **13**(2), 3–10 (2012)
18. Zhang, Z., Yimit, A.: Design of a two-point-contact fingertip tactile force feedback device. In: 2017 2nd International Conference on Cybernetics, Robotics and Control, Chengdu, China, pp. 71–74 (2017)

UnrealHaptics: A Plugin-System for High Fidelity Haptic Rendering in the Unreal Engine

Marc O. Rüdel, Johannes Ganser, Rene Weller$^{(\boxtimes)}$, and Gabriel Zachmann

University of Bremen, Bremen, Germany
weller@informatik.uni-bremen.de
http://cgvr.informatik.uni-bremen.de/

Abstract. We present UNREALHAPTICS, a novel set of plugins that enable both 3-DOF and 6-DOF haptic rendering in the Unreal Engine 4. The core is the combination of the integration of a state-of-the-art collision detection library with support for very fast and stable force and torque computations and a general haptics library for the communication with different haptic hardware devices. Our modular and lightweight architecture makes it easy for other researchers to adapt our plugins to their own requirements. As a use case we have tested our plugin in a new asymmetric collaborative multiplayer game for blind and sighted people. The results show that our plugin easily meets the requirements for haptic rendering even in complex scenes.

1 Introduction

With the rise of affordable consumer devices such as the Oculus Rift or the HTC Vive there has been a large increase in interest and development in the area of virtual reality (VR). The new display and tracking technologies of these devices enable high fidelity graphics rendering and natural interaction with the virtual environments. Modern game engines like Unreal or Unity have simplified the development of VR applications dramatically. They almost hide the technological background from the content creation process so that today, everyone can click their way to their own VR application in a few minutes. However, consumer VR devices are primarily focused on outputting information to the two main human senses: seeing and hearing. Also game engines are mainly limited to visual and audio output. The sense of touch is widely neglected. This lack of haptic feedback can disturb the immersion in virtual environments significantly. Moreover, the concentration on visual feedback excludes a large number of people from the content created with the game engines: those who cannot *see* this content, i.e. blind and visually impaired people.

The main reasons why the sense of touch is widely neglected in the context of games are that haptic devices are still comparatively bulky and expensive. Moreover, haptic rendering is computationally and algorithmically very challenging. Although many game engines have a built-in physics engine, they are

© Springer Nature Switzerland AG 2018
P. Bourdot et al. (Eds.): EuroVR 2018, LNCS 11162, pp. 128–147, 2018.
https://doi.org/10.1007/978-3-030-01790-3_8

most usually limited to simple convex shapes and they are relatively slow: for the visual rendering loop it is sufficient to provide 60–120 frames per second (FPS) to guarantee a smooth visual feedback. Our sense of touch is much more sensitive with respect to the temporal resolution. Here, a frequency of preferably 1000 Hz is required to provide an acceptable force feedback. This requirement for haptic rendering requires a decoupling of the physically-based simulation from the visual rendering path.

In this paper, we present UNREALHAPTICS to enable high-fidelity haptic rendering in a modern game engine. Following the idea of decoupling the simulation part from the core game engine, UNREALHAPTICS consists of three individual plugins:

- A plugin that we call HAPTICO: it realizes the communication with the haptic hardware.
- The computational bottleneck during the physically-based simulation is the collision detection. Our plugin called COLLETTE builds a bridge to an external collision detection library that is fast enough for haptic rendering.
- Finally, FFORCECOMP computes the appropriate forces and torques from the collision information.

This modular structure of UNREALHAPTICS allows other researchers to easily replace individual parts, e.g. the force computation or the collision detection, to fit their individual needs. We have integrated UNREALHAPTICS into the Unreal Engine 4 (UE4). We use a fast, lightweight and highly maintainable and adjustable event system to handle the communication in UNREALHAPTICS.

As a use case we present a novel asymmetric collaborative multiplayer game for sighted and blind players. In our implementation, HAPTICO integrates the CHAI3D library that offers support for a wide variety of available haptic devices. For the collision detection we use the state-of-the-art collision detection library CollDet [27] that supports complexity independent volumetric collision detection at haptic rates. Our force calculation relies on a penalty-based approach with both 3- and 6-degree-of-freedom (DOF) force and torque computations. Our results show that UNREALHAPTICS is able to compute stable forces and torques for different 3- and 6-DOF devices in Unreal at haptic rates.

2 Related Work

Game engines enable the rapid development with high end graphics and the easy extension to VR to a broad pool of developers. Hence, they are usually the first choice when designing demanding 3D virtual environments. Obviously, this is also true for haptic applications. Consequently, there exist many (research) projects that already integrated haptics into such game engines, e.g. [2],[15], [14] to name but a few. However, they usually have spent a lot of time in developing single use approaches which are hardly generalizable and thus, not applicable to other programs.

Actually, there exist only a very few approaches that provide comfortable interfaces for the integration of haptics into modern game engines. We only found [11] and [22] that provide plugins for UE4 that serve as interfaces to the *3D Systems Touch* (formerly *SensAble PHANToM Omni*) [16] via the *OpenHaptics* library [1]. OpenHaptics is a proprietary library that is specific to 3D Systems' devices, which means that other devices cannot be used with these plugins. Furthermore, the plugins are not actively maintained and seem to not be working with the current version of UE4 (version 4.18 at the time of writing). Another example is a plugin for the PHANToM device presented in [20], also based on the OpenHaptics library. Like the other plugins, it is no longer maintained and was even removed from Unity's asset store [21]. During our research, we could not find any actively maintained plugin for a commonly used game engine that supports 3- or 6-DOF force feedback.

Outside the context of game engines, there are a number of libraries that provide force calculations for haptic devices. A general overview is given in [10]. One example is the CHAI3D library [4]. It is an open-source library written in C++ that supports a variety of devices by different vendors. It offers a common interface for all devices that can be extended to implement custom device support. For its haptic rendering, CHAI3D accelerates the collision detection with mesh objects by using an axis-aligned bounding box (AABB) hierarchy. The force rendering is based on a finger-proxy algorithm. The device position is proxied by a second, virtual position that tries to track the device position. When the device position enters a mesh the proxy will stay on the meshes surface. The proxy tries to minimize the distance to the device position locally by sliding along the surface. Finally, the forces are computed by exerting a spring force between the two points [3]. Due to this method's simplicity, it only returns 3-DOF force feedback, even though the library generally allows for also passing torques and grip forces to devices. Nevertheless we are using CHAI3D in our use case, but only for the communication with haptic devices.

A comparable, slightly older library is the H3DAPI library [7]. Same as CHAI3D, it is extensible in both the device and algorithm domain. However by default H3DAPI supports less devices and likewise does not provide 6-DOF force feedback.

A general haptic toolkit with a focus on web development was presented by Ruffaldi et al. [18]. It is based on the eXtreme Virtual Reality (XVR) engine, utilising the CHAI3D library, in order to allow rapid application development independent from the specific haptic interface. Unfortunately, the toolkit has not been further developed and there is no documentation to be found, since their homepage went down.

All approaches mentioned above are limited to 3-DOF haptic rendering. Sagardia et al. [19] present an extension to the *Bullet* physics engine for faster collision detection and force computation. Their algorithm is based on the Voxmap-Pointshell algorithm [12]. Objects are encoded both in a voxmap that stores distances to the closest points of the object as well as point-shells on the object surface that are clustured to generate optimally wrapped sphere trees. The penetration depth from the voxmap is then used to calculate the forces and torques. In contrast to Bullet's build-in algorithms this approach offers full 6-DOF haptic rendering for complex scenes. However, the Voxmap-Pointshell algorithm is known to be very memory intensive and susceptible to noise [23].

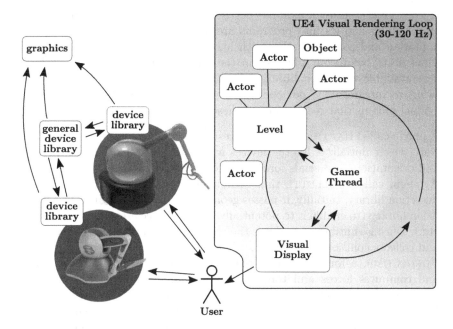

Fig. 1. A typical haptic integration without UNREALHAPTICS. Left: different haptic devices available with their libraries. Right: Scheme of UE4, which we want to integrate the devices with.

3 UNREALHAPTICS

The goal of our work was to develop an easy-to-use and simultaneously adjustable and generalizable system for haptic rendering in modern game engines. This can be used in games, research or business related contexts, either as whole or in parts. We decided to use the Unreal Engine for development because of several reasons:

- it is one of the most popular game engines with a large community, regular updates and a good documentation,
- it is free to use in most cases, especially in a research context where it is already heavily used [13,17],
- it is fully open-source, thus can be examined and adapted,
- it offers programmers access on the source code level while game designers can use a comfortable graphical editor in combination with a graphical scripting system called *Blueprints*. Thus, it combines the advantages of open class libraries and extensible IDEs

- it is extendable via plugins,
- and finally, it is build on C++, which makes it easy to integrate external C++-libraries. This is convenient because C++ is still the first choice for high-performance haptic rendering libraries.

Our goals directly imply a modular design for our system. The main challenges when including haptics into programs are fast collision detection, stable force computation and communication with hardware devices. Figure 1 presents the previous state before our plugins: on the one side, there are different haptic devices available with their libraries. On the other side, there is UE4 in which we want to integrate the devices. Consequently, our system consists of three individual plugins that realizes one of these tasks. In detail these are:

- A plugin called HAPTICO, which realizes the communication with haptic hardware, i.e. it initializes haptic devices and during runtime receives positions and orientations and sends forces and torques back to the hardware.
- A plugin called COLLETTE that communicates with an (external) collision detection library. Initially, it passes geometric objects from Unreal to the collision library (to enable it to potentially compute acceleration data structures etc.). During runtime, it updates the transformation matrices of the objects and collects collision information.
- FORCECOMP, a force rendering plugin which receives collision information and computes forces and torques that are finally send to HAPTICO. The force calculation is closely related to the collision detection method because it depends on the provided collision information. However, we decided to separate the force and torque computation from the actual collision detection into separate plugins because this allows an easy replacement, e.g. if the simulation is switched from penalty-based to impulse-based.

The list of plugins already suggest that communication plays an important role in the design of our plugin system. Hence, we will start with a short description on this topic before we detail the implementations of the individual plugins.

3.1 Unreal Engine Recap

UE4 is a game engine that comprises the engine itself as well as a 3D editor to create applications using the engine. We will start with a short recap of UE4's basic concepts.

UE4 follows the component-based entity system design. Every object in the scene (3D objects, lights, cameras, etc.) is at its core a data-, logic-less entity (in the case of UE4 called *actors*). The different behavior between the objects stems from *components* that can be attached to these actors. For example, a `StaticMeshActor` (which represents a 3D object) has a mesh component attached, while a light source will have different components attached. These components contain the data used by UE4's internal systems to implement the behavior of the composed objects (e.g. the rendering system will use the mesh components, the physics system will use the physics components etc.).

UE4 allows its users to attach new components to actors in the scene graph which allows extending objects with new behavior. Furthermore, if a new class is created using UE4's C++-dialect, variables of that class can be exposed to the editor. By doing so, users have the ability to easily change values of an instance of the class from within the editor itself, which minimizes programming effort.

UE4 not only provides a C++ interface, but also a visual programming language called *Blueprints*. Blueprints abstract functions and classes from the C++ interface and present them as "building blocks" that can be connected by execution lines. It serves as straightforward way to minimize programming effort and even allows people without programming experience to create game logic for their project.

When extending the UE4 with custom classes, the general idea is noted in [6]: programmers extend the existing systems by exposing the changes via blueprints. These can be used by other users to create game behavior. Our plugin system follows this ideas.

Furthermore, UE4 allows developers to bundle their code as plugins in order to make the code more reusable and easier to distribute [5]. Plugins can be managed easily within the editor. All classes and blueprints are directly accessible for usage in the editor (Fig. 2). We implemented our system as a set of three plugins to make the distribution effortless and allow the users to choose which features they need for their projects.

Finally, UE4 programs can be linked against external libraries at compile time, or dynamically loaded at runtime, similar to regular C++ applications. We are using this technique to base our plugins on already existing libraries. This ensures a time-tested and actively maintained base for our plugins.

3.2   Design of the Plugin Communication

As described above, our system consists of three individual plugins that exchange data. Hence, communication between the plugins plays an important role. Following our goal of flexibility, this communication has to meet two major requirements.

- The plugins need to communicate with each other without knowledge about the others' implementation because users of our plugins should be able to use them individually or combined. They could even be replaced by the users' own implementations. Thus, the communication has to run on an independent layer.
- Users of the plugins should be able to access the data produced by the plugins for their individual needs. This means that it must be possible to pass data outside of the plugins.

To fulfill both these requirements, we implemented a messaging approach based on *delegates*. A *delegator* is an object that represents an event in the system. The delegator can define a certain function signature by specifying parameter types. *Delegates* are functions of said signature that are bound to the delegator. The delegator can issue a broadcast which will call all bound delegates. Effectively, the delegates are functions reacting to the event represented by the delegator. A delegator can pass data to its delegates when broadcasting, completing the messaging system.

Fig. 2. Unreal's editor view of the game. On the left side, you see the Phantom player in the virtual environment. In front of him are the virtual tool (pen) and a `ColletteStaticMeshActor` to be recognized (crown). On the right, the scene graph is displayed with our custom classes.

The setup of the delegates between the plugins can be handled for example in a custom controller class within the users' projects. We describe the implementation details for such a controller in Sect. 3.6.

Our Light Delegate System. UE4 provides the possibility to declare different kinds of delegates out of the box. However, these delegates have a few drawbacks. Only Unreal Objects (declared with the `UOBJECT` macro etc.) can be passed with such delegates, limiting their use for more general C++ applications. They also introduce several layers of calls in the call stack since they are implemented around UE4's reflection system. This may influence performance when many delegates are used. Finally, we experienced problems at runtime: UE4-delegators temporarily forgot their bound functions which led to crashes when trying to access the addresses of these functions.

To overcome these problems we implemented our own lightweight `Delegator` class. It is a pure C++ class that can take a variable number of template arguments which represent the parameter types of its delegates. A so called *callable* can be bound with the `addDelegate(...)` function. Our solution supports all common C++-callables (free functions, member functions, lambdas etc.). The delegates can be executed with the `broadcast()` function which will execute delegates one after another with just a single additional step in the call stack. The data is always passed around as references internally, preventing any additional copies.

3.3   HAPTICO Plugin – Haptic Device Interface

HAPTICO enables game developers to use haptic devices directly from UE4 without implementing a connection to the device manually. It automatically detects a connected haptic device and allows full control via either Blueprints or C++ Code. This includes the retrieval of positions and orientations from the device and the sending of forces and torques to the device, thanks to the underlying CHAI3D library.

HAPTICO consists of mainly three parts: The haptic manager, the haptic thread and the haptic device interface. The haptic manager is the only user interface and represented as an UE4 actor in the scene. It provides functions to apply forces and torques to the device and to get informations such as position and rotation of the end effector. To be used for haptic rendering the execution loop of the plugin must be separated from UE4's game thread which runs at a low frequency. The plugin uses its own haptic thread internally. The haptic thread reads the positional and rotational data from the device, provides it for the haptic manager and applies the new force and torques retrieved from the haptic manager to the device in every tick. When new haptic data is available a delegator-event `OnTransform` is broadcasted, which passes the device data to the haptic manager in every tick. Users of the plugin can easily hook their own functions to this event, allowing to react to the moved device. A second delegator-event `ForceOnHapticTick` is broadcasted, which allows users to hook force calculation functions into the haptic thread. Our own FORCECOMP plugin uses this mechanism, which is further described in Sect. 3.6.

3.4   COLLETTE – Collision Detection Plugin

The physics module included in UE4 has two drawbacks that makes it unsuitable for haptic rendering:

1. It runs on the main game thread, which means it is capped at 120 FPS.
2. Objects are approximated by simple bounding volumes, which is very efficient for game scenarios but too imprecise to compute the collision data needed for haptic rendering.

This leads to the realization that for haptic rendering, UE4's physics module has to be bypassed.

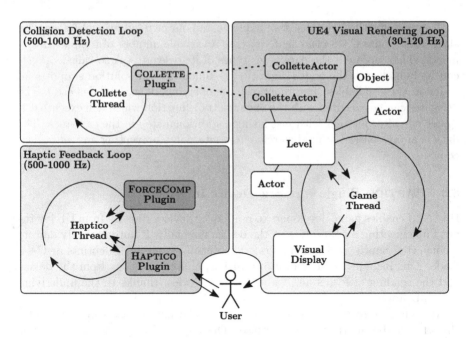

Fig. 3. The basic structure of our plugin system with three threads. Right: The UE4 game thread that is responsible for the visual feedback and runs with up to 120 Hz. Left: The haptic rendering thread and the collision detection thread. The haptic rendering that included the HAPTICO and the FORCECOMP plugin runs at 1000 Hz for a stable haptic feedback. We decided to put the collision detection in its own thread in order to not disturb the haptic rendering e.g. in case of deep collisions that require more computation time than 1 ms. The collidable objects in the Unreal scenegraph are represented as `CardetteStaticMeshActors` that are derived from Unreal's built in `StaticMeshActors`.

Our COLLETTE plugin does exactly that. We do not implement a collision detection in this plugin, but provide a flexible wrapper to bind external libraries. In our use case we show an example how to integrate the CollDet library (see Sect. 4.2). Like HAPTICO, COLLETTE can run in its own thread. Thus, the frequency needed for haptic rendering can be achieved.

The plugin uses a `CardetteStaticMeshActor` to represent collidable objects. This is an extension to UE4's `StaticMeshActor`. It supports loading additional pre-computed acceleration data structures to the actor's mesh component when the 3D asset is loaded. For instance, in our use case we load a pre-generated sphere tree asset from the hard drive which is used for internal representation of the underlying algorithm.

The collision pipeline is represented by a `CardetteVolume`, which extends the UE4 `VolumeActor`. We decided to use a volume actor because it allows to restrict collision detection checks to defined areas in the level. This is especially useful for asymmetric multiplayer scenarios as described in Sect. 4.

To register collidable objects with the pipeline, they can be registered with an `AddCollisionWatcher(...)` blueprint function to the collision detection pipeline. The function takes references to the `ColletteVolume` as well as two `ColletteStaticMeshActors`.

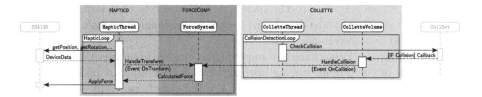

Fig. 4. A simplified sequence diagram of the communication of FORCECOMP, COLLETTE and HAPTICO in case of a collision: HAPTICO receives the current position and orientation from the device and informs FORCECOMP via a `OnTransform` event. `ColletteVolume` in COLLETTE evokes an `OnCollision` event and passes the collision data to FORCECOMP. FORCECOMP computes appropriate forces and torques and passes them back to HAPTICO that finally, applies them to the device. Please note, due to space constrains, we did not include transformations that are send from HAPTICO to the respective `ColletteStaticMeshActors`. Moreover, we omitted the `EventHandler` in this example.

During runtime, the collision thread checks registered pairs with their current positions and orientations. If a collision is determined, the class `ColletteCallback` broadcasts an `OnCollision` delegator-event. Users of the plugin can easily hook their own functions to this event, allowing reactions to the collision. Blueprint events cannot be used here as they are also executed on the game thread and thus run at a low frequency. The event also transmits references to the pair of `ColletteStaticMeshActors` involved in the collision, as well as the collision data generated by the underlying algorithm. This data can then be used for example to compute collision response forces.

3.5 FORCECOMP Plugin

The force calculation is implemented as a free standing function which accepts the data from two `ForceComponents` that can be attached especially to `ColletteStaticMeshActors` and depends on the current transform of the `ColletteStaticMeshActor`. The `ForceComponent` provides UE4 editor properties needed for the physical simulation of the forces: For instance the mass of the objects, a scaling factor or a damper (see Sect. 4.2). We have separated the force data from the collision detection. This allows users to use the COLLETTE plugin without the force computation.

3.6 Controlling Data Flow via Events

We already mentioned that we use a delegate-based event system to organize the data flow between the three plugins. In order to mange the events we use an

EventHandler actor. This guarantees a maximum of flexibility and avoids that the plugins depend on the specific implementation. Basically, the EventHandler has references to all involved components and game objects like actors and events. Our EventHandler supports drag-and-drop in the Unreal editor window, hence, there is no coding required to establish these references. For instance, if we want to attach an mesh to the haptic device to use it as a virtual tool. In this case, we simply have to drag a ColletteStaticMeshActor instance on the EventHandler instance in the editor window.

In addition, the EventHandler implements various functions that it binds to the events of the plugins during initialization. For example, it provides functions for the two most important events: the OnTransform event sent by the haptic thread and for the OnCollision event of the ColletteVolume actor. The OnTransform event broadcasts the position and orientation data to the virtual tool automatically. This has the same effect as if the virtual tool would be updated directly in the haptic thread. Moreover, the OnTransform event also evokes a second delegate function from FORCECOMP that computes the collision forces based on this data. When finished, it passes the forces back to the HapticManager, which applies them to the associated haptic device (see Fig. 4 for a simplified example).

The OnCollision delegator event of the ColletteVolume actor sends the collision data to the attached function of the EventHandler and finally stores it in shared variables. By doing this, the haptic thread will execute the delegate after it has updated the virtual tool's transform. The delegate itself reads the data from the shared variables and

With this solution however, we keep the concrete implementations of the plugins separate from each other. Figure 5 shows and example for the event handling between FORCECOMP and HAPTICO.

Overall, a typical setup with our plugin system consists of three threads: one for the main game loop including the visual rendering in Unreal, one for the haptic rendering, that covers HAPTICO and FORCECOMP and one for the collision detection. We decided to run collision detection independently in it's own thread in order to guarantee stable haptic rendering rates even in the case of deep interpenetrations where the collision detection could exceed the 1ms time frame. Figure 3 shows this three-thread scenario. However, it is easy to use COLLETTE also in the haptic rendering thread (or to even spend a fourth thread for FORCECOMP) by simply adjusting the configuration in the EventHandler.

This modular and customizable approach guarantees a very flexible data flow between the different plugins that can be easily defined by the user within the editor.

4   Use Case

We applied the UNREALHAPTICS to a real-world application with support for haptic rendering. This example shows how actual collision detection libraries, force rendering and communication libraries can be integrated into our plugin system. Our use case is an asymmetric virtual reality multiplayer game [9]

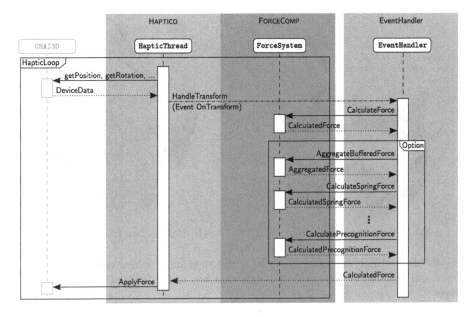

Fig. 5. A simplified sequence diagram of the communication of FORCECOMP, HAPTICO and our textttEventHandler that also shows the flexibility of our system. Initially, HAPTICO reads the configuration from the haptic library and evokes an `OnTransform` event. This is passed to the `EventHandler` that calls the callable `HandleTransform` function that has initially registered for this event. It is easy to register more than one functions for the same event, e.g. to toggle friction or virtual coupling. The results are finally transferred back to HAPTICO via the `EventHandler`.

where a visually impaired and a seeing player can interact collaboratively in the same virtual environment. While the seeing person uses a head mounted display (HMD) and tracked controllers like the HTC Vive hand controllers, the blind person operates a haptic force feedback device, like the PHANToM Omni.

4.1 Game Idea

An extensive research involving interviews with visually impaired people was done to understand their perspective for a good game before going into development phase. It turned out that most people we interviewed attach great importance to a captivating storyline and ambiance. Therefore we included believable recordings and realistic sound effects to achieve an exciting experience.

The game takes place in a museum owned by a dubious relics collector. A team of two professional thieves, Phantom and Vive, attempt to break into the museum in order to steal various valuable artifacts. The blind player takes control over Phantom, a technician, particularly skilled in compromising security systems and an expert for forgeries. Vive is played by the sighted player using an HMD. He is a professional pickpocket and a master of deceiving people.

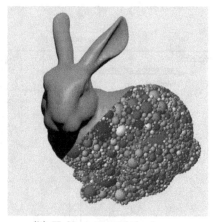

(a) Half-section of the crown   (b) Half-section of the bunny

Fig. 6. Objects from our game application and their inner sphere representations: A crown and a model of the Stanford bunny that has to be detected by the Phantom player.

For every exhibit in the museum, there are several fake artifacts that look exactly the same as the real ones. Since Vive is incapable of differentiating between real and fake artifacts, it is the job of Phantom to apply his skills here. Also, several guards patrol in the premises for possible intruders (see Fig. 7). Vive has to be careful not to get spotted or make too much noise as these guards are highly sensitive to sounds. Vive's job is to break the displays, collect the artifacts while distracting the guards and bring them to Phantom. Phantom's job on the other hand is to recognize the right artifact using his shape recognition expertise. The goal of the game is to steal and identify all the specified artifacts before the time runs out.

In order to identify objects and the differences between fake and real objects in the game, the Phantom player uses a haptic force feedback device to sweep over the virtual collected objects. As soon as the virtual representation of the haptic device collides with an object, UNREALHAPTICS detects these collisions and renders the resulting forces back to the haptic device. It is therefore possible for visually impaired people to perceive the object similarly to how they would in real life. Adding realistic sounds to this sampling could further improve this experience.

Even if the gameplay is in the foreground in our current use case, it is obvious that almost the same setup can be easily extended to perform complex object recognition tasks or to combine HMD and haptic interaction for the sighted player.

Fig. 7. In-game screenshot of our implemented game. The Phantom player sits at the table recognizing objects. A guard (right) is patrolling the room.

4.2   Implementation Details

The concept behind UNREALHAPTICS is explained in Sect. 3. The following sections will give an insight into our concrete implementations for the individual plugins.

Device Communication via CHAI3D. The basis for HAPTICO is the CHAI3D library. As already mentioned in Sect. 2, this library supports a wide variety of haptic devices, including the PHANToM and the *Haption Virtuose* [8] which we used for testing. CHAI3D is linked by HAPTICO as a third-party library at compile time. We primarily use CHAI3D's *Devices* module as an interface to the hardware devices, especially to set and retrieve positions and rotations. We did not use CHAI3D's force rendering algorithms as they do not support 6-DOF force calculation.

Collision Detection with CollDet. CollDet is a collision detection library written in C++ that implements a complete collision detection pipeline with several layers of filtering [27]. This includes broad-phase collision detection algorithms like a uniform grid or convex hull pre-filtering as well as several narrow phase algorithms like a memory optimized version of an AABB-tree, called Boxtree [25], and DOP-trees [26]. For haptic rendering, the *Inner Sphere Trees* data structure fits best. Unlike other methods, ISTs define hierarchical bounding volumes of spheres *inside* the object based on a polydisperse sphere packing (see Fig. 6). This approach is independent of the object's triangle count and it has shown to be applicable to haptic rendering. The main advantage, beyond the performance, is the collision information provided by the ISTs: they do not simply deliver a list of overlapping triangles but give an approximation of the objects' overlap volume. This guarantees stable and continuous forces and torques [23]. The source code is available under an academic-free license.

Collette's CanletteVolume is, at its core, a wrapper around CollDet's pipeline class. Instead of adding CollDet objects to the pipeline, the plugin abstract this process by registering the ColletteStaticMeshActors with the volume. Internally, a ColletteStaticMeshActor is assigned a ColID from the CollDet pipeline through its ColletteStaticMeshComponent, so that each actor represents a unique object in the pipeline. When the volume moves the objects and checks for collisions in the pipeline, it passes the IDs of the respective actors to the CollDet functions which implement the collision checking. Like with CHAI3D, Collette links to the CollDet library at compile time.

Force Calculation. Force and torque computations for haptics usually rely on penalty-based approaches because of their performance. The actual force computation method is closely related to the collision information that is delivered from Collette. In case of the ISTs this is a list of overlapping inner spheres for a pair of objects. In our implementation we apply a slightly modified volumetric collision response scheme as reported by [24]:

Fig. 8. In order to evaluate the performance of our plugins, we used a complex test scene where the user controls a gemstone with the Phantom device to touch the 3D Stanford bunny.

For an object A colliding with an object B we compute the restitution force $\boldsymbol{F}_A$ by

$$
\begin{aligned}
\boldsymbol{F}_A &= \sum_{j \cap i \neq \varnothing} \boldsymbol{F}_{A_i} \\
&= \sum_{j \cap i \neq \varnothing} \boldsymbol{n}_{i,j} \cdot \max\left(vol_{i,j} \cdot \left(\varepsilon_c - \frac{vel_{i,j} \cdot \varepsilon_d}{\text{Vol}_{total}} \right), 0 \right)
\end{aligned}
\tag{1}
$$

where (i, j) is a pair of colliding spheres, $\boldsymbol{n}_{i,j}$ is the collision normal, $vol_{i,j}$ is the overlap volume of the sphere pair, Vol_{total} is the total overlap volume of all colliding spheres, $vel_{i,j}$ is the magnitude of the relative velocity at the collision center in direction of $\boldsymbol{n}_{i,j}$. Additionally, we added an empirically determined scaling factor ε_c for the forces and applied some damping with ε_d to prevent unwanted increases of forces in the system.

Only positive forces are considered to prevent an increase in the overlapping volume of the objects. The total restitution force is then computed simply by summing up the restitution forces of all colliding sphere pairs.

Torques for full 6-DOF force feedback can be computed by

$$
\boldsymbol{\tau}_A = \sum_{j \cap i \neq \varnothing} (C_{i,j} - A_m) \times \boldsymbol{F}_{A_i}
\tag{2}
$$

where $C_{i,j}$ is the center of collision for sphere pair (i, j) and A_m is the center of mass of the object A. Again, the total torques of one object are computed by summing the torques of all colliding sphere pairs [24].

4.3   Performance

We have evaluated the performance of our implementation in the game on an Intel Core i7-6700K (4 Cores) with 64 GB of main memory and a NVIDIA GeForce GTX 1080 Ti running Microsoft Windows 10 Enterprise.

We used a typical test scene from our game: the user explores the surface of an object (in our example, the Stanford bunny) with a Phantom device. In our example, we represented the end effector by a gemstone (see Fig. 8).

We achieved almost always a frequency of 500-1K Hz for the force rendering and haptic communication thread. It only dropped slightly in case of situations with a lot of intersecting pairs of spheres. The same appears for the collision detection that slightly dropped to 500 Hz in situations of heavy interpenetrations. This is similar to the results reported in [23] where a simple OpenGL test scene was used and it shows that our architecture does not add significant processing overhead (see Fig. 9).

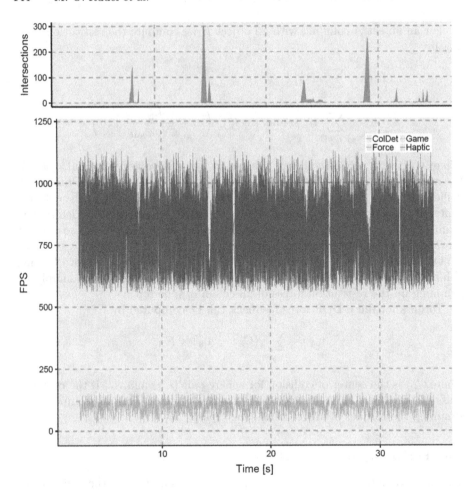

Fig. 9. Performance of our plugins in a typical exploration scene of about 35 seconds total duration in our game. We achieved haptic frame rates even in situations with large penetrations.

5   Conclusions and Future Work

We have presented a new plugin system for integrating haptics into modern plugin-orientated game engines. Our system consists of three individual plugins that cover the complete requirements for haptic rendering: communication with different hardware devices, collision detection and force rendering. Intentionally we used an abstract design of our plugins. This abstract and modular setup makes it easy for other developers to exchange parts of our system to adjust it to their individual needs. In our use case, a collaborative multiplayer VR game for blind and sighted people, we have demonstrated the simplicity of integrating external C++-libraries with our plugins, namely CHAI3D for the communication with the hardware and the collision detection library CollDet. Our results show that our plugin system works stably and the performance is well suited for haptic rendering even for complex non-convex objects.

With our plugin system, future projects have an easy way to provide haptic force feedback in haptic enabled games, serious games, and business related applications. Even though other developers may decide to use different libraries for their work, we are confident that our experiences reported here in combination with our high-level UE4 plugin system will simplify their integration effort enormously. Moreover, our system is not limited to haptic rendering but it can be also used to integrate general physically-based simulations.

However, our system, and the current CHAI3D and CollDet-based implementation also have some limitations that we want to solve in future developments: currently, our system is restricted to rigid body interaction. Further work may entail the inclusion of deformable objects. In this case, a rework of the interfaces is necessary because the amount of data to be exchanged between the plugins will increase significantly; instead of transferring simple matrices that represent the translation and orientation of an object we have to augment complete meshes. Direct access to UE4s mesh memory could be helpful to solve this challenge.

Also, our use case offers interesting avenues for future works. Currently, we plan a user study with blind video game players to test their acceptance of haptic devices in 3D multiplayer environments. Moreover, we want to investigate different haptic object recognition tasks, for instance with respect to the influence of the degrees of freedom of the haptic device or with bi-manual vs single-handed interaction. Finally, other haptic interaction metaphors could also be interesting, e.g. the use of the haptic devices as a virtual cane to enable orientation in 3D environments for blind people.

References

1. 3D Systems: Geomagic OpenHaptics Toolkit (2018). https://www.3dsystems.com/haptics-devices/openhaptics
2. Andrews, S., Mora, J., Lang, J., Lee, W.S.: Hapticast: a physically-based 3D game with Haptic feedback (2006)
3. CHAI3D: CHAI3D Documentation – Haptic Rendering (2018) http://www.chai3d.org/download/doc/html/chapter17-haptics.html
4. CHAI3D (2018). http://www.chai3d.org/
5. Epic Games: Plugins (17112017). https://docs.unrealengine.com/latest/INT/Programming/Plugins/index.html
6. Epic Games: Introduction to C++ Programming in UE4 (2018). https://docs.unrealengine.com/en-US/Programming/Introduction
7. H3DAPI. http://h3dapi.org/
8. Haption SA: Virtuose 6D desktop. https://www.haption.com/pdf/Datasheet_Virtuose_6DDesktop.pdf
9. Juul, J.: The game, the player, the world: looking for a heart of gameness. PLURAIS-Revista Multidisciplinar, vol. 1, no. 2 (2010)
10. Kadleček, P., Kmoch, S.P.: Overview of current developments in haptic APIs. In: Proceedings of CESCG (2011)

11. Kollasch, F.: Sirraherydya/phantom-omni-plugin (11122017). https://github.com/SirrahErydya/Phantom-Omni-Plugin

12. McNeely, W.A., Puterbaugh, K.D., Troy, J.J.: Six degree-of-freedom haptic rendering using voxel sampling. In: Proceedings of the 26th Annual Conference on Computer Graphics and Interactive Techniques, SIGGRAPH 1999, pp. 401–408. ACM Press/Addison-Wesley Publishing Co., New York (1999). https://doi.org/10.1145/311535.311600

13. Mól, A.C.A., Jorge, C.A.F., Couto, P.M.: Using a game engine for VR simulations in evacuation planning. IEEE Comput. Graph. Appl. **28**(3), 6–12 (2008). https://doi.org/10.1109/MCG.2008.61

14. Morris, D., Joshi, N., Salisbury, K.: Haptic battle pong: high-degree-of-freedom haptics in a multiplayer gaming environment (2004). https://www.microsoft.com/en-us/research/publication/haptic-battle-pong-high-degree-freedom-haptics-multiplayer-gaming-environment-2/

15. de Pedro, J., Esteban, G., Conde, M.A., Fernández, C.: HCore: a game engine independent OO architecture for fast development of Haptic simulators for teaching/learning. In: Proceedings of the Fourth International Conference on Technological Ecosystems for Enhancing Multiculturality, pp. 1011–1018. ACM (2016)

16. The Phantom of the Opera: SensAble technologies, Inc. http://www.sensable.com

17. Reinschluessel, A.V., et al.: Virtual reality for user-centered design and evaluation of touch-free interaction techniques for navigating medical images in the operating room. In: Proceedings of the 2017 CHI Conference Extended Abstracts on Human Factors in Computing Systems, CHI EA 2017, pp. 2001–2009. ACM, New York (2017). https://doi.org/10.1145/3027063.3053173

18. Ruffaldi, E., Frisoli, A., Bergamasco, M., Gottlieb, C., Tecchia, F.: A Haptic toolkit for the development of immersive and web-enabled games. In: Proceedings of the ACM Symposium on Virtual Rreality Software and Technology, pp. 320–323. ACM (2006)

19. Sagardia, M., Stouraitis, T., Silva, J.L.e.: A new fast and robust collision detection and force computation algorithm applied to the physics engine bullet: method, integration, and evaluation. In: Perret, J., et al. (eds.) EuroVR 2014 - Conference and Exhibition of the European Association of Virtual and Augmented Reality. The Eurographics Association (2014). https://doi.org/10.2312/eurovr.20141341

20. The Glasgow School of Art: Haptic demo in Unity using OpenHaptics with Phantom Omni (2014). https://www.youtube.com/watch?v=nmrviXro65g

21. The Glasgow School of Art: Unity Haptic Plugin for Geomagic OpenHaptics (HLAPI/HDAPI) (2018). https://assetstore.unity.com/packages/templates/unity-haptic-plugin-for-geomagic-openhaptics-hlapi-hdapi-19580

22. User ZeonmkII: Zeonmkii/omniplugin (1732016). https://github.com/ZeonmkII/OmniPlugin

23. Weller, R., Sagardia, M., Mainzer, D., Hulin, T., Zachmann, G., Preusche, C.: A benchmarking suite for 6-DOF real time collision response algorithms (2010). https://doi.org/10.1145/1889863.1889874. http://dl.acm.org/ft_gateway.cfm?id=1889874&type=pdf

24. Weller, R., Zachmann, G.: A unified approach for physically-based simulations and Haptic rendering. In: Davidson, D. (ed.) Sandbox 2009, p. 151. ACM, New York (2009). https://doi.org/10.1145/1581073.1581097

25. Zachmann, G.: The BoxTree: exact and fast collision detection of arbitrary Polyhedra. In: SIVE Workshop, pp. 104–112, July 1995

26. Zachmann, G.: Rapid collision detection by dynamically aligned DOP-trees. In: Proceedings of IEEE Virtual Reality Annual International Symposium, VRAIS 1998, Atlanta, Georgia, pp. 90–97, March 1998
27. Zachmann, G.: Optimizing the collision detection pipeline. In: Procedings of the First International Game Technology Conference (GTEC) (2001)

Distributed Signal Processing Architecture for Real-Time Convolution of 3D Audio Rendering for Mobile Applications

Yukio Iwaya[1,2(✉)] and Brian F. G. Katz[2]

[1] Tohoku Gakuin University, Tajao, Miyagi, Japan
yukio@iwaya-lab.org
[2] Sorbonne Université, CNRS, Institut Jean Le Rond ∂'Alembert, Paris, France
brian.katz@sorbonne-universite.fr

Abstract. By convolving an audio stream with a given pair of impulse responses between a source position and the two ears, virtual sound scenes can be created over headphones. Typically, the set of these filters for an ensemble of spatial positions, termed the Head-Related Impulse Response (HRIR) is used to render position information of a sound object to a listener. However, HRIRs are measured in free-field conditions, ignoring room reflections. In the real world, multiple reflections and reverberation exist, producing complex rich sound spaces. Including room reflections and reverberation with the HRIR results in a binaural room impulse response (BRIR). The length of a given BRIR depend on the shape and volume of the room, with BRIRs having typical duration of several seconds, resulting in computationally long processing. When the virtual environment is updated in response to head/body movement, BRIRs need to be updated according to the relative direction of a sound object within the perceptual detection threshold of system latency. This poses complications for mobile devices where processing power is limited, such as the case of augmented reality. In this paper, the architecture of a new signal processing method by distributed computers is proposed for convolution of BRIRs applicable to such conditions.

Keywords: Three-dimensional sound rendering
Binaural room impulse responses · Distributed signal processing
Real-time rendering

1 Introduction

Virtual sound spaces can be rendered over headphones/loudspeakers, providing a high sense of presence in virtual and augmented reality situations. Such audio rendering is termed virtual auditory display (VAD), which provides three-dimensional acoustic information to a listener's ears [11]. VAD can be constructed as a binaural rendering system through the use of headphones. In binaural rendering, the system is portable, with hardware costs being lower and

© Springer Nature Switzerland AG 2018
P. Bourdot et al. (Eds.): EuroVR 2018, LNCS 11162, pp. 148–157, 2018.
https://doi.org/10.1007/978-3-030-01790-3_9

installation simpler than with spatial audio loudspeaker array systems [3,9,15]. The virtual sound space is synthesized by convolution of an audio stream with a pair of impulse responses (IRs) between a sound source's position and both ears. Usually, IRs used in VAD are Head-Related Impulse Responses (HRIRs), or their frequency domain transfer function equivalent (HRTF) [4]. HRIRs can be used to render a sound object at a precise and determined position in space around the listener. HRIRs are defined in a free-field, therefore, any reflections or room reverberation are not included. In such a context, HRIRs have a duration on the order of a dozen milliseconds, for which HRIRs can easily be rendered with the current computation power of a common PC or mobile device.

In the real world, however, reflections and room reverberation exist. Such additional information provides a more complex, rich sound space and offers a more immersive feeling to the listener. Therefore, it is advantageous if we can render sound spaces including reflections and room reverberation. Including such information in the HRIR results in the binaural room impulse response (BRIR). The duration of a BRIR depends on the volume and shape of the virtual room, and can often have a duration of several seconds. As a result, additional computational power is required to render virtual spaces via BRIR than a simple sound via HRIR convolution.

Moreover, VAD systems which are responsive to head movement (VAD/RHM) can improve the accuracy of sound localization and the realism of the presented virtual acoustic space [6,7]. In a VAD/RHM system, IRs should be updated/swapped according to changes of relative sound position to the listener. An additional system latency is then present due to the update of the new position due to changing IRs. Yairi et al. [20] estimated detection threshold (DT) of system latency of VAD/RHM to be around 75 ms. Stitt et al. [18] showed that the latency detection threshold increased by 10 ms when comparing simple vs. complex sound scenes. To avoid perceptual artifacts, the total system latency in VAD/RHM systems should be shorter than DT. In current mobile devices, many sensors can be available, such as camera, microphone, compass, gyroscope, etc., some of which are available for sensing head movement. Therefore, these mobile devices are suitable for VAD/RHM. However, they have limited computation power and, in consequence complex, real-time rendering of sound fields such as via convolution with BRIRs cannot be realized.

Various projects in the past have attempted to provide real-time audio scene rendering [1,5,17], with some of them gearing towards mobility conditions with headphones. Warusfel and Eckel [19] employed a solely remote architecture with computed binaural transmitted over tracked wireless headphones to listeners. Mariette et al. [14] proposed a distributed rendering architecture using the remote computing of Ambisonic audio which was then streamed to client mini-PCs which performed the Ambisonic to binaural conversion locally using local head-tracking data. Finally, Katz et al. [12] proposed a purely local binaural rendering using a lightweight mobile PC in a backpack to perform binaural rendering using GPS and head-tracking data.

To take advantage of the combined computational power of modern mobile devices and larger remote machines, we have developed a VAD system (VAD-NR) responsive to listener head movements, where elements of the acoustic rendering are performed on a remote server and transmitted via the computer network while time-critical elements of the rendering are performed locally [10].

From the evaluation of the system in the network in our laboratory, the system latency for HRIR rendering was about 100 ms. The latency was slightly longer than the detection threshold. On the other hand, this latency includes buffering time in a client (android OS), transfer time of relative position from the client, and transfer time of rendered sound from a server. These times are just waiting times for the client computer, and they are useless. Therefore, the client may contribute to signal processing during these times.

In this paper, we propose a new rendering method for real-time sound scenes which can employ BRIRs within the latency detection threshold. We anticipate a maximum duration of BRIRs to be about 3 s (44.1 kHz sampling frequency), which is longer than the reverberation time of typical concert halls [2]. In our method, the convolution of BRIRs is realized by collaborative signal processing of distributed PCs. In the following sections, we describe the proposed algorithm and it's architecture, an example of implementation, and latency evaluation of the method.

2   Fast Convolution Method by Distributed Signal Processing

In this section, we describe the proposed method, which is realized by rendering long-duration impulse responses by distributed convolution via a computer network. Some conventional methods related to the proposed method are explained in Sects. 2.1–2.3. The proposed method is further described in 2.4.

2.1   Linear Convolution with FFT/IFFT

When an input signal $x(n)$ is rendered with an impulse response $h(n)$, the output signal $y(n)$ can be obtained from Eq. 1,

$$y(n) = x(n) * h(n), \tag{1}$$

where $*$ indicates linear convolution. The signal length N_y can be expressed by

$$N_y = N_x + N_{ir} - 1, \tag{2}$$

where N_x and N_{ir} express the length of $x(n)$ and $ir(n)$, respectively. When N_x and N_{ir} are the same number N, we can obtain the same result of Eq. (1) using Eq. 3:

$$y(n) = \text{IFFT}\left(X(k)IR(k)\right), \tag{3}$$

where $X(k)$ and $IR(k)$ are the Fourier transforms of $x(n)$ and $h(n)$, respectively. To prevent circular convolution, zeros of length N are added to both $x(n)$ and $h(n)$. By using Eq. 3, therefore, we can obtain the results faster than via Eq. 1, when N is large. The length of the result in Eq. 3 is $2N$.

2.2 Overlap-Add Method (OA)

In actual implementation, a long input signal $x(n)$ is divided into blocks of a fixed length, and the results of partial convolutions are appropriately added to their corresponding time positions in buffers. This is generally known as the *overlap-add* method [16]. In this case, $y(n)$ in Eq. 1 can be expressed as

$$y(n) = \sum_{i=0}^{M_{in}-1} y_i(n - iN_x), \qquad (4)$$

where

$$y_i(n) = x_i(n) * h(n), \qquad (5)$$

where $x_i(n)$ is the i-th block of the input signal, N_x is a fixed length of one block, M_{in} is the number of blocks of the input signal, and $y_i(n)$ is the partial convolution result of $x_i(n)$ and $h(n)$.

2.3 Double Overlap-Add Method (DOA)

When $h(n)$ in Eq. 4 has a long duration, it may take a excessive time to obtain the early output signals because of the need to compute the whole impulse response convolution. In such a case, the impulse response $h(n)$ can also be divided into blocks, and the output signal $y(n)$ can be expressed by Eq. 6:

$$y(n) = \sum_{i=0}^{M_{in}-1} \sum_{j=0}^{M_{ir}-1} y_{i,j}(n - iN_x - jN_{ir_b}), \qquad (6)$$

where $y_{i,j}(n) = x_i(n) * h_j(n)$, where $h_j(n)$, N_{ir_b}, M_{ir}, $y_{i,j}(n)$ indicate the j-th block of impulse response, length of the partial block of impulse response, number of blocks in the impulse response, and partial convolution result of i-th block of input and j-th block of impulse response, respectively. In such case, the length of the entire impulse response $N_{ir} = M_{ir} \times N_{ir_b}$. From Eq. 6, we obtain output signals when results of partial convolution $y_{i,j}(n)$ are added to buffers. This method is known as double overlap-add method [8].

2.4 Distributed Double Overlap-Add Method (DDOA)

In this subsection, we explain our proposed method. In actual implementation of Eq. 6, we need a lot of partial convolutions among blocks. Therefore, sufficient computation power is required. When using a low performance device, such as a mobile phone, to render a virtual sound space, computation power may be insufficient. Furthermore, a VAD/RHM system requires rapid swapping of IRs in the convolution buffer, according to head movements, achievable within the detection threshold of system latency.

It is necessary to calculate the partial convolution of the early part of the IR earlier than that of late response. Therefore, we distribute the set of partial convolutions between the client and server. On the client side, the partial convolution of the early blocks of the IRs are calculated. The remaining partial convolutions of the late blocks of the IRs are calculated on the server and transferred to the client while the early portions are being rendered as audio. In this case, the block size may be different between the server and client. The impulse response is divided into blocks, such that the early part of IR has length N_{cl} and late responses have a fixed length of N_{sv}. We can rewrite Eq. 6 as

$$
y(n) = \underbrace{\sum_{i=0}^{M_{in}-1} y_{\mathrm{cl},i}(n - iN_x)}_{\text{Calc. on Client}}
$$
$$
+ \underbrace{\sum_{i=0}^{M_{in}-1} \sum_{j=0}^{M_{ir}-1} y_{\mathrm{sv},i,j}(n - iN_x - N_{\mathrm{cl}} - jN_{\mathrm{sv}})}_{\text{Calc. on Server}}, \tag{7}
$$

where

$$
y_{\mathrm{cl},i}(n) = x_i(n) * h_{\mathrm{early}}(n), \tag{8}
$$
$$
y_{\mathrm{sv},i,j}(n) = x_i(n) * h_{\mathrm{late},j}(n), \tag{9}
$$

where $h_{\mathrm{early}}(n)$ and $h_{\mathrm{late},j}(n)$ are the early portion of IR of length N_{cl} and the j-th late portion of IR of length N_{sv}, respectively. In this case, the length of the entire impulse response is expressed by $N_{ir} = N_{\mathrm{cl}} + M_{ir} \times N_{\mathrm{sv}}$. Eqs. 8 and 9 are calculated on the client and server, respectively. Results of the partial convolutions of Eq. 9 are transferred from the server to the client. Finally, all partial convolutions are added to the audio buffer based on Eq. 7. Rendered sound of both ears are calculated simultaneously and delivered to a listener. This method is hereinafter referred to as the *distributed double overlap-add* method (DDOA). The architecture of the DDOA method is shown in Fig. 1.

In the DDOA method, convolution output signals of early portions of the IRs can be obtained rapidly on the client without any communication with the server. On the other hand, output signals of the later blocks are calculated on the server while the early portions are being rendered as audio to the listener. This type of collaborative processing between server and client is currently drawing attention in the field of IoT (Internet of Things) under the term 'Edge-computing'. Linear convolutions of partial data can be performed with different data sizes between client and server. Therefore, it is possible to calculation times on the server, when a larger FFT block is used.

3   Implementation Example of DDOA Method

In this section, we present an implementation example of the proposed method. Common PCs were used to confirm proper behavior of the method via a

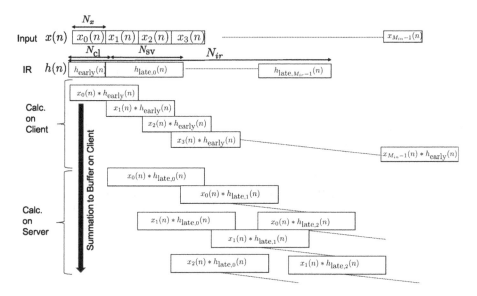

Fig. 1. Overview of the processing architecture of the distributed double overlap-add method (DDOA).

wired network. Two PCs were used for the system: the server (Microsoft Windows 10 Pro, Intel(R) Core(TM) i7-6770HQ CPU, 32 GB memory), and client (Microsoft Windows 10 Pro, Inter(R) Core(TM) i5-3210M CPU, 8 GB memory). They were connected with a wired network through a switching HUB (1 Gbps). Implementation was carried out using Microsoft Visual Studio 2015. A USB audio interface (Steinberg: UR 22) was connected to the client and was controlled through a low latency ASIO driver.

Several different threads were used to transfer data between PCs as follows:

- 1 thread to transfer position data from the client to the server,
- 1 thread to transfer original sound data from the server to the client, and
- M_{ir} threads to transfer rendered sound data blocks of the late portions of the BRIRs from the server to the client,

where M_{ir} is the number of partial convolutions on the server. All partial convolutions between input signal blocks and IR blocks were performed as multiplications in the frequency domain followed by an inverse-Fast Fourier Transform. Sampling frequency, f_s, was set to 44.1 kHz. The partial convolutions that could not be received "in time" on the client were discarded, *i.e.* if the partial convolution was not added to the convolution buffer in time, the client emitted the sound without the partial convolution contribution from the server.

3.1   Confirmation of Completion of Convolution

In this subsection, we investigate the success in completing the full convolution for the following IR conditions:

1. *First-1* Cond.: First sample of the IR $= 1$, remaining samples $= 0$. This case confirms if the input stream can be convolved on the client,
2. *Last-1* Cond.: Last sample of the IR $= 1$, remaining samples $= 0$. Confirms if the last data of IR can be convolved and transferred from the server.

Other parameters, such as N_{cl}, N_{SV}, and M_{ir}, were set to confirm distributed signal processing was adequately adjusted (see Table 1). Table 1 summarizes the results of this evaluation for the different conditions. For two of the four case configurations, both *First-1* and *Last-1* conditions resulted in satisfactory audio output of processing results without delay artifacts. From these results, it can be concluded that the system is capable of performing convolutions of BRIRs of 3 s (case 2). While BRIRs of the same length could not be convolved using 4 (instead of 8) threads (case 3). In Case 3, because the convolution block N_{SV} on the server side was too large, computation time of the partial convolutions became too large and they could not be convolved in time. It therefore appears necessary to correctly choose processing parameters between client and server in order to properly perform convolutions.

Table 1. Test case parameters and results summary to confirm system behavior of DDOA $f_s = 44.1$ kHz for *First-1* and *Last-1* conditions. ✓ indicates successful processing, × indicates failure to process in real-time.

Case ID	Client block length N_{cl}	Server block length N_{SV}	# of threads M_{ir}	IR length N_{ir}	*First-1*	*Last-1*
Case 1	2048 pt 46.4 ms	16384 pt 371 ms	4	67584 pt 1.53 s	✓	✓
Case 2	2048 pt 46.4 ms	16384 pt 371 ms	8	133120 pt 3.02 s	✓	✓
Case 3	2048 pt 46.4 ms	32768 pt 743 ms	4	133120 pt 3.02 s	✓	×
Case 4	2048 pt 46.4 ms	32768 pt 743 ms	8	264192 pt 5.99 s	×	×

3.2   Evaluation of System Latency When Changing IRs

We evaluated system latency in changing IRs according to relative position caused by head movement. However, there were no position sensors to capture head movement on the client PC in the current system. We measured system latency by following procedures.

Two IRs were prepared, $h_1(n)$ and $h_2(n)$, in which only the first data point was 1 and 0.5, respectively. The rest were zeros. Both IRs were used for both channels of headphones. Sinusoidal wave of one-minute-duration was used as an original sound. As a result, when IRs was changed, the amplitude of emitted

sinusoidal wave varied. On the other hand, when the new position was transferred from the client to the server, current data on buffer was set to zero by the
next new position on the right channel. We measured the time between beginning of zeros on the right channel to amplitude changing time of left channel as
a system latency. An example of measurement was shown in Fig. 2. Length of
all IRs was 133,120 pt (sampling frequency of 44.1 kHz), resulting in a duration
of IRs of approximately 3 s. The system latency was measured for 60 repetitions.
The average observed system latency was 32.7 ms. The maximum, minimum,
and standard deviation of the latency measurements were: 57.0 ms, 4.0 ms, and
14.8 ms, respectively. Using the detection threshold of system latency reported
in [20] of 75 ms, it can be confirmed that the system latency of the tested configuration was significantly less than the DT.

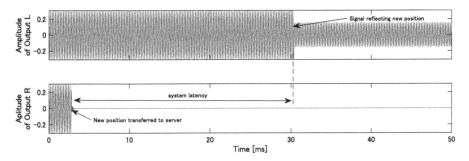

Fig. 2. Example of system latency measurement.

4   Summary

In order to present listeners with an immersive virtual sound space responsive
to head movements and presenting a high sense of presence, a fast convolution
and switching method for rendering spatial scenes via convolution with binaural
impulse responses comprising significant room reverberation decays is needed.
In this paper, we have proposed a new distributed convolution method utilizing
collaborative computation between a client and a server base employing the concept of *edge-computing* [13]. In the presented method, the early and late portions
of convolution impulse responses are rendered seperately on distributed computers. The system was validated as capable of real-time rendering with BRIRs on
the order of 3 s with an observed average system latency for IR swapping of
32.7 ms. This latency is shorter than reported latency detection thresholds [20].
In consequence, the proposed method would appear useful for the construction
of high definition VAD systems.

In future works, the system will be extended by implementing the client side
of the architecture on a mobile device. This step of using a lower capacity processor, as well as moving from a wired-network to wireless WiFi network communications will likely result in differences in treatment of sound buffers and communication latencies when compared to the currently present system architecture.

We fully anticipate being able to address these problems. The proposed architecture requires a high-speed network. In the current preliminary evaluation, a wired network was used. However, in the mobile scenario, will likely be a WiFi network. For example, in Case 2 in Table 1, at least $9 \times 1.4\,\text{Mbps} = 12.7\,\text{Mbps}$ data are exchanged between the client and server. These data exchange rates are easily achievable with current WiFi networks. The processing capability of the mobile device is a key point of the system. A short impulse response filter such as an HRIR can be processed in real-time on the client. Therefore, we should investigate whether data exchange and the addition of the partial convolution would be possible or not on the mobile device. Realizable BRIR lengths may need to be reduced compared to the current example for real-time convolution of the impulse response, due to reduced processing power of the mobile client device.

In addition to processing power, the system requires a set of BRIR according to each source and listening pair position combination. These data sets may be very large as it is necessary to consider various head directions for a given sound source position. To synthesize a fully interactive environment, a large RAM space may be required, which may cause issues, albeit on the server side where such limitations are not difficult to address. When high-resolution BRIR based on physical measurement are available, the proposed method can render these virtual sound fields with higher physical accuracy than conventional methods, such as ambisonic-based systems, to listeners.

The ability to provide immersive interactive spatially detailed 3D sound fields can be expected to develop in the following mobile applications: (1) auditory augmented reality art projects or museum visits, (2) multi-user shared VAR environments or game-play within interior spaces, and (3) architectural space navigation training and echolocation training for visually impaired people.

Acknowledgements. The authors would like to thank Mr. S. Ito, Mr. H. Nojiri, K. Saito, and Ms. J. Chiba for their contributions in implementation of the system. A part of this study was supported by JSPS Kakenhi (26280078) and by SCOPE from Ministry of Internal Affairs and Communications, Japan.

References

1. Assenmacher, I., Kuhlen, T., Lentz, T., Vorlaender, M.: Integrating real-time binaural acoustics into VR applications. In: Eurographics Conference on Virtual Environments, pp. 129–136 (2004)
2. Beranek, L.: Concert and Opera Halls: Music, Acoustics, and Architecture, 2nd edn. Springer, New York (2004). https://doi.org/10.1007/978-0-387-21636-2
3. Berkhout, A.J., de Vries, D., Vogel, P.: Acoustic control by wave field synthesis. J. Acoust. Soc. Am. **93**(5), 2764–2778 (1993)
4. Blauert, J.: Spatial Hearing. MIT Press, Cambridge (1997)
5. Funkhouser, T., Min, P., Carlbom, I.: Real-time acoustic modeling for distributed virtual environments. In: Conference on Computer Graphics and Interactive Techniques. SIGGRAPH, pp. 365–374 (1999). https://doi.org/10.1145/311535.311590

6. Hendrickx, E., Stitt, P., Messonnier, J.C., Lyzwa, J.M., Katz, B.F., de Boishraud, C.: Improvement of externalization by listener and source movement, using a "binauralized" microphone array. J. Audio Eng. Soc., pp. 589–599 (2017). https://doi.org/10.17743/jaes.2017.0018

7. Hendrickx, E., Stitt, P., Messonnier, J.C., Lyzwa, J.M., Katz, B.F., de Boishraud, C.: Influence of head tracking on the externalization of speech stimuli for non-individualized binaural synthesis. J. Acoust. Soc. Am. **141**(3), 2011–2023 (2017). https://doi.org/10.1121/1.4978612

8. Iiboshi, H., Yanagida, M.: Double overlap processing for convolving a long impulse response with an infinite length signal. In: Proceedings of FIT, pp. 11–12 (2004). (in Japanese)

9. Ise, S.: A principle of sound field control based on the Kirchhoff-Helmholtz integral equation and the theory of inverse systems. Acta Acust. United Acust. **85**(1), 78–87 (1999)

10. Iwaya, Y., Otani, M., Tsuchiya, T., Li, J.: Virtual auditory display on a smartphone for high-resolution acoustic space by remote rendering. In: International Conference on Intelligent Information Hiding and Multimedia Signal Processing (IIHMSP), pp. 368–371 (2015)

11. Iwaya, Y., Suzuki, Y.: Sound localization and virtual auditory display. J. IEICE **89**(1), 1091–1095 (2006). (in Japanese)

12. Katz, B.F., et al.: NAVIG: augmented reality guidance system for the visually impaired. Virtual Real. **16**(4), 253–269 (2012). https://doi.org/10.1007/s10055-012-0213-6

13. Lopez, P.G., et al.: Edge-centric computing: vision and challenges. ACM SIGCOMM Comput. Commun. Rev. **45**(5), 37–42 (2015)

14. Mariette, N., Katz, B., Boussetta, K., Guillerminet, O.: SoundDelta: a study of audio augmented reality using WiFi-distributed Ambisonic cell rendering. In: Audio Engineering Society Convention 128, London, pp. 1–15 (2010). http://www.aes.org/e-lib/browse.cfm?elib=15420

15. Poletti, M.: Three-dimensional surround sound systems based on spherical harmonics. J. Audio Eng. Soc. **23**, 1004–1025 (2005)

16. Proakis, J.G., Manolakis, D.K.: Digital Signal Processing, 3rd edn. Prentice-Hall, Englewood Cliffs (1996)

17. Schissler, C., Manocha, D.: Interactive sound rendering on mobile devices using ray-parameterized reverberation filters. CoRR abs/1803.00430 (2018). http://arxiv.org/abs/1803.00430

18. Stitt, P., Hendrickx, E., Messonnier, J.C., Katz, B.F.G.: The influence of head tracking latency on binaural rendering in simple and complex sound scenes. In: Audio Engineering Society Convention 140, Paris, pp. 9591:1–8, June 2016. http://www.aes.org/e-lib/browse.cfm?elib=18289

19. Warusfel, O., Eckel, G.: LISTEN - augmenting everyday environments through interactive soundscapes. In: Workshop VR for Public Consumption, IEEE VR, Chicago (2004). http://resumbrae.com/vr04/warusfel.pdf

20. Yairi, S., Iwaya, Y., Suzuki, Y.: Estimation of detection threshold of system latency of virtual auditory display. Appl. Acoust. **68**(8), 851–863 (2007)

Perception and Cognition

A Virtual Reality Investigation of the Impact of Wallpaper Pattern Scale on Qualitative Spaciousness Judgments and Action-Based Measures of Room Size Perception

Governess Simpson[1], Ariadne Sinnis-Bourozikas[2], Megan Zhao[3], Sahar Aseeri[1], and Victoria Interrante[1(✉)]

[1] University of Minnesota, Minneapolis, MN 55455, USA
{simps422,aseer002,interran}@umn.edu
[2] Bard College, Annandale-on-Hudson, NY 12504, USA
ariadne.sinnisbourozikas@gmail.com
[3] Carleton College, Northfield, MN 55057, USA
zhaom@carleton.edu

Abstract. Visual design elements influence the spaciousness of a room. Although wallpaper and stencil patterns are widely used in interior design, there is a lack of research on how these surface treatments affect people's perception of the space. We examined whether the dominant scale of a wallpaper pattern (i) impacts subjective spaciousness judgments, or (ii) alters action-based measures of a room's size. We found that both were true: participants reported lower subjective ratings of spaciousness in rooms covered with bolder (larger scale) texture patterns, and they also judged these rooms to be smaller than equivalently-sized rooms covered with finer-scaled patterns in action-based estimates of their egocentric distance from the opposing wall of the room. This research reinforces the utility of VR as a supporting technology for architecture and design, as the information we gathered from these experiments can help designers and consumers make better informed decisions about interior surface treatments.

Keywords: Virtual environments · Wallpaper patterns
Spaciousness perception · Egocentric distance judgments · Interior design

1 Introduction

As increasing research emerges on the interaction between architectural design and the perceptual human experience, interior designers and architects have begun to consider the visual attributes that affect user perception of architectural quality. Studies show that, among these attributes, spaciousness is an important quality on which people base their descriptions and assessments of the environment [5]. Ozdemir's research [12] also indicates a positive correlation between people's satisfaction and their sense of spaciousness of the environment. Therefore, a knowledge of architectural attributes that

© Springer Nature Switzerland AG 2018
P. Bourdot et al. (Eds.): EuroVR 2018, LNCS 11162, pp. 161–176, 2018.
https://doi.org/10.1007/978-3-030-01790-3_10

cause a perception of increased spaciousness will contribute to the future efforts of architects and interior designers.

There has been extensive research on how the presence of various architectural attributes, such as windows and lighting, can affect the perception of spaciousness. However, there have been very few studies on the subject of wallpaper patterns, which is a crucial element of interior design. A lack of knowledge in this area may cause inaccurate judgement in interior environment quality due to professional bias or the absence of user input in design selection [4]. Such judgment can lead to negative interior experience and thus affect people's everyday life.

To assist architects to design pleasing interior environments and to establish a basis for further research in this area, we investigated the potential relationship between the scale of a wallpaper pattern and people's perception of the environment's spaciousness. By using immersive virtual reality technology, we were able to easily manipulate the main factors of metric room size and wallpaper pattern scale and at the same time fully control for other features that could potentially affect the sense of spaciousness of the room, such as lighting, ceiling height, windows, etc.

2   Previous Work

There are many previous studies that suggest that certain architectural and design features impact our visual perception of a space. In examining how the physical characteristics of a room affect its perceived spaciousness, researchers have found a positive correlation between the horizontal area and/or ceiling height of a room and its perceived spaciousness [15]. Changing the aspect ratio of a room can also lead to an altered perception of spaciousness even though the total floor area remains constant. Experiments have found that elongated rooms – spaces with a higher ratio of length to width – are judged as less spacious than square rooms of equivalent size [14]. The manipulation of furnishing within a room can also affect the visual perception of spaciousness; the more objects that take up a room, the more crowded and cramped a room can feel, which results in a decrease in perceived room spaciousness [1]. It has also been found that rooms with lighter-colored walls appear bigger, and that lighter-colored ceilings feel taller, which in turn increases people's spaciousness ratings of a space, while the luminance of the floor doesn't appear to affect spaciousness judgments [11, 12]. Designers have also opined that certain stripes and patterns can subjectively widen or narrow a space [6].

From the aforementioned previous work, we have learned that an abundance of architectural design elements can influence our perceived sense of the spaciousness of a room. However, quantitative studies regarding whether wallpaper patterns impact our judgment of room proportions – particularly in an immersive virtual environment – have yet to be thoroughly explored and performed. We were able to use immersive virtual reality to control for many other variables that would be almost impossible to do in real physical rooms and look at how the scale of the elements in wallpaper pattern affects the sense of a room's spaciousness and size.

It is important to also acknowledge that there is an abundance of research in the virtual reality and psychology fields showing that people tend to systematically underestimate egocentric distances when viewing virtual environments using head-mounted displays [9] and the root cause of this problem is still not well-understood [13]. While researchers are actively investigating potential methods for facilitating more veridical spatial judgments in VR [7], and we cannot yet assume that spaciousness judgments made in VR will exactly match spaciousness judgments made in the real world, we nevertheless feel that virtual reality can provide a robust platform for studying potential differences in subjective and objective measures of room size and spaciousness caused by differences in surface treatments [3].

3   Experiment

Our experiment consisted of two parts. In the first part, we asked participants to provide subjective ratings of spaciousness in seven differently-sized rooms, each with five different interior surface treatments (four differently-scaled texture patterns and a solid color that represented the average intensity of the texture). In the second part, we asked participants to make action-based estimates [8] of their egocentric distance from the opposing wall in four differently-sized rooms, each with four differently-scaled texture patterns.

Our hypotheses were that (1) the scale of the wallpaper texture would affect people's perceived sense of spaciousness in a room, but that (2) their action-based judgments of the metric size of the room would not be affected.

3.1   Participants

A total of 14 participants from our local community completed the study (7 m., 7f., ages 19–30, $\mu = 21.3 \pm 2.7$). We had recruited 15 overall, but one participant experienced cybersickness halfway through the second block of trials and was unable to continue; their data was not included in the analysis. Two of the participants were members of our lab, though they were not involved in the design or implementation of the experiment. However, they did have some prior knowledge about the hypotheses being tested. We recruited by word of mouth among personal contacts and students from other Research Experience for Undergraduates (REU) programs. All participants who were not lab members were compensated with a $10 Amazon gift card; participants who were members of our lab were not compensated, to avoid conflict of interest. The experiment was approved by the Institutional Review Board at the University of Minnesota, and all participants gave written informed consent.

3.2   Materials

We created a set of nine different sized square-shaped rooms, the largest and smallest of which were only shown once and used to anchor participants' spaciousness judgments. We chose to use seven room sizes for testing so that the participants couldn't easily store the size of each room in their short term memory. The room sizes were: 4.00 m × 4.00 m, 4.33 m × 4.33 m, 4.67 m × 4.67 m, 5.00 m × 5.00 m, 5.33 m 5.33 m, 5.67 m × 5.67 m and 6.00 m × 6.00 m. All rooms had a ceiling height of

2.743 m. The range was chosen to be wide enough that participants could easily differentiate between the largest and smallest sizes, but with small enough increments that the difference between rooms adjacent in size could potentially be mistaken. Each room had a textureless white ceiling and neutral grey floor. We applied five different types of surface treatments to the four walls of each room: a wallpaper texture featuring small (11.60 cm), medium (15.55 cm), large (23.30 cm), or extra large (46.65 cm) diamond-shaped elements, or a solid grey color representing the average of all pixel colors in the wallpaper used. This resulted in a total of 35 different rooms. Figure 1 shows the nine different room sizes rendered with the solid color and Fig. 2 shows what each of the different wallpaper patterns looked like on the same-sized room.

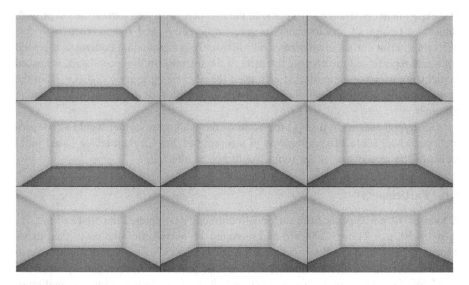

Fig. 1. Top row: 3.67 m, 4.00 m, 4.33 m; Middle row: 4.67 m, 5.00 m, 5.33 m; Bottom row: 5.67 m, 6.00 m, 6.33 m.

We built the rooms in Google SketchUp and then imported them into the Unreal Engine to apply the textures, wall colors, and lighting. The wallpaper texture was inspired by an example from Pinterest[1], recreated using Powerpoint and Photoshop, then proportionally scaled in the Unreal Engine to achieve the four different sizes used. We chose a design featuring oblique elements in order to avoid any inadvertent visual synchrony between the wallpaper pattern and the horizontal and vertical lines formed by the edges between the walls, ceiling, and floor. The individual elements were offset from each other to ensure that smaller elements did not visually group when viewed from far away to form larger elements, such as dominant lines going through the pattern. The diamond shape was chosen because there is no scale intrinsically

---

[1] https://ar.pinterest.com/pin/366269382190103454/.

associated with that element (e.g. unlike a rectangle, which might be intuitively associated with a standard sized brick) and because when grouped together they do not evoke any horizontal or vertical lines. The lighting was done as emissive lighting in the Unreal Engine, meaning that there was no direct light source, although there was some darkening in the corners achieved via ambient occlusion. This was done in order to ensure that the lighting was consistent in all of the differently-sized rooms. We chose a black-and-white color scheme to achieve maximum pattern contrast.

Fig. 2. The four differently-scaled wallpaper patterns applied to the 4 m room.

Participants were immersed in the virtual environment using an HTC Vive head-mounted display and their viewpoint was tracked using the Valve's Lighthouse Tracking system. The HTC Vive head-mounted display weighs about one pound and offers a 110° field of view. It has two OLED displays, each with a resolution of 1080 × 1200 pixels.

This study took place in our lab space of approximately 8.83 m × 9.14 m. The HTC Vive automatically shows a boundary square on the ground when one nears the edge of what the system has predetermined to be the edge of the tracked space. In reality, the Valve's Lighthouse Tracking system provides accurate tracking beyond this space, and in the second part of the experiment, participants often walked beyond these bounds.

3.3   Procedure

Participants were scheduled individually by appointment so that no participant was exposed to the any activity of any other participant. Each participant was welcomed into the lab by the same experimenter and screened for adequate visual acuity, defined by the ability to successfully read lines of letters corresponding to 20/70 or above on a wall-mounted eye chart from a distance of 20'. Next, participants were screened for stereo vision by asking them to describe the contents of two different random dot stereograms presented on the HTC Vive. The ability to pass both of these screenings determined a participant's eligibility to participate in the experiment. All participants passed both the visual and stereo acuity tests. After they passed the screenings, participants were asked to sign an informed consent form and were given written instructions for the first half of the experiment. Written instructions for the second half of the experiment were provided after participants had completed the first part.

For the first half of the experiment, participants were asked to stand at a predefined location in the real-world environment that was marked by a piece of tape on the floor. For each trial, the Unreal engine set the virtual camera to be at a random coordinate in the horizonal direction between two-sevenths and five-sevenths of the room's width while maintaining a constant 0.95 m distance from the wall at their back. We chose 0.95 m so that participants could have a fairly wide view of the virtual room in front of them while not being able to touch the walls of the real lab space behind them. At the start of the experiment, participants were shown two rooms to anchor their spaciousness ratings. They were shown a 3.67 m × 3.67 m room (smaller than any other room in the experiment) and told that they should consider this room to be a 1 on the spaciousness scale, and a 6.33 m × 6.33 m room (bigger than any other room in the experiment) and told that they should consider this to be a 10 on the spaciousness scale. Both of these rooms had solid colored walls, the same grey that was the average of all the pixels in the wallpaper used in the experiment. Next, the 35 different rooms were shown to the participant in a randomized order that was unique for each participant. For each room, the participant was asked to verbally rate the room's spaciousness on the scale of 1–10. Each room was faded in from black, the participant gave a spaciousness rating, and then the room was faded out to black and after a very brief delay the next room was faded in. The purpose of this transition was to discourage participants from making comparative judgments. When each room faded in, the participant found themselves at a slightly different spot in the room but always the same distance from the wall. Figure 3 shows the leftmost and rightmost extents of the interval across which the viewpoint was randomly distributed. The rating process took about 10–15 min in total for the 35 rooms. After finishing the first block of trials, participants were given a five minute break during which they had to take off the headset. The same process was then repeated for a second time. The participants then removed the headset after this second block of trials and took a ten minute break before beginning the second half of the experiment.

Fig. 3. These images illustrate the maximum extent of the random sideways shift that was applied to the participant's position in the room between each trial.

In the second half of the experiment, the participants were asked to make action-based judgments of egocentric distance in a subset of the original 35 rooms. This subset consisted of the rooms that were 4.00 m × 4.00 m, 4.67 m × 4.67 m, 5.33 m 5.33 m and 6.00 m × 6.00 m, each with all of the different sized wallpapers (not including the solid-colored condition) for a total of 16 rooms. We chose to limit the number of trials to 16 in this part of the experiment so as to not exhaust the participant. During this part of the experiment, the participants wore noise cancelling headphones to block out ambient sounds that might otherwise have provided audio cues to their location in the physical world. Each room faded in with the participant standing at a point where two-thirds of the room's width was in front of them and the walls on each side were equidistant. We chose this configuration so as to keep the participant within the tracked space during the course of each trial. For each trial, the participant was told that they should close their eyes, after which time the walls of the room would be removed, and that they should then walk through the room until they feel that their body is at the exact location where the opposite wall used to be. The experimenter pressed a key to record the starting position of the participant when the room as faded in, and when the participant had stopped walking the experimenter pressed another key to record their ending position. To ensure that the participant could not see where they were in relation to the room, the visuals were turned to black when the participant indicated that they were ready to walk. We recorded their starting and ending coordinates using the Valve's Lighthouse Tracking system to calculate the distance they walked. To avoid allowing the participants to familiarize themselves with the space, we verbally guided them on a random, circuitous path back to the starting position. The experiment ended after the participant had completed these 16 trials.

4 Results

The first result from our first experiment is the observation that people's spaciousness judgments increased linearly with the room size. A two-way ANOVA (7 room sizes × 5 texture scales) found a significant main effect of room size on spaciousness judgments {$F(6, 455) = 205.15$, $p < 0.001$}, and all pairwise differences were found to be significant at $\alpha = 0.05$ according to the Tukey HSD test, except between the two largest rooms. The number of degrees-of-freedom reflects the fact that each participant's repeated ratings (between the first and second blocks of trials) were averaged to a single value before performing the statistical analysis. Figure 4 shows these results. This finding, while expected, provides a robust sanity check on the overall validity of the experimental procedure.

Since each participant made spaciousness ratings for each room twice, we were able to assess the consistency of their ratings. We found that two participants had a median difference of 3 in their ratings between the blocks of trials, and a maximum difference of 9, meaning that on at least one occasion they had rated the same room as having a spaciousness of 1 in one block and a spaciousness of 10 in the other block. Two additional participants had a median inter-block difference of 2 in their subjective spaciousness ratings, and maximum differences of 7 and 8. Each of the remaining 10 participants had a median difference of 1 in their spaciousness ratings between blocks

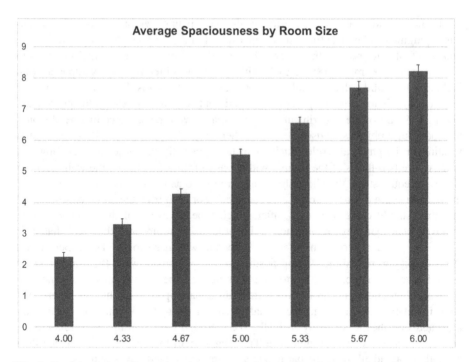

Fig. 4. Participants' spaciousness ratings, averaged over all surface treatments for each room size presented. The error bars represent ±1 standard error.

and a maximum difference of between 3–5. Overall, while some rating inconsistencies did occur, they do not appear to have significantly affected the outcome of the experiment.

The most interesting finding from our first experiment is that participants' spaciousness ratings are inversely related to the scale of the wallpaper texture. The same two-way ANOVA also found a significant main effect of texture scale on room spaciousness judgments $\{F(4, 455) = 32.30, p < 0.001\}$. The Tukey HSD test found that the rooms with the largest-size texture elements (XL) were judged to be significantly less spacious than equivalently-sized rooms textured with the small (S) and medium sized (M) elements as well as the solid colored room ($p < 0.01$), and the rooms with the next-to-largest texture elements (L) were judged to be significantly less spacious than rooms with the finest-scale texture elements (S) ($p < 0.05$). These results support the first part of our hypothesis that as the wallpaper texture scale increases, people's subjective perception of the spaciousness of the room decreases. Figure 5 shows a plot of these findings.

The two-way ANOVA did not find any significant interaction between room size and texture scale $\{F(24, 455) = 0.711, p = 0.842\}$.

The first result from the second part of our experiment is the finding that people walked longer distances when the wall was farther away from them. A two-way ANOVA (4 room sizes × 4 texture scales) found a statistically significant main effect of room size on distance walked $\{F(3, 208) = 49.14, p < 0.001\}$, and Tukey HSD

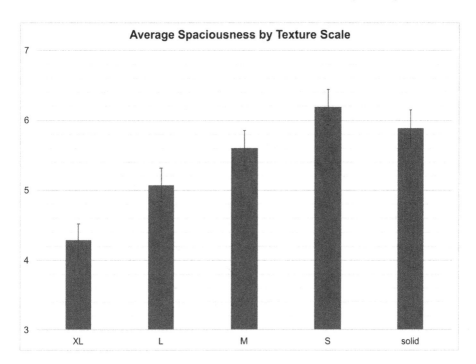

Fig. 5. Participants' spaciousness ratings, averaged over all room sizes for each texture scale. The error bars represent ±1 standard error.

post-hoc tests found that all pairwise differences were also significant at $p < 0.05$. This result provides a reassuring sanity check on the validity of the experimental process.

Figure 6 shows a scatter plot of each individual distance judgment, with a bold line showing the linear trend. As can be seen from this figure, most people walked significantly shorter than the actual distance of the virtual wall. The overall average amount of distance underestimation, computed across all participants, all rooms, and all textures, was 29.7%. This finding is consistent with classical reports of systematic distance underestimation in virtual environments [13].

The most interesting finding from our second experiment is that, on average, people tended to physically underestimate distances more as the scale of the wallpaper pattern increased. The same two-way ANOVA found a significant main effect of texture scale on distance walked {$F(3, 208) = 8.21$, $p < 0.01$}, and Tukey HSD post-hoc tests found that people walked significantly shorter in the rooms with the two largest scale wallpaper textures (L, XL) than in the room with the finest scale pattern (S), with $p < 0.05$ and $p < 0.01$, respectively. Figure 7 shows these results.

The two-way ANOVA did not find a significant interaction between room size and texture scale {$F(9,208) = 1.694$, $p = 0.092$}. However we observed a slight trend towards the texture scale having a stronger effect on distance walked as the rooms became larger.

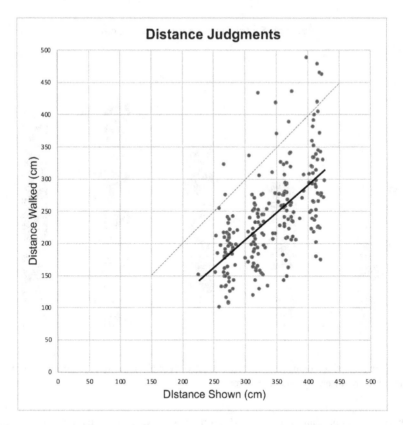

Fig. 6. A scatter plot showing each distance judgment made by each participant. The slight variation in the distances shown is due to participants not starting exactly at the prescribed starting location used to define the initial relationship between the viewer and the room in our software. The bold trendline plots the linear trend in the data; the light grey line shows where ideal performance would lie.

In a separate statistical test, we verified that there was no significant difference {F (3, 220) = 0.038, p = 0.99} in the overall average distance shown (from the observer to the far wall of the room) between texture conditions, as might have potentially occurred because participants did not stand exactly on the starting line at the start of each trial.

The results from our second experiment refute the second part of our hypothesis that the size of the wallpaper texture would not affect people's action-based egocentric judgement of the size of the room. Rather, they extend our first hypothesis – that people's perception of the spaciousness of a room will decrease as the scale of the wallpaper pattern increases – to an effect on metric size judgments as well.

5 Discussion

Our findings – that the dominant scale of a wallpaper texture pattern can have a significant impact both on people's subjective feeling of the spaciousness of a room and on their action-based judgments of the actual locations of the walls of the room – make sense in the context of our everyday experience of the statistics of built environments. In 2003, Torralba and Oliva [16] showed that in a collection of hundreds of images, the characteristics of the dominant spatial frequencies varied systematically with the distance of the camera from the imaged scene, on a scale ranging from less than one meter to a kilometer or more. In indoor or external views of man-made environments, they found that images taken from closer views tended to be dominated by lower spatial frequency content, and that as camera distances increased, the images' spectral signatures reflected a greater presence of higher spatial frequencies, particularly in the horizontal and vertical directions. It may be that people have developed an intuitive sense of the typical range of spatial frequencies associated with their experience of being in close-in versus larger spaces, and that texture patterns with "unnaturally" bold features may feel somehow enlarged, evoking an impression that they are closer than they really are.

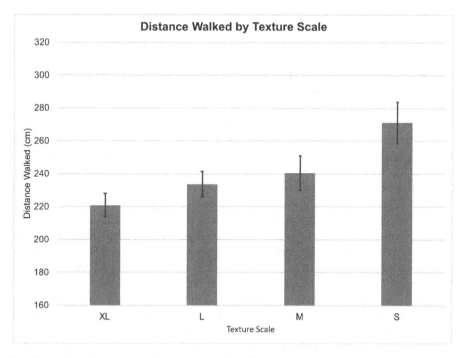

Fig. 7. A plot of the average distance walked by all participants, averaged over all room sizes, for each texture scale. The error bars represent ±1 standard error.

It could also be that as the dominant features in the wallpaper pattern get larger, they become more individually noticeable and thereby create a greater sense of clutter that could also make a room feel less spacious. We deliberately chose to use a starkly contrasting pattern in our present study to allow the texture's scale to be readily apparent across a wide range of distances. It might be interesting to explore a wider range of pattern contrasts in future work, as lower-contrast patterns might have less impact on people's sense of the spaciousness of a room regardless of the dominant scale of the texture.

It is important to note that the pattern of the smallest scale texture appeared slightly blurry when viewed through the head-mounted display. Particularly, the lines making up each of the elements of the smallest patterned wallpaper were notably less distinct on the opposite side of the room than on the more nearby walls. This effect is due to the limited resolution of the OLED displays on the current HTC Vive, as only 1200 pixels are available to subtend 110° of visual angle in the vertical direction, while the naked eye can resolve two points of light separated by a visual angle of one arc minute (1/60°), a difference of 5.5×. The phenomenon of decreasing clarity with increasing distance is a hallmark of atmospheric attenuation, a recognized cue to depth [2]. It is therefore possible that the greater apparent blurriness of smaller texture features could evoke a heightened impression that those surfaces are located farther away than comparable surfaces on which the texture features appear more distinct.

In Fig. 5, it may be noted that the solid-colored rooms appear to have been rated, on average, as slightly less spacious than the rooms featuring the finest wallpaper pattern. This suggests the possible potential of using very finely-textured wallpaper to enhance the sense of spaciousness in a room. However, we must emphasize that our experiment did not find these differences to be statistically significant, and further studies with more participants would be necessary to support any claim that a room's sense of spaciousness might have the potential to be enhanced, rather than diminished, by the application of an appropriately chosen wallpaper pattern.

Finally, we acknowledge the possibility that some participants may have disregarded the written instructions provided to them. We observed one participant in particular verbally counting steps during the second half of the experiment, even though the written instructions (which can be seen in the appendices to this paper) had explicitly requested that they avoid doing so and warned that using such artificial strategies would interfere with the research goals of the study. It is additionally possible that other participants could have been counting steps non-verbally, without our being aware of it. We did not debrief participants to find out what strategies they had used to reach the target because our written instructions had so clearly specified the process we wanted them to use that we did not anticipate non-compliance. Also, even though participants were explicitly told to keep their eyes closed at all times during the second part of the experiment except when viewing the room at the very beginning of each trial, the possibility remains that some participants might have opened their eyes as they walked. In such an event, they might have been able to see the bounding line of the Vive's tracking space, which would appear as a dark grey square on the ground whenever the participant traveled farther than 2.79 m beyond the designated starting position. However, our data do not show any evidence of a change in error rates at longer distances; the proportion of distance underestimation in the largest rooms is similar to that in the smaller ones where the grid would not have been active.

6 Conclusions and Future Work

This study provides potentially useful insights to architects and interior designers by showing that the scale of a wallpaper pattern can not only affect people's subjective impression of spaciousness in a room, which is primarily an emotional sensation [5], but that it can also affect their action-based judgments of how far away from them the walls of a room are located. This understanding of how the dominant scale of a wallpaper pattern impacts spatial judgments can be deployed when designing spaces to make them seem more spacious or, alternatively, more cozy. In addition to wall treatments, there are many other features of a room's design that can affect its perceived spaciousness, and we plan to continue our efforts to use virtual reality technology to explore other design-related hypotheses and to better support an informed design process overall.

Acknowledgments. This work was supported by the National Science Foundation through grants CHS: Small: Transforming the Architectural Design Review Process through Collaborative Embodiment in HMD-based Immersive Virtual Environments (1526693), by REU Site: Computational Methods for Discovery Driven by Big Data (1757916), by the Computing Research Association's Committee on the Status of Women in Research (CRA-W) through its Distributed Research Experiences for Undergraduates (DREU) program, by Carleton College's Summer Internship Funding, and by the Linda and Ted Johnson Digital Design Consortium Endowment.

Appendix A: Written Instructions (Part 1)

You will be asked to perform two simple tasks multiple times for this experiment. Please try to perform each task at a natural and consistent pace. To make things easier to remember, we will give you the instructions for each task separately.

Preparation: If you look at the carpet in our lab, you will see a red colored tape mark. Please stand on top of the tape so that your heels align with the back edge of the tape mark. (Note, you will not see this tape in the virtual reality environment). Once you are in the correct position, we will ask you to put on a head mounted display (HTC Vive). Please take some time to adjust the straps on the device so that it fits your head comfortably. We will then ask you to go through a brief calibration procedure to optimize the visuals for your individual head shape.

Task: We will show you a series of virtual rooms and will ask you to rate how spacious they feel to you using a scale from 1 to 10. We will start out by showing you two rooms that you can use to help anchor this scale; you can consider the first room to be an example of a place that has a spaciousness of "1" and the second room to be an example of a place that has a spaciousness of "10". We will then show you, one at a time, a series of 35 different rooms. As each room becomes visible, please briefly look around (without taking any steps) and then verbally tell us the number that best corresponds to how spacious the room feels to you. After we record your rating, the screen will briefly turn black and then a different virtual room will become visible. Please note that you will be seeing each room from a slightly different position. After you have provided a verbal rating for each of the 35 rooms we will ask you to take off the head-mounted display and have a short break. Following this break, we will show you a different set of 35 rooms and will ask you to provide another set of spaciousness ratings. If at any point, during any of the trials, you start to feel tired, distracted, impatient, or otherwise uncomfortable or unhappy, please let us know and we will pause the experiment to let you rest.

It is important for us to stress that there are no right or wrong answers in any part of this task. We are just very interested to know how each room makes you feel. What is important to the integrity of our experiment is that you treat each judgment independently and devote the same level of attention and care to all of the judgments you make. We expect that this portion of the experiment will take about 20–30 min in total, and after this part is completed we will give you a long break.

Please remember that you are always free to discontinue your participation in this experiment at any time, for any reason. In that event you would still be compensated with a gift card of value proportional to the time you spent.

Thank you in advance for your participation. Please ask us if you have any questions at any time.

Appendix B: Written Instructions (Part 2)

Task: In this part of the experiment, we will ask you to wear a set of headphones (playing an ambient sound track) in addition to wearing the head-mounted display. Please start out by standing at the same red tape mark as before. After you have put on the head-mounted display, we will show you a series of 16 different virtual rooms. In each room, we will ask you to take visual aim at the opposite wall of the room (located directly in front of you), then close your eyes. After you have closed your eyes, please say "ready" and we will remove the walls of the room. We then ask that you keep your eyes closed and physically walk through the room that you remember until you feel that you have reached the exact location of where the wall used to be. Please stop walking when you feel that your head and eyes would be exactly inside of the wall, if the wall were still there. When you believe you have reached the target location, please keep your eyes closed and wait a few moments for us to record your position. We will then verbally direct you to walk, with your eyes still closed, in a circuitous path back to a different starting point for the next trial. Please be sure to keep your eyes closed for the entire time until we explicitly tell you to open them again.

In each trial, as you walk from your starting point to the wall, please try to imagine what the virtual room would look like as you move through it. It is very important to the integrity of our experiment that you do not use any artificial strategies to reach the wall, such as numerically estimating the distance from the starting point and then counting steps, or referring back to your memory of a previous room and abstractly pre-deciding to just take more or fewer steps than you did before, as that would invalidate our research. We need to stress that our goal in this experiment is not to "judge" the task performance of any individual against any sort of benchmark. Our goal is to better understand how the human brain interprets 3D space as people physically walk around with their eyes closed in virtual reality, and we cannot do that properly unless the described protocol is carefully followed. What is most important to us is that you let your intuition guide you, on each trial independently, in knowing when you have reached the wall of each virtual room. We expect that this portion of the experiment will take about 30–40 min.

End: All data will be de-identified before it is analyzed, so we will not be able to share your individual results with you, as we will have no way to know them ourselves. But we will be happy to share our overall findings with you after the experiment has been completed. If you would like to receive a copy of any eventual publication on this experiment, please let us know.

Within two weeks from the completion date of the experiment, we will ask the Department of Computer Science to order a $10 Amazon gift card for you, in compensation for your participation. The email containing the gift certificate will come directly from amazon.com and will be sent to the email address you provided on the consent form. The gift card will not expire. If for any reason you fail to receive the email with the gift card, or you inadvertently lose the email before having a chance to use the gift card, you can always contact us to have the gift card re-issued, even after a delay of many months or years.

Please remember that you are always free to discontinue your participation in the experiment at any time, for any reason. In that event you would still be compensated with a gift card of value proportional to the time you spent.

Thank you in advance for your participation. Please ask us if you have any questions at any time.

References

1. Castell, C.V., Oberfeld, D., Hecht, H.: The effect of furnishing on perceived spatial dimensions and spaciousness of interior space. PLoS ONE **9**(11), e113267 (2014)
2. Cutting, J.E., Vishton, P.M.: Perceiving layout and knowing distances: the integration, relative potency, and contextual use of different information about depth. In: Epstein, W., Rogers, S. (eds.) Perception of Space and Motion, pp. 69–117. Academic Press (1995)
3. Franz, G., von der Heyde, M., Bülthoff, H.: An empirical approach to the experience of architectural space in virtual reality – exploring relations between features and affective appraisals of rectangular indoor spaces. Autom. Constr. **14**(2), 165–172 (2005)
4. Hershberger, R.G., Clements, R.C.: A study of meaning and architecture. Rev. Res. Vis. Environ. Educ. **1**(1), 75–82 (1973)
5. Imamoglu, V.: Assessing the spaciousness of interiors. METU J. Fac. Archit. **7**(2), 127–142 (1986)
6. Jaglarz, A.: The application of optical illusions in interior design in order to improve the visual size and proportions of the rooms. In: Vink, P. (ed.) 2012 International Conference on Applied Human Factors and Ergonomics (AHFE), San Francisco, USA. Advances in Social and Organizational Factors, vol. 12. CRC Press (2012)

7. Kelly, J.W., Cherep, L.A., Klesel, B., Siegel, Z.D., George, S: Comparison of two methods for improving distance perception in virtual reality. ACM Trans. Appl. Percept. **15**(2), 11 p. (2018). Article no. 11

8. Loomis, J.M., DaSilva, J.A., Fujita, N., Fukusima, S.S.: Visual space perception and visually directed action. J. Exp. Psychol. Hum. Percept. Perform. **18**(4), 906–921 (1992)

9. Loomis, J., Knapp, J.: Visual perception of egocentric distance in real and virtual environments. In: Hettinger, L.J., Haas, M.W. (eds.) Virtual and Adaptive Environments, pp. 21–46. Lawrence Erlbaum Associates Publishers (2003)

10. Oberfeld, D., Hecht, H., Gamer, M.: Surface lightness influences perceived room height. Q. J. Exp. Psychol. **63**(10), 1999–2011 (2010)

11. Oberfeld, D., Hecht, H.: Fashion versus perception: the impact of surface lightness on the perceived dimensions of interior space. Hum. Factors: J. Hum. Factors Ergonom. Soc. **53**(3), 284–298 (2011)

12. Ozdemir, A.: The effect of window views' openness and naturalness on the perception of rooms' spaciousness and brightness: a visual preference study. Sci. Res. Essays **5**(16), 2275–2287 (2010)

13. Renner, R.S., Velichkovsky, B.M., Helmert, J.R.: The perception of egocentric distances in virtual environments - a review. ACM Comput. Surv. 46(2), 40 p. (2013). Article no. 23

14. Sadalla, E.K., Oxley, D.: The perception of room size. Environ. Behav. **16**(3), 394–405 (1984)

15. Stamps, A.E.: Effects of area, height, elongation, and color on perceived spaciousness. Environ. Behav. **43**(2), 252–273 (2010)

16. Torralba, A., Oliva, A.: Statistics of natural image categories. Netw.: Comput. Neural Syst. **14**(3), 391–412 (2003)

Context-Dependent Memory in Real and Virtual Reality

Maik Lanen(iD) and Maarten H. Lamers(✉)(iD)

Leiden Institute of Advanced Computer Science, Leiden University,
Leiden, The Netherlands
maiklanen@gmail.com, m.h.lamers@liacs.leidenuniv.nl

Abstract. Context-dependency effects on memory exist, whereby people's context influences their ability to recall items from memory. This effect was not previously studied when considering VR as an environmental context. We show that adverse effects on memory exist when changing between virtual and real environments. The effect was not present when memorizing and recall were both done in VR; it appears caused by the change of environmental context. This previously unknown result challenges how we use VR in education and training. It undermines the paradigm that VR can be effectively used for learning information whereby later recall of that information in a real environment is important. In a memory-recall experiment ($n = 51$) participants that underwent a context change involving VR after memorizing performed significantly worse on 24-hour later item recall than those who did not change context (17% lower accuracy, $p < 0.001$). In particular memorizing in VR as opposed to a real environment lowers accuracy of recall in a real environment (24% lower, $p = 0.001$).

Keywords: Virtual reality · Memory · Context-dependency

1 Introduction

It is possible that you have had to memorize words for learning a secondary language. Sitting at home you memorize the given words until you are able to recall them well. The next day at school, you are quizzed on your ability to recall the words and you find yourself forgetting a portion of the words. Is it because you have started studying too late? Is it because you did not study hard enough? However, upon your return home, when sitting behind your desk again, somehow you can recall most of the "forgotten" words. How is that possible?

This could be caused by an effect known as *context-dependent memory*, wherein your context influences the ability to recall items from your memory. For example, in 1975 Godden and Baddeley [1] let two groups of divers memorize words in different contexts, namely under water and on land. Later, all participants were asked to recall the words while being in either the same or the other context. It was found that subjects asked to recall in the other context than the one in which they had memorized the items did so significantly worse than those who were asked to recall them in the same

© Springer Nature Switzerland AG 2018
P. Bourdot et al. (Eds.): EuroVR 2018, LNCS 11162, pp. 177–189, 2018.
https://doi.org/10.1007/978-3-030-01790-3_11

context. Apparently a change in context negatively affected the ability to recall items learned. This effect was later found to exist for other context changes also.

The relation of context-dependent memory and virtual reality is an interesting topic to research as the role of VR has become more prevalent in society. For example, consider search-and-rescue workers who learned the position of potential victims in a virtual environment. Will they recall these positions in reality as well as in training, or will the change of context from VR to reality affect their recall ability? An analogous case could be argued in light of increasing use of VR in education. Our study aims to uncover knowledge about context-dependent memory and its relation to VR.

To uncover whether the change of context from VR to real environment and vice-versa affects our ability to recall items memorized, we hypothesize that such a change negatively affects our ability to recall when compared to an unchanged context, analogous to effects shown in prior studies. To test our hypothesis, we constructed and realized an empirical study ($n = 51$), based on methods and findings from prior studies. Our analyses take into account potential effects caused by the use of VR as a context and focus on the effects of context change.

We firstly explore the most relevant related work done to-date, specifically in relation to memory, context-dependency, and VR. Based on the review of prior studies we construct the experiment, of which all choices are described in Sect. 3. Analyses of the results are presented and discussed in light of our hypothesis and potential implications of our findings.

2   Related Work

Here we concisely sketch an overview of prior results that are of interest to our hypothesis. For sake of brevity, selected prior research is mentioned, not aiming to be exhaustive.

2.1   Memory and Context

In a famous study of 1969, Goodwin et al. performed an experiment [2] whereby participants performed four different memory tasks while being sober or being under the influence of alcohol. After twenty-four hours, the participants were tested under both the conditions. Results showed that participants were better in recalling memorized items when being tested in the same state they learned in. Their ability to recognize had not been altered by the different states; thus, not all sub-forms of memory were affected. The memorization and recall tasks applied by Goodwin et al. form the basis of our own experimental design, as is explained in a further section.

As mentioned in our Introduction, Godden and Baddeley [1] showed that the context-dependency effect on memory extends to the external environment also, i.c. under water versus on land. From this it was concluded that the disruption in moving from one environment to another negatively influences the ability to recall memory learned in the first environment.

This outcome firmly underlies our own study, as we also study potential context-dependency effects on memory caused by moving from one environment to another.

Specifically we consider disruption caused by moving from a real to a similar but virtual environment, and vice-versa.

Other prior results include an outcome that no context-dependency was found in a memory-recall task that considered different tastes as contexts – one context being created by chewing mint-flavored gum, the other by chewing flavorless gum [3]. Also a change of mood (happy/sad) was found to adversely affect ability to recall memorized items [4], as opposed to when mood was unchanged. When given a task that relies less on contextual information, but more on introspective thought for example, then context-dependency effects on memory-recall tasks are less strong [5].

2.2 Memory and Virtual Reality

The validity of using VR to assess learning and memory skills in brain-injured and healthy individuals was studied by Matheis *et al.* [6]. The authors found a significant correspondence between their VR-based assessment of memory and a standard neuropsychological measure. From this they conclude that VR "provides a viable medium for measuring learning and memory".

A study that compared potential effects on memory between active and passive participation in a virtual environment [7], found that participants with active participation tested as having a better memory for spatial layouts while participants who passively participated tested higher in object recall.

Naturally, how realistic a virtual environment is, is an interesting aspect to consider in relation to memory recall tasks. This was studied by Dinh *et al.* [8] by way of a multi-modal experience wherein subjects could smell, feel and hear a virtual environment. Results showed that by offering tactile input, the quality of presence in VR was enhanced, making it easier for the participants to remember objects in the virtual environment. Auditory and olfactory stimuli only increased the feeling of being present in the virtual world, but had no effect on memorization.

Perhaps less related to our work are studies in which personal demographics (e.g. age [9]), medical conditions (e.g. non-progressive brain injury [10]) or mental parameters (e.g. depression [11]) act as different contexts for memorization and spatial recall tasks in VR.

2.3 Virtual Reality and Context-Dependent Memory, an Unexplored Area

We have shown that prior studies have compared VR and real environments with respect to their effects on memory. Moreover, VR was shown to be suitable for memory-recall assessment within the VR environment itself. However, no prior study was done to uncover possible context-dependency effects on memory when changing between virtual and real environmental contexts. It is exactly that knowledge gap which our study aims to fill.

3   Method

Our experimental design considers four randomly assigned groups of participants who must memorize and recall items in either the same or a different context. Twenty-four hours after memorizing, participants are assessed on their ability to recall the memorized items (cf. [2] and other studies). Since in practice, assessing all participants after exactly twenty-four hours may be difficult, the exact memorizing and recall times are noted and used to check for possible confounding effects of retention duration.

3.1   Real and Virtual Environments

We aim to make the real and virtual environments, which form the contexts for our study into context-dependent memory, as similar in experience as possible. By doing so we focus on uncovering potential effects of a change between a real and similar virtual environment, as opposed to effects caused by unnecessary large discrepancies between both environments. Naturally, in the hypothetical case that the virtual environment is indistinguishable from the real environment, we would not expect such effects to exist. To be relevant with regards to the current state of VR technology, we create a likeness between real and virtual environments that is exemplary of said current state.

As the scenario that forms the context of our memory-recall study, participants are seated in an office chair behind a desk. A book is placed centered on the desk in front of them. A potted plant stands on the left side of the desk surface. Wooden divider boards surround the desk's left, right and opposing ends. A poster is hung on the right divider board, at eye's height. The plant and office chair are the same in both the real and virtual scenarios and the divider boards and poster as similar as possible. In both the real and virtual contexts participants are seated in front of the real desk on the real office chair (Fig. 1).

Fig. 1. Photograph of a participant in the real experimental setting (left) and overview from an observer's point-of-view of the virtual experimental environment created in Unity (right). (Color figure online)

In the virtual context, participants are outfitted with an HTC Vive headset and a single HTC Vive controller, enabling them to look around and interact with the virtual book on the desk. Turning a page of the virtual book is done by moving the virtual hand towards the top right corner of the book, clicking and holding the trigger on the controller and making an overturning movement to thereafter release the trigger. In VR, the test persons can see their own avatar's arm that is dressed in a blue sleeve and has light toned skin (as we expected most test participants to have light toned skin).

Participants are asked to have the same interaction with the real environment as in the virtual world. Both in the real and virtual environments they are only allowed to look around and turn over pages of the book in front of them. The experiment is executed in two different locations, namely in the office environment of a sports retail company in the city of Leiden and in an educational environment within a building of the Rotterdam University of Applied Sciences. Both memorizing and recall occur at the same experimental location for each participant.

3.2 Language and Demographics

Participants are given two language options from which they can choose to perform the experiment in: Dutch and English. We provide both language options because during a small pilot study some Dutch participants were observed to have difficulties performing the experiment in English. Since a lack of fluency in a language could affect memory recall, participants can only participate in the experiment when they are fluent in Dutch or English, as assessment that is made by participants themselves.

Several demographic variables are collected via self-report from participants, namely gender, age, prior experience with VR, and education level. Demographic questions are formulated by the standards of the PGA Group [12], questions about education are formulated by the European Qualifications Framework [13].

3.3 Orientation Task

After being introduced to their given context (real or VR), participants are verbally instructed to execute a simple orientation task within the given context. It is intended to make participants familiar with the given context and to ensure that the participant is proficient enough technologically to participate in the experiment. The orientation task consists of (1) looking around at different objects (plant, poster, and book) and (2) executing an example task wherein the participant interacts with the book on the table by turning one page, either in reality or VR. On the day of recall, participants were asked to do the same orientation task as on the day of memorizing.

The orientation task is considered successfully completed if the participant is able to perform the requested interactions. If not, then the supervisor will try to help the participant to master the interactions. If the participant is then not able to master the interactions, then s/he is excluded from the experiment.

3.4   Rote-Learning Task

After the introduction and orientation task, participants must complete three tasks which were based on studies by Goodwin *et al*. [2] and Marks *et al*. [14]. These tasks are a rote-learning task, an association task and a recognition task. The resulting recall scores from the three tasks are averaged to form an overall "recall score" per participant. Here we start with describing the rote-learning task.

Memorizing. The rote-learning task consists of saying four 5-word sentences/lists (Table 1) with varying meaningfulness out loud, repeatedly, for the duration of two minutes (cf. [3]). Participants are asked to remember the sentences as they will be assessed on their ability to recall them after twenty-four hours.

There are four types of sentences/lists: a normal sentence (arbitrarily obtained from a magazine), an anomalous sentence (obtained from a paper by Chomsky [15]), an anagram list (obtained from online anagram generator litscape.com), and a word list (obtained from online tool textfixer.com). All were translated from English to Dutch, except for the anagram list (obtained from Dutch online tool mijnwoordenboek.nl). The sentences are provided in the real or virtual book.

Table 1. Four English and Dutch five-word sentences/lists used in the rote-learning task.

Type	English	Dutch
Normal sentence	I walk to the station	Ik loop naar het station
Anomalous sentence	Colourless green ideas sleep furiously	Kleurloze groene ideeën slapen woedend
Anagram list	Drawer, Redraw, Reward, Warder, Warred	Mentors, Stormen, Stromen, `n Stomer, `t Morsen
Word list	Flatness, Iron, Harbor, Crab, Thief	Vlakheid, IJzer, Haven, Krab, Dief

Recall. Participants were asked to recall the sentences/lists learned within two minutes (cf. [1]). Participants must say the sentences out loud while their voice is being recorded. Participants are prohibited to ask the supervisor for hints regarding the memorized sentences.

Assessment. Recall performance is measured in terms of the number of sequence and omission errors. It is possible that participants recall a sentence or list differently than learned, but the meaning is nearly the same. We applied an online tool (provided by explosion.ai) that gives scores based on assessed similarity. E.g. comparing "*I walk to the station*" and "*I walked to the station*" results in a similarity score of 0.97. For the word list and anagram list we use the fraction of correct answers. If a participant recalls a word that is close to the learned word, then we asses this differently. E.g. if a participant recalls the word list (Table 1) as "*Flat, Iron, Harbor, Crab, Thief*", we asses "*Flat*" as a semi-correct recall, resulting for this recall sequence in a score 0.9. It is also possible that a participant might say the recalled sentence with slight variance several times. We decided to only assess the last verbal submission to prevent lucky guesses. Every recalled sentence/list yields a score between zero and one. The final score for the rote-learning task is the average of the scores for all four memorized sentences/lists.

3.5   Association Task

Memorizing. Participants are asked to say out loud the first word that comes to mind in reaction to each of ten given low-association words (obtained from a study by Burke *et al.* [16]). For Dutch speaking participants, these words were translated to Dutch (Table 2).

Table 2. Ten English and Dutch low-association words used in the association task.

English (from [16])	Dutch (translated from English)
Chance, cruel, lazy, melt, narrow, money, now, size, time, tall	Kans, wreed, lui, smelten, smal, geld, nu, maat, tijd, lang

Recall. Given the same stimulus words as provided during memorizing, participants must recall the self-associated word and say them out loud.

Assessment. Only the final submission for each given stimulus word is assessed – previous submissions are not assessed. Scoring is done conform the assessment procedure for the rote-learning task.

3.6   Recognition Task

Memorizing. Participants are asked to memorize twenty different pictures, displayed in randomized order each on an individual page of the book. Ten pictures have emotional content (5 female and 5 male cover models from erotically themed magazines) and ten pictures have neutral content (5 female and 5 male mail-order catalog models), cf. the study by Goodwin *et al.* [2]. Participants are allowed to browse the images for a maximum duration of five minutes.

Recall. Participants are asked to select maximally twenty memorized pictures from forty pictures shown in the book, after browsing through the pictures for maximally ten minutes. The twenty newly added pictures are of similar nature and distribution as the memorized pictures.

Assessment. The recognition task is scored as the fraction of memorized pictures correctly recalled. If participants change their mind during the recall period, then their last submission is considered the final submission.

4 Results

Within seven weeks (Spring 2018) 57 participants voluntarily did the memorizing tasks, of which 51 also returned for the recall tasks. The six non-returning subjects (two memorized in VR, four in the real environment) were not contacted and no reason for their absence is known. Their data was discarded and not expected to introduce selection bias. All participants opted for the Dutch language tasks, and all successfully completed the orientation tasks before both memorizing and recall.

Table 3 compares the mean recall scores[1] across various demographic sub-samples of the total sample ($n = 51$). From the resulting p-values we conclude that participant gender, experimental testing location, occupational status and prior experience with VR did not significantly affect the mean recall score.

Table 3. Outcomes (p-values) of multiple independent samples Student's T-tests, comparing recall scores across various demographic sub-samples.

Sub-group	n	Normally distr.	Mean (SD) recall score	p
Females	21	Yes	0.635 (0.146)	0.516
Males	30	Yes	0.660 (0.126)	
Tested at retail offices	19	Yes	0.638 (0.157)	0.641
Tested at education location	32	Yes	0.657 (0.121)	
Students	41	Yes	0.646 (0.128)	0.722
Waged staff	10	Yes	0.664 (0.163)	
Prior VR experience	27	Yes	0.647 (0.130)	0.839
No VR experience	24	Yes	0.653 (0.142)	

Not all participants could perform the recall tasks exactly twenty-four hours (1440 min) after the memorizing tasks. Figure 2 illustrates the correlation between retention duration in minutes (*mean* = 1455, *SD* = 104, normally distributed) before recall and recall score (*mean* = 0.650, *SD* = 0.134, normally distributed). No evidence of significant correlation was found, leading us to conclude that variation in retention duration as found in our sample does not affect recall score.

As mentioned earlier participants were randomly assigned to one of four context conditions: R+R when both memorizing and recalling in the real context, V+R when memorizing in the virtual context and recalling in the real context, etcetera. By joining groups R+R with V+V and groups R+V with V+R we obtain two new groups of participants: one for whom the contexts during memorizing and recall were the same, and one for whom the context changed.

---

[1] Throughout this paper statistical significance is defined as $p < 0.05$ and indicated with *. Student's T-tests are all two-tailed and assume equal variances. Normality is assessed through Shapiro-Wilk testing with $p < 0.05$ indicating deviation from normality.

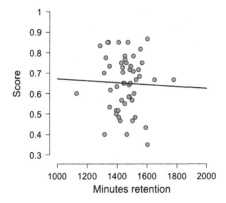

Fig. 2. Scatter plot correlating retention duration (in minutes) and recall score of all participants ($n = 51$, Pearson's $r = -0.037$, $p = 0.797$). Note that 24 h equals 1440 min.

Figure 3 and Table 4 compare mean recall scores across combinations of these groups. Participants whose environmental context changed score on average significantly lower ($p < 0.001$) than those for whom the context did not change; 17% lower in fact. This result confirms our main hypothesis that context-dependency effects as found in prior research exist for environments of real and virtual nature also.

When comparing recall scores for context-conditions R+R and V+R the relative decrease in recall accuracy is 24% when memorizing in the virtual as opposed to the real environment. This result is particularly striking in face of current interests in VR as a learning environment. This difference is statistically significant (Student's T-test $p = 0.001$, not included in Table 4).

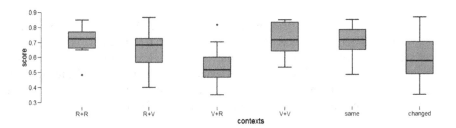

Fig. 3. Boxplots of recall scores for different context groups (detailed values in Table 4).

Table 4. Outcomes (*p*-values) of multiple independent samples Student's T-tests, comparing recall scores across various memorizing and recall context-conditions. Normality of distribution is indicated under column "Norm."

Memorizing context	Recall context	*n*	Norm.	Mean (SD) recall score	*p*
Real	Real	12	Yes	0.708 (0.094)	0.901
Virtual	Virtual	13	Yes	0.713 (0.109)	
Real	Virtual	13	Yes	0.642 (0.133)	0.058
Virtual	Real	13	Yes	0.540 (0.128)	
Same context		25	Yes	0.711 (0.100)	<0.001*
Changed context		26	Yes	0.591 (0.138)	

Through an additional ANOVA test we compared recall scores using the memorizing and recall contexts as fixed factors. Outcomes (Table 5) tell us that the contexts in which memorizing and recall are done do not by themselves affect the recall score in a statically significant manner. However, the interaction between both factors is statistically significant, supporting our hypothesis that recall scores are affected by context change and not by the memorizing or recall context itself.

Table 5. Outcomes (*p*-values) of two-way ANOVA test using memorizing and recall context-conditions as factors.

Tested factor	*p*
Memorizing context	0.148
Recall context	0.111
Interaction between memorizing and recall contexts	<0.001*

When we consider the separate memory tasks (Table 6), then we observe that a context change negatively affects all mean task-specific recall scores. However, statistical significance of this outcome is found for the rote-learning task and the recognition task, but not for the association task. Deviation from normality of the recognition scores was visually scrutinized and found to be caused by their tendency to be on average near the maximum score, yet with substantial variance.

Table 6. Comparison (independent samples Student's T-test *p*-values) of mean recall scores for separate memory tasks, per context-changed and -unchanged group. Normality of distribution is indicated under column "Norm."

| Task | Same context | | | Changed context | | | |
	n	Norm.	Mean (SD) recall	*n*	Norm.	Mean (SD) recall	*p*
Rote-learning	25	Yes	0.473 (0.221)	26	Yes	0.294 (0.225)	0.006*
Association	25	Yes	0.792 (0.144)	26	Yes	0.715 (0.185)	0.106
Recognition	25	No*	0.868 (0.104)	26	No*	0.763 (0.214)	0.032*

5   Discussion

This study investigates the previously unexplored area of context-dependency effects on memory when changing between virtual and real environments. The outcomes of our experiment clearly show that significant and substantial adverse effects on memory exist. Reviewing the results, we conclude that they are valid to base conclusions on. Memory recall scores do not appear to be influenced by demographic factors in our sample and prior experience with VR. All participants were native Dutch speakers, meaning that no language effects are expected.

Our hypothesis that a change in environmental context between VR and real environment has an adverse effect on the ability to recall after twenty-four hours is supported by a highly significant ($p < 0.001$) difference in recall scores between groups with and without a change of environmental context. The group with a context change scored 17% lower on item recall accuracy. This main result is novel, yet corresponds with prior research findings regarding other environmental contexts (e.g. under water and on land [1]) and mental states (e.g. under the influence of alcohol and sober [2]).

Another highly significant result is that the ability to accurately recall items in a real environment is 24% lower when these items were memorized in VR when compared to memorization in a real environment ($p = 0.001$). This previously unknown result challenges how we use VR in education and training. It undermines the generally accepted paradigm that VR can be effectively used for learning when accurate recall of that information in a real environment is important. One could conjecture that memorizing in VR is more difficult than memorizing in the real environment. Excitement for or novelty of VR might make it more difficult for participants to memorize in the VR context. However, if this conjecture were to hold, then one would hypothesize the V+V context group to score lower than the R+R group, which was not the case. Moreover, two-way ANOVA testing showed that memorizing and recall contexts separately do not significantly affect recall scores, but that their interaction does ($p < 0.001$). As such the alternative explanation for the findings, posed in this paragraph, is unsupported and the low recall performance under V+R condition is attributed to content-change.

We provided an example in our introduction of search-and-rescue workers who must learn the position of potential victims. Do the uncovered effects imply that it is unwanted to use VR for this task? We cannot answer this question with certainty. However, our findings do mean that we are less certain that VR can be effectively used for memorizing information whereby recall in reality is important.

Recall scores of the rote-learning task and the recognition task were significantly affected by a change in environmental context, while the negative effect of context change on the association task recall was not strong enough to be significant. In the association task, participants create self-generated content which must be memorized. Perhaps the association task recall is influenced less by a context change because it is more focused on generating content than on learning given content. It is possible that self-generated memory is less susceptive to a context-dependency effect, a finding that may relate to effects of introspective thought found by Smith et al. [5]. We can conclude that not all sub-forms of memory are equally sensitive to the effect (confirming prior finding, e.g. [2]).

A final matter worthy of further attention is that in this work we only considered short-term context-dependency effects on memory – we did not take long-term effects into account, which is something that further research could explore. Also context-dependency effects caused by changing graphic and immersive qualities of the VR environment remain open for investigation. One could hypothesize that as VR immersion and realism approach that of the real world, that context-dependent memory effects become less dominant, if not absent.

References

1. Godden, D.R., Baddeley, A.D.: Context-dependent memory in two natural environments: on land and underwater. Br. J. Psychol. **66**(3), 325–331 (1975)
2. Goodwin, D.W., Powell, B., Bremer, D., Hoine, H., Stern, J.: Alcohol and recall: state-dependent effects in man. Science **163**(3873), 1358–1360 (1969)
3. Johnson, A.J., Miles, C.: Chewing gum and context-dependent memory: the independent roles of chewing gum and mint flavour. Br. J. Psychol. **99**(2), 293–306 (2008)
4. Bower, G.H., Monteiro, K.P., Gilligan, S.G.: Emotional mood as a context for learning and recall. J. Verbal Learn. Verbal Behav. **17**(5), 573–585 (1978)
5. Smith, S.M., Vela, E.: Environmental context-dependent memory: a review and meta-analysis. Psychon. Bull. Rev. **8**(2), 203–220 (2001)
6. Matheis, R.J., Schultheis, M.T., Tiersky, L.A., DeLuca, J., Millis, S.R., Rizzo, A.: Is learning and memory different in a virtual environment? Clin. Neuropsychol. **21**(1), 146–161 (2007)
7. Attree, E.A., Brooks, B.M., Rose, F.D., Andrews, T.K., Leadbetter, A.G., Clifford, B.R.: Memory processes and virtual environments: I can't remember what was there, but I can remember how I got there. Implications for people with disabilities. In: Proceedings of the First European conference on Disability, Virtual Reality and Associated Technologies, University of Reading, pp. 117–122 (1996)
8. Dinh, H.Q., Walker, N., Hodges, L.F., Song, C., Kobayashi, A.: Evaluating the importance of multi-sensory input on memory and the sense of presence in virtual environments. In: Proceedings of the Virtual Reality Annual International Symposium, pp. 222–228 (1999)
9. Plancher, G., Gyselinck, V., Nicolas, S., Piolino, P.: Age effect on components of episodic memory and feature binding: a virtual reality study. Neuropsychology **24**(3), 379–390 (2010)
10. Sweeney, S., Kersel, D., Morris, R.G., Manly, T., Evans, J.J.: The sensitivity of a virtual reality task to planning and prospective memory impairments: group differences and the efficacy of periodic alerts on performance. Neuropsychol. Rehabil. **20**(2), 239–263 (2010)
11. Gould, N.F., et al.: Performance on a virtual reality spatial memory navigation task in depressed patients. Am. J. Psychiatry **164**(3), 516–519 (2007)
12. Standardized Survey Classifications - Individuals. http://www.pgagroup.com/standardized-survey-classifications.html. Accessed 19 Mar 2018
13. Descriptors defining levels in the European Qualifications Framework (EQF) - Learning Opportunities and Qualifications in Europe - European Commission. https://ec.europa.eu/ploteus/en/content/descriptorspage. Accessed 19 Mar 2018

14. Marks, L.E., Miller, G.A.: The role of semantic and syntactic constraints in the memorization of English sentences. J. Verbal Learn. Verbal Behav. **3**, 1–5 (1964)
15. Chomsky, N.: Three models for the description of language. IRE Trans. Inf. Theor. **2**(3), 113–124 (1956)
16. Burke, D.M., Peters, L., Harrold, R.M.: Word association norms for young and older adults. Soc. Behav. Sci. Doc. **17**(2) (1987)

Evaluation of AR Inconsistencies on AR Placement Tasks: A VR Simulation Study

Romain Terrier[1,4(✉)], Ferran Argelaguet[1], Jean-Marie Normand[3], and Maud Marchal[1,2]

[1] Univ. Rennes, Inria, CNRS, IRISA, Rennes, France
{romain.terrier,ferran.argelaguet,jean-marie.normand,
maud.marchal}@irisa.fr
[2] INSA, Rennes, France
[3] Ecole Centrale de Nantes, AAU UMR CNRS 1563, Nantes, France
jean-marie.normand@ec-nantes.fr
[4] IRT b<>com, Rennes, France
romain.terrier@b-com.com

Abstract. One of the major challenges of Augmented Reality (AR) is the registration of virtual and real contents. When errors occur during the registration process, inconsistencies between real and virtual contents arise and can alter user interaction. In this paper, we assess the impact of registration errors on the user performance and behaviour during an AR pick-and-place task in a Virtual Reality (VR) simulation. The VR simulation ensured the repeatability and control over experimental conditions. The paper describes the VR simulation framework used and three experiments studying how registration errors (e.g., rotational errors, positional errors, shaking) and visualization modalities (e.g., transparency, occlusion) modify the user behaviour while performing a pick-and-place task. Our results show that users kept a constant behavior during the task, i.e., the interaction was driven either by the VR or the AR content, except if the registration errors did not enable to efficiently perform the task. Furthermore, users showed preference towards an half-transparent AR in which correct depth sorting is provided between AR and VR contents. Taken together, our results open perspectives for the design and evaluation of AR applications through VR simulation frameworks.

Keywords: Registration errors · Augmented Reality
VR simulation · Interaction

1 Introduction

Current advances in Augmented Reality (AR) technology (e.g., Microsoft HoloLens or Meta 2 glasses) as well as in tracking capabilities [5] (with e.g., the release of Apple's ARKit and Google's ARCode SDKs) are showing the potential of AR applications in consumer grade applications (e.g., entertainment, education or maintenance). However, despite these recent advances, AR is

© Springer Nature Switzerland AG 2018
P. Bourdot et al. (Eds.): EuroVR 2018, LNCS 11162, pp. 190–210, 2018.
https://doi.org/10.1007/978-3-030-01790-3_12

still confronted to a number of challenges such as occlusion management between virtual and real objects, limitations in the field-of-view of AR devices or, as it is the main focus in this paper, registration errors. Registration is generally referred to as the process of finding in real-time the position and orientation of virtual objects so that they can be integrated in a plausible way in the real world. When errors occur during this process, inconsistencies between real and virtual objects can arise. Such inconsistencies can be constant (e.g., fixed errors on position and orientation) or irregular (e.g., shakiness of the virtual content), and can potentially hinder user interaction or alter users' behavior. Furthermore, as mentioned by Azuma and Bishop [2] *"The human visual system is very good at detecting even small misregistrations [...]. Errors of just a few pixels are noticeable"*. As of today, most AR applications or SDKs still face many of these inconsistencies, especially when the user modifies the scene through direct interaction with real or virtual objects.

Studying how registration issues affect users when interacting with AR is of great importance but remains difficult to achieve. Indeed, since AR is typically presented on hand-held devices (tablets, phones) or Head-Mounted Displays (HMDs), it generally remains complex to propose repeatable and controlled user studies in AR environments. To that purpose, Virtual Reality (VR) provides a promising tool to evaluate, not only AR interfaces, but also to explore how current limitations of AR systems influence users' behaviors and interaction capabilities [12]. Carrying out controlled VR experiments enables to explore a particular subset of limitations while perfectly simulating other AR features (e.g., ensuring a perfect tracking).

In this paper, we explore, through a VR simulation of AR, how user behavior and performance is altered when registration errors occur. Indeed, while it has been shown that the perception of the co-existence of virtual and real objects can be altered by registration accuracy (e.g., misregistration distorts spatial relationships [15]), little is known of their impact on the interaction process. Through three different experiments participants were confronted with different degrees of registration errors and AR visualizations in a VR simulation environment while performing a pick-and-place task (a common manipulation task). The main goal of the experiments were (1) to explore how the intensity of registration errors alters the behavior of users, in particular, whether real or augmented content drive their interactions, and (2) to measure how irregular registration errors impact users' accuracy.

The remainder of the paper is structured as follows: Sect. 2 provides an overview on registration errors in AR as well as on how VR simulation is used to study AR systems. Then, Sect. 3 presents the VR simulation platform we used in our experiments. Sections 4, 5 and 6 detail three different experiments aiming to analyze the impact of registration errors on users' behaviors and performance. Finally, Sect. 7 presents a global discussion and Sect. 8 concludes the paper.

2   Related Work

2.1   Categorization of Registration Errors in AR

A critical issue in AR applications is when virtual information is misaligned with the real environment [3]. This misalignment is also called registration errors [10]. From the users' viewpoint, registration errors can be seen as if the AR information floats and can break the illusion that real and virtual objects co-exist [15].

Registration should be stable both spatially (virtual objects must be collocated in rotation and position with real objects) and temporally (motion of virtual and real objects should be synchronous). In the literature, several classifications of registration errors have been presented [3,9]. Holloway [9] gives a precise definition of registration errors by decomposing them into four main metrics: linear, lateral, angular and depth registration errors. In contrast, the classification proposed by Azuma [3] focused on whether or not AR objects or the user's viewpoint were static (static) or in motion (dynamic). The remainder of this section is structured following the taxonomy of Azuma [3] where static errors represent a spatial incoherence between AR and real content while dynamic errors represent a temporal incoherence.

Static Errors. Static errors are visible even if the user does not move his/her viewpoint (or the hand-held device) or when the real environment remains immobile. From the user's viewpoint, the AR content seems to be floating near its real position. Static registration errors are due to either optical distortions, tracking errors, mechanical misalignments or incorrect viewing parameters (i.e., field of view, tracker-to-eye position and orientation, inter-pupillary distance) [3]. Most of the time users perceive static errors as a constant gap between the desired and the actual position/orientation of the AR information even if the AR content has a perfect shape (see Fig. 3 for examples of static errors).

There are several ways to reduce static errors: improve calibration [1] or improve tracking techniques [11]. Nevertheless, the huge variability of environments (e.g., indoor, outdoor) and behaviors of tracked objects (e.g., static, in motion, slow, fast) makes it complex to provide error-prone solutions [19].

Dynamic Errors. On the other hand, dynamic errors are only visible when the user's viewpoint or when objects are moving. Dynamic errors are mainly due to the latency of the system when there is a motion [3]. This delay (or latency) is the time between the moment when the tracking system computes the new position and rotation of the viewpoint and the moment when the virtual information is rendered at this position. This delay implies that virtual objects are not displayed with the right position and orientation at the right time. In order to reduce dynamic errors, four methods exist [3]: reduce system lag, reduce apparent lag, match temporal streams and predictive methods. Another characteristic of registration errors is that they are hard to predict. Such uncertainty introduces a strong bias when evaluating AR systems as replicability is compromised. In order to overcome such limitations, VR has been proposed to simulate AR systems and thus evaluating them.

2.2 Simulating AR in VR

Virtual reality is a powerful tool to evaluate AR systems as it allows to simulate in a controlled way many AR features, enabling repeatable user studies. Several studies conducted in VR environments simulate AR systems in order to evaluate features such as latency [15,16], field of view [17,18] or visual realism [14].

Regarding latency, Lee et al. [13] replicated an AR study [6] in a VR simulation context. Their results showed that users' performance when moving a virtual ring along a virtual path was comparable between the simulated AR and the real AR studies. The VR simulator provided the feeling that the AR content was real thanks to a restricted transparent window in which the AR simulated content was displayed. Moreover, on top of the internal latency of the simulator due to tracker latency, computation time, render time and display time, Lee et al. [12] proposed to include "artificial latencies" between virtual objects and the real world. This enabled to add controlled latency to the simulated AR content and to analyze its effect. Other studies also linked latency with interaction performance showing a degradation of performance as latency increases [15]. Finally, Ragan et al. [16] studied the impact of jitter (visual shakiness of AR content) and showed that it is predominant over visual latency.

The Field of View (FOV) is a distinctive feature of HMDs that has also been evaluated in VR simulations. While comparing different AR HMDs with different FOV is prone to bias due to confounding factors (e.g., other HMDs characteristics) VR simulations enable to only alter the FOV parameter while minimizing confounding factors. For example, Ren et al. [17] showed that a wider FOV is better because it allows to display more information (2D annotations in their case) and to explore it more quickly. Moreover, a wider FOV also reduces users' head movements in the search task. Another important factor related to FOV corresponds to where guidance information regarding objects of interest is displayed (e.g., within the FOV, outside of the FOV, on the object, etc.). Users better focus during a manipulation task if AR guidance is drawn as a line connecting the hand of the user to the center of the searched object [18]. In another study, Baričević et al. [4] proposed to use VR to simulate user perspective rendering in AR (the view is rendered according to the user's point of view) in order to study its benefits over the classical device perspective (the view is rendered according to the point of view of the device's camera) for AR applications.

Furthermore, visual realism is also an important factor that simulated AR has to deal with. Lee conducted a study [14] about the impact of the realism of the VR environment (photo-realistic, etc.) on a user task. Results did not show relevant effects and the necessity to design a realistic VR environment has not been proved in this case. Finally, AR content presentation (transparency of the virtual content or occlusion management) has also been shown to impact interaction with AR systems [7,8]. In order to study its impact, we integrated those conditions into our experiments.

As a conclusion, although registration is a major challenge of AR, there is still a lack of studies on its impact in the interaction process. Such studies are complex to perform using existing AR systems since it is nearly impossible to ensure experimental conditions comparable across participants (e.g., registration errors will be hardly reproducible). To this end, inspired by existing works, we propose to study the impact of registration errors in a VR simulation of an AR interaction task.

3   Experimental Platform: VR Simulation of AR

As mentioned above, in order to be able to carry out repeatable and fully controlled user experiments, we chose to simulate our AR environments in VR. Our VR environment was designed to replicate a pick-and-place task of an AR application where the user has to position a cube ($10 \times 10 \times 10$ cm) precisely onto a target. The cube and the target were lying on a table and both could be augmented (see Fig. 1, bottom).

In our VR simulation, some virtual objects played the role of real objects in while others represented AR objects (*i.e.* virtual objects inserted into a real scene). As a consequence the virtual environment consisted of a set of "real objects", or simulated Real (sReal) objects, and AR objects, or simulated AR (sAR) objects. The sReal objects could also be augmented by sAR objects.

Additionally, we could also manipulate the virtual AR FOV in the simulation. This allowed the simulation of both a device-based and of an HMD-based AR environment by adapting the size of a virtual window with a slightly different color. In our experiments, the virtual AR FOV covered ~90% of the VR HMD's FOV. We chose this value so that users would not be disturbed in their interaction with the sAR content. Figure 1 (bottom) shows two first person views of the virtual environment were sAR and sReal objects co-exist.

The following subsections detail the different simulated conditions in terms of registration errors and AR content presentation. Only sAR objects were affected by registration errors (see Fig. 2) and sAR visualization conditions (see Fig. 3).

3.1   Registration Errors

In order to study how registration errors would affect user interaction and performance in an AR pick-and-place task, we propose to simulate two different kinds of registration errors (see Fig. 2): constant and irregular. For ours experiments, we make the choice to focus the analysis on errors with only a rotation of the sAR content with respect of the sReal content around the Y-axis. Those errors are called rotational errors. The choice is motivated by the simplicity of the error that has only one degree of freedom. Translation errors are not in the scope of our study.

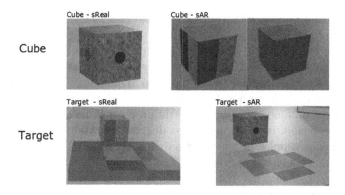

Fig. 1. Depiction of the different simulated objects (Top - cube; Bottom - target). The depiction is either sReal (Left) or sAR (Right). When the cube is sReal and the target is sAR, colored dots are painted on the sReal cube to indicate the orientation of the cube. When there is a sReal cube with its sAR cube and a sReal target, the sReal cube has no colored dot. The orientation is given by the sAR cube. The sAR objects have different conditions of visualization (transparency condition and opacity condition). (Color figure online)

Constant registration errors introduce a constant misalignment between sAR and sReal objects (either in position or orientation). In this condition, no matter how the user manipulates the sReal cube, its sAR counterpart is always misaligned by the same amount either in position or rotation. We do not use the term "Static" registration errors proposed by Azuma [3] (that only happen when the user's viewpoint does not move) since in VR we can simulate a constant error even with a dynamic environment (objects in motion or user's changing his/her viewpoint). For simplicity, and due to the nature of the pick-and-place task, in order to avoid inter-penetrations we only considered rotation errors on

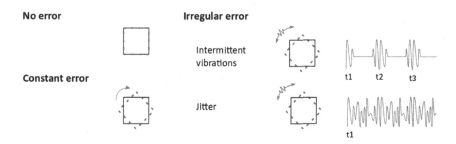

Fig. 2. Simulation of AR rotational errors. A black solid square (resp. red dotted) represents a sReal (resp. sAR) object. Top-Left: no rotational error. sAR and sReal objects are perfectly aligned. Bottom-Left: constant error. The angle between sReal and sAR objects is constant over time. Right: two states, intermittent vibrations (rotational vibration that occurs from time to time, Top-Right) and jitter (rotational vibration around a position that constantly occurs, Bottom-Right). (Color figure online)

the vertical axis (Y-axis). sAR content is rotated on its own Y-axis with respect to the sReal object.

Irregular registration errors are dynamic and variable over time. There are two kinds of such errors that we chose to name *jitter* and *intermittent vibrations*. Here again we chose not to use the term "Dynamic" [3] since the registration errors we simulate are not due to latency or delay but we rather wanted to study the effect on a non-constant registration error in a dynamic environment.

Intermittent vibrations are defined as discrete vibrations of the sAR object. More specifically, a pulse is generated on the sAR object's Y-axis for a certain amount of time (e.g., for 0.1s every 1s). The pulse follows a noise function f (see Eq. 1) with x_1, x_2 being two real values $\in [0, 1]$, and k a real positive constant which determines the maximum absolute rotation error (in radians).

$$f(x_1, x_2) = \frac{\sin(2\pi x_2) * \sqrt{-2\log(x_1)}}{3k} \tag{1}$$

On the other hand, *"jitter"* refers to a continuous vibration of the sAR object around it's Y-axis. The *"jitter"* is generated continuously for a certain amount of time and follows the same function f as *intermittent vibrations*.

3.2   AR Content Presentation

The second aspect of the simulation we wanted to evaluate was the presentation of the AR content. Although numerous rendering styles could have been considered, we decided to focus on transparency of the AR content and occlusion management (whether or not AR objects were correctly occluded by real objects) of sAR objects, as illustrated in Fig. 3. In particular the two considered conditions were:

1. "Transparency" of the sAR content. A transparency of 100% makes the sAR object invisible while a transparency of 0% makes it completely opaque.
2. "Occlusion" management. This allows us to control whether the sAR content was properly (Occlusion ON) or not (Occlusion OFF) occluded by the sReal content.

4   Experiment 1: Analyzing the Effect of Constant Registration Errors in User Behaviour

The goal of the first experiment was to explore how registration errors influence the perception of co-existing sAR and sReal objects. In particular, the experiment aimed at determining which object is used as a *reference* (sAR or sReal) or in other words, which content drives the users' actions. Furthermore, as different AR visualizations might play an important role on users' behaviour, different sAR visualizations were evaluated.

4.1   Apparatus and Participants

Experiments were performed using an HMD (HTC Vive) and users were able to interact with the environment through a controller (an HTC Controller). During the experiment, the users were comfortably seated in an office chair. The experiment was conducted using the platform described in Sect. 3 which was implemented in Unity (5.6).

Twelve right-handed users (1 female, 11 males) participated in this experiment (age: $M = 22.83; SD = 2.66$). All participants had previous experience with AR and/or VR.

4.2   Experimental Protocol

Upon arrival participants read and signed a consent form which briefly described the experiment and their rights. The consent form did not provide any information that could bias the users during the experiment. At the end of the experiment additional information was provided regarding the real purpose of the experiment. Users were told that they should consider the VR environment as their reality (*i.e.* with sReal objects) and that the AR content (*i.e.* sAR objects) which is displayed in the brown window is the AR. In addition, users had to fill out a pre-experiment questionnaire to gather background information (*e.g.* age, VR and AR experience, headset experience, laterality, visual impairment). Once users fully understood the experimental task, the experimenter equipped them with the HMD and they were immersed in the virtual experimentation room.

The experimental task was a pick-and-place. Users had to pick a sReal cube augmented with an sAR cube (see Fig. 4) and place it at the center of a colored target (also a sReal object). Users had to orient the cube to match the color code, (*e.g.* the blue face of the sAR cube should face the blue marker on the target, etc., see Fig. 4). The field of view of the AR window was enough to ensure that all cubes fit the AR display. Participants were asked to be as precise as possible and no indication was given regarding which cube (sAR or sReal) had to be aligned on the target. Users performed several trials grouped in four blocks (see Sect. 4.3).

The users' virtual hand was represented as a green sphere to let them focus on the manipulation and not on their appearance. The green sphere was controlled with the HTC Vive controller (the trigger enabled to grab the sReal cube). Once users were pleased with the location of the cube, they had to signal the end of the trial by pressing the touchpad of the Vive controller. Basic physical simulation capabilities were enabled (gravity and collision detection with the virtual table). At the end of each block, participants had to fill out a questionnaire to gather their subjective impressions.

4.3   Experimental Design

In order to assess the effect of registration errors, we artificially considered a different range of constant registration errors. In particular, we considered seven rotational mismatches $\{15, 10, 5, 0, -5, -10, -15\}°$. In addition, we also considered four different visualizations for sAR objects. The visualization was by two independent variables (*transparency* and *occlusion*) with two levels each (see Fig. 3) in order to analyze whether they biased the relationship between sAR and sReal content. The *transparency* of the sAR content was set to either 0% or 50%. *Occlusion* of the sAR content also had two options: ON (the sAR content is always visible) or OFF (the sAR content is correctly occluded by sReal objects depending on which object is closer to the user's viewpoint). To sum up, the experiment had a $7 \times 2 \times 2$ factorial design with 4 repetitions for each condition, resulting in a total of 112 trials. The four combinations of transparency and occlusion were split into four blocks and counterbalanced using a Latin-Square design. For each block (28 trials), the order of the registration mismatch was randomized.

Fig. 3. AR presentation conditions. Each row corresponds to a *transparency* condition (50% and 0%). Each column corresponds to an *occlusion* condition (precise depth sorting vs. sAR always on top).

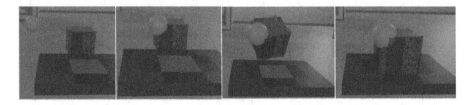

Fig. 4. Depiction of the first experiment's task. The user, using a virtual hand metaphor (see Sect. 4.2) had to pick and place the sAR/sReal cube on a target. Only the sAR cube was displayed in the AR overlay. (Color figure online)

The dependent variables were the task-completion time (s), the position accuracy (cm) and the rotational accuracy (degrees). The task-completion time was measured from the moment the user grabs the cube until he/she validates the placement. The position accuracy was computed as the distance between the center of the sReal cube (sReal and sAR cubes shared the same center position)

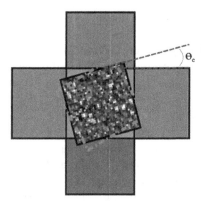

Fig. 5. Depiction of how rotational error θ_e is calculated. The blue, orange and red cross is the target. The textured square is the sReal cube. The green dotted line square is the sAR cube. In this example, the error is the angle between the sReal cube and the sReal target and not between the sAR cube and the sReal target because the angle of the error between the two sReal objects is the lowest.

with respect to the center of the perfect placement position. The rotation accuracy was computed as the minimum angle between the sReal and sAR cubes with respect to the perfect placement rotation (see Fig. 5). Participants had no explicit instruction whether hey have to align the sReal or the sAR cube, considering the minimum provides a more insightful result. Positional and rotational accuracies are measured for each trial upon user validation of the placement.

Regarding subjective information, participants had to fill out a questionnaire after each block and at the end of the experiment. The aim of the after-block questionnaires was to observe the progression of the state of the participants (i.e., tiredness, visual discomfort and task difficulty). A 7-point Likert scale was used where 1 meant "not at all" and 7 "meant completely". The final questionnaire was designed to understand the behaviour of the participants and their impression on their performance. Therefore, the participants answered which reference they chose and if they placed the cube in relation to the sAR content or in relation to the sReal content. Then participants quantified the variability of the choice about the picked reference. Additionally, the participants evaluated on a scale of one (never) to seven (always) how often their choice changed. Finally, participants ranked the 4 conditions from their most preferred to their least preferred one. In the final questionnaire, we use the term "AR cube" to refer to the sAR cube and the term "real cube" to refer to the sReal one. Given this experimental design, we hypothesized that:

H1.1 Smaller registration errors will result in lower rotation accuracy. The bigger is the mismatch the lower will be the ambiguity.

H1.2 When the sAR content is semitransparent (*i.e.* Transparency 50%) the task completion time will be higher. Seeing sAR and sReal contents at the same time can be distracting.

H1.3 When the sAR content is displayed on top (*i.e.* Occlusion ON) it will result in lower task completion times due to the same reasoning as H1.2.

H1.4 As only rotational accuracy is considered and the sReal and sAR cubes share the same center position, no significant difference in positional accuracy is expected.

4.4   Results

Regarding the objective measures, the analysis of the data (ANOVA analysis with post-hoc Tukey tests ($\alpha > 0.05$)) showed that the different independent variables had no impact on the dependent variables. All comparisons were not-significant. For the sake of simplicity we only report the two-way ANOVA analysis for the factors *Transparency* and *Occlusion*, pooling the data from the different levels of rotation mismatch. Anderson Darling tests were performed to ensure the normal distribution of the data.

Rotation Accuracy. No significant main effect was found for *Transparency* ($F_{1,11} = 0.77$, $p = 0.399$, $\eta_p^2 = 0.06$) nor for *Occlusion* ($F_{1,11} = 0.83$, $p = 0.382$, $\eta_p^2 = 0.07$). In overall, participants were extremely precise $M = -0.12°$; $SD = 0.93°$ no matter the *reference* and the condition. In addition, as previously stated, the amount of registration mismatch did not influenced rotation accuracy. Thus, results do not support **H1.1**.

Task-Completion Time. No significant main effect was found for *Transparency* ($F_{1,11} = 1.27$, $p = 0.284$, $\eta_p^2 = 0.10$) nor for *Occlusion* ($F_{1,11} = 2.83$, $p = 0.121$, $\eta_p^2 = 0.20$). In overall, participants required $M = 10.086\,\mathrm{s}$; $SD = 5.927\,\mathrm{s}$ to complete the task. Although the mean task completion time was considerably high considering the nature of the task, we have to note that participants were requested to perform the task as accurately as possible. Thus, we cannot accept neither **H1.2** nor **H1.3**.

Position Accuracy. No significant main effect was found for *Transparency* ($F_{1,11} = 2.31$, $p = 0.156$, $\eta_p^2 = 0.17$) nor for *Occlusion* ($F_{1,11} = 0.36$, $p = 0.560$, $\eta_p^2 = 0.03$). In overall, participants were extremely accurate $M = 0.15\,\mathrm{cm}$; $SD = 0.07\,\mathrm{cm}$ no matter the visual condition. These results support **H1.4**. Yet, if any difference exists, considering the level of accuracy, it would be non-relevant.

4.5   Reference Cube

After analyzing users' behaviors, we observed that the majority of participants had a different yet consistent behaviour during the entire experiment. In particular, we computed the object (sAR or sReal cube) that was considered as the *reference* by the user. The *reference* cube is the cube (sAR or sReal) that minimizes the error to the target orientation at the moment the user validates the

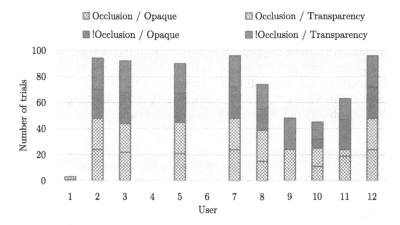

Fig. 6. Bar plot showing the number of trials in which for each participant the sReal cube was calculated as the *reference* object.

trial. Figure 6 shows the amount of time the sReal cube was chosen as *reference* for each user and for each condition. Cases in which the rotation mismatch was 0 were not considered as they do not provide any information. Six out of twelve users considered the sReal cube as the main *reference* (users 2, 3, 5, 7, 8, and 12), three users considered the sAR cube as the main *reference* (users 1, 4 and 6), one user (user 10) did the task considering that both cubes were the *reference* (minimizing the error between both cubes) and two users (9 and 11) changed *reference* in the middle of the experiment.

4.6   Subjective Questionnaires

After-Block Questionnaires. Concerning the task difficulty, users considered the task relatively easy $M = 2.54; SD = 1.18$ no matter the visual condition. Interestingly, small misalignments (e.g., $\pm 5°$) were reported to increase the difficulty of the task. Three users reported that "With small misalignments it was harder". Moreover, some users felt confused about the task: "I had the impression of making wrong choices" or "I was confused and a little bit disturbed because of misalignments". Concerning visual discomfort, it remained constant during the entire experiment $m = 2.90; SD = 1.43$, which shows that the task and the set-up do not cause strong visual discomforts. Finally regarding tiredness, the mean value is almost constant and below 3 $M = 2.85; SD = 0.92$.

Post-Experiment Questionnaire Nine users (75%) stated that they picked a *reference* and kept it during all the experiment, whereas three users (25%) reported to change their *reference*. Six users out of twelve (50%) chose the sReal cube, three chose the sAR cube and the others changed during the manipulation. Only one user picked all the time an imaginary cube placed at the mid-position between the sAR cube and the sReal cube. These results confirm results from the previous section. Globally users pick a reference and keep it during all the task. According to users, the choice of the *reference* was made because the task seems easier for them with their choice of *reference*: "With AR it was more practical". Finally, regarding user preferences on sAR visualization, the condition in which the sAR content was always visible and opaque was the less preferred one. Seven out of twelve participants (58.33%) answered that it was their less preferred choice. Yet, results do not show a clear user preference.

4.7   Discussion

The main outcome of this experiment is that constant registration errors did not alter the way users performed the task nor their performance. The analysis of users' behaviors as well as questionnaires showed that participants have a strong preference when choosing the main *reference* (either sReal or sAR) no matter the registration mismatch nor the visualization. Interestingly, while we hypothesized that the occlusion would have an influence on users' behavior, it was not the case, nor any other visualization condition. One explanation could be that users did not need to change their *reference* (there was no significant effect on accuracy) since in all cases they were able to accurately place the chosen cube.

Another interesting finding is that there was no significant difference in task-completion time for the different sAR visualization conditions. As users were requested to be as accurate as possible, there was a moderate user variability. This could have decreased the power of the analysis. Nevertheless, we were expecting strong differences and it was not the case. Finally, the condition that we hypothesized to be the less optimal (no transparency and no occlusion) was the condition users preferred less.

5   Experiment 2: Analyzing the Effect of Irregular Registration Errors in User Behaviour

The results of the previous experiment shown that when constant registration errors occur, they do not have a strong influence on users' behavior, as the *reference* chosen by users rarely changed during the experiment. In order to explore in depth users' behavior, we performed a follow up experiment in which we explored the effects of irregular registration errors. The goal of this second experiment was to analyze the tolerance to irregular registration errors and measure if there was a threshold that triggers a shift in the selected *reference*. The experimental protocol and the apparatus of the experiment were the same as the first experiment. Upon their arrival, participants read and signed a consent form which briefly described the experiment and their rights. After users fully understand the experimental task, the experimenter equipped them with the HMD.

5.1 Participants

Twelve right-handed users (2 females, 10 males) participated in this follow up experiment ($M = 23.25; SD = 2.22$). Seven never had any experience with VR, five never had any experience with AR and six never used a HMD before.

5.2 Experimental Design

Participants had to perform the same pick-and-place as in the first experiment task while varying the intensity of the registration error. We considered five different levels of intensity, defined by the amplitude of the vibration (the k parameter of Eq. 1) and the time (discrete vs. continuous). The registration errors were presented by increasing intensity:

L1. No Error: Perfect registration between sAR and sReal objects.

L2. Low intensity intermittent vibration: a pulse of 0.11 s is generated every 1 s with $k = 0.3$ rad.

L3. High intensity intermittent vibration: a pulse of 0.11 s is generated every 0.5 s with $k = 0.3$ rad.

L4. Low intensity jitter: a continuous vibration is generated with $k = 0.05$ rad.

L5. High intensity jitter: a continuous vibration is generated with $k = 0.3$ rad.

Only one sAR visualization was considered which corresponded with the most preferred condition of the first experiment (50% transparency and Occlusion OFF). For each intensity level, participants performed 5 repetitions of the pick-and-place task. To better account for users' choice of *reference*, constant registration errors were also introduced for each intensity level (four repetitions randomly chosen between $\{-10, 10\}°$ and one repetition had no constant registration error). The target is a sReal object once again. We were only interested in measuring the *reference* chosen for each trial, which we determined following the same approach as in the first experiment, choosing the object (sReal or sAR) which minimized the placement accuracy. We hypothesized that:

H2.1 As the intensity of the irregular registration error increases the users will have the tendency to shift their *reference* towards the sReal object.

5.3 Results

Similar to the first experiment, the ANOVA analysis did not show any significant differences among, participants were extremely precise in the placement task (position accuracy: $M = 1.65$ mm; $SD = 0.9$ mm and rotation accuracy: $M = 0.86°; SD = 0.95°$). Also, participants followed a similar behavior: once participants chose the *reference* (typically in the first few trials), they tend to keep it during the entire experiment (see Fig. 7 right). Six users had a clear tendency towards choosing the sAR cube as *reference* while the remaining six users chose the sReal cube as *reference*.

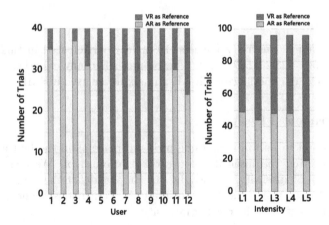

Fig. 7. Choice of *reference* during the second experiment. (Left) Bar plot showing the choice of *reference* for each participant. (Right) Bar plot showing the choice for each condition.

Regarding the strength of registration errors (see Fig. 7), we observed a change in behaviour for some users who chose the sAR reference in the L5 condition. Seven out of twelve users (58.33%) explained that they picked a *reference* and kept it during all the experiment. Four users (33.33%) said they changed their *reference*, explicitly mentioning that the change occurred at the beginning of the last condition (L5, high intensity jitter). Thus, in the presence of strong registration errors, and due to the inability to perform the task, the *reference* object was changed to the more reliable *reference*.

5.4   Discussion

Results of the second experiment tend to reinforce the fact that users make a strong reference choice at the beginning of the experience. Even with the addition of irregular registration errors, participants are reluctant to change their *reference*. However, if the error can discourage the completion of the task, they have the tendency to shift towards a more stable *reference*. In conclusion, **H2.1** is validated only in the presence of high intensity of jitter.

6   Experiment 3: Analyzing the Effects of Irregular Registration Errors on User Performance

One common element of the first two experiments is that sAR content augmented sReal objects (*i.e.* a sAR cube was displayed on top of a sReal cube). However, in AR applications pure virtual objects (*i.e.* without any relation to real objects) are commonly used. In such situations, the pure virtual object will always be considered as the *reference* as there is no ambiguity. This third experiment explores the impact of irregular registration errors on user performance when the task is driven just by AR content. Can users perform effectively and efficiently in presence of irregular registration errors in such context? The participants in this experiment were the same group which participated in the second experiment.

6.1   Experimental Protocol

Upon their arrival, participants read and signed a consent form which briefly described the experiment and their rights. After users fully understand the experimental task, the experimenter equipped them with the HMD. The task was a variation of the pick-and-place task of the first experiment. In this case, the sReal cube was not augmented, and the target location was a sAR object. Users had to pick the sReal cube and place it at the location indicated by the sAR target. sReal colored stickers were placed on the sReal cube to display the correspondence with the sAR target (see Fig. 8). At the end of the experiment participants had to fill out a questionnaire to gather their subjective impressions.

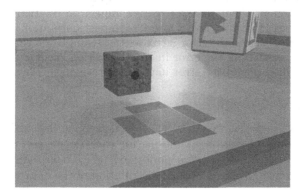

Fig. 8. Task description of the third experiment. The user had to place the sReal cube onto the sAR target by aligning the colored stickers placed on the sReal cube with the sAR target's colors. (Color figure online)

6.2   Experimental Design

The experiment had two independent variables which defined the *intensity* of the irregular registration error and the sAR *visualization*. Only the sAR target is affected by vibrations. Regarding registration errors, we considered (and simulated) the following five different levels of intensity (sorted by increasing intensity):

L1. No Error is applied to the target.
L2. Low intensity intermittent vibration: a pulse of $0.11\,\text{s}$ is generated every $2\,\text{s}$ with $k = 0.33\,\text{rad}$.

L3. Medium intensity intermittent vibration: a pulse of 0.11 s is generated every 1 s with $k = 0.33$ rad.

L4. High intensity intermittent vibration: a pulse of 0.11 s is generated every 0.5 s with $k = 0.33$ rad.

L5. High intensity jitter: a continuous vibration is generated with $k = 0.33$ rad.

Regarding the sAR visualization, we only considered the occlusion condition with two levels, either the sAR content is occluded (Occlusion ON) or not (Occlusion OFF) by the real content. For both conditions the sAR target was displayed with a 50% transparency. The experiment had a 5×2 factorial design, each combination being repeated six times (60 trials per participant). To avoid ordering effects, the experiment was divided in four blocks in which the order of the sAR visualization was counterbalanced. For each block order the intensity level was randomized. The dependent variables were the task-completion time, the position accuracy and the rotation accuracy.

According to this experimental design, our hypotheses were that:

H3.1 Occlusion OFF will have a negative impact on task-completion time.
H3.2 Occlusion OFF will have a negative impact on position accuracy.
H3.3 Occlusion OFF will have a negative impact onrotation accuracy.
H3.4 as the intensity of the error increases task-completion time will increase.
H3.5 as the intensity of the error increases position accuracy will decrease.
H3.6 as the intensity of the error increases rotation accuracy will decrease.

6.3   Results

Two-way ANOVA analysis were performed to determine the significance of registration errors and Occlusion conditions for each dependent variable. When needed, post-hoc Tukey tests were performed ($\alpha > 0.05$). Anderson-Darling tests were performed to ensure normal distribution of the data.

Task-Completion Time. The ANOVA analysis showed a main effect on Intensity ($F_{4,44} = 5.34$, $p < 0.001$, $\eta_p^2 = 0.33$), but there was no effect on Visualization ($F_{1,11} = 0.49$, $p = 0.498$, $\eta_p^2 = 0.04$) nor on interaction effect ($F_{4,44} = 0.76$, $p = 0.557$, $\eta_p^2 = 0.06$). Post-hoc tests showed that participants significantly required more time to perform the task for L5 than for the other conditions (see Fig. 9, left). These results do not support **H3.1** and only partially support **H3.4**.

Position Accuracy. The ANOVA analysis showed a main effect on Intensity ($F_{4,44} = 47.66$, $p < 0.001$, $\eta_p^2 = 0.82$) and in Visualization ($F_{1,11} = 15.16$, $p < 0.01$, $\eta_p^2 = 0.59$). No interaction effect was found. Post-hoc tests showed that the intensity level L5 resulted in significantly lower accuracy compared to the other four intensities (see Fig. 9, center), and that when the sAR content is not occluded by the sReal content ($M = 1.97$ mm; $SD = 1.05$ mm) significantly (although slightly) decreased position accuracy compared to the opposite condition ($M = 1.57$ mm; $SD = 1.04$ mm). These results support **H3.2** and only partially support **H3.5**.

Rotational Accuracy. The ANOVA analysis showed only a main effect for Intensity $(F_{4,44} = 9.18,\ p < 0.001,\ \eta_p^2 = 0.46)$. No main effect for Visualization $(F_{1,11} = 0.34,\ p = 0.572,\ \eta_p^2 = 0.03)$ and no interaction effects were found $(F_{4,44} = 1.39,\ p = 0.300,\ \eta_p^2 = 0.10)$. Post-hoc tests showed that for the Intensity variable, the L5 level induced significantly lower rotation accuracy than the other levels (see Fig. 9, right). These results do not support **H3.3** and only partially support **H3.6**.

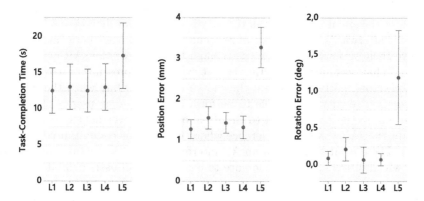

Fig. 9. Confidence intervals (95%) of the mean for each dependent variable. Left: task-completion time. Center: position accuracy. Right: rotation accuracy.

6.4 Subjective Questionnaires

Eleven users out of twelve (91.66%) preferred when the sAR content was occluded by sReal objects (*i.e.* the Occlusion ON condition). Most of the users felt perturbed when the occlusion was not computed correctly: "it was easier to see edges and borders of the cube when the AR target did not hide the real cube" and "when objects that should be behind everything appear in the foreground, it is not natural". Regarding the amount of jitter, as in the second experiment, users only complained when the registration error did not allowed them to perform the task efficiently (i.e., the L5 level).

6.5 Discussion

Results of this experiment show that low to moderate levels of irregular (see Sec. 3.1) registration errors (L1 to L4) do not have a noticeable impact on user performance and accuracy. Surprisingly, no significant effects were found between levels L1 to L4. Indeed, this result shows a relatively strong tolerance of users towards registration errors. Furthermore, in terms of user preferences of the sAR visualization, although the objective results did not present any significant differences, the visualization minimizing the perceptual conflicts (i.e., correct occlusion management) was preferred.

7   General Discussion

In this paper, we have presented three experiments focusing on the impact on registration errors in an AR pick-and-place task. In order to ensure controlled and repeatable experimental conditions, the AR environment was simulated in VR. Data analysis has mainly focused on user behavior (how registration errors alter the way users interact) and user performance (how users can account for registration errors).

The first two experiments shown that participants chose a reference (the sAR content or the sReal content) from the very beginning and they were reluctant to change it afterwards. This choice of reference impacted their performance since it drove their actions (e.g., they either align the sReal or the sAR cube on the target). What was more interesting is that even in the presence of irregular registration errors, participants kept the chosen reference. Only when the task was compromised (e.g., when unable to perform the task) some users shifted their reference from the sAR content to the sReal content. Nevertheless, several users still kept the sAR content as reference when the task was compromised (L5 condition). These results show that an AR interface designer should unambiguously define which objects serve as reference to ensure that all users exhibit the same behavior.

In contrast, the third experiment focused on the impact of irregular registration errors on user performance, and more importantly on how users tolerate them. Results showed that, for the tested errors, the tolerance was high, and that errors of low to medium intensity did not significantly altered users' performance. These results show that users had a strong adaptation to adverse situations.

Along the different experiments, a secondary goal was to assess the impact of how AR content is presented. Simulating AR in VR enabled us to test a wide range of visualizations which were difficult or almost impossible to achieve with current AR systems. The preference results are not ground-breaking: users prefer a perceptually-correct integration (e.g., correct occlusion management) as they provide a non-ambiguous layout. Yet, when occlusion management cannot be achieved (e.g., due to technical limitations) semi-transparent visualizations should be considered as they minimize perceptual conflicts. Regarding the impact on performance, interestingly, we did not find any significant difference between visualizations (i.e., transparency and occlusion). This result shows that for all conditions users were able to recover enough information from the sAR and sReal contents to successfully perform the task (e.g., a fully visible edge or corner of the cube).

8   Conclusion

Although registration algorithms are continuously being perfected, inconsistencies between sReal and sAR contents are still a major issue in AR applications. Results obtained our three user studies show that visual inconsistencies generated by registration errors can alter users' behavior as they require a subjective interpretation. According to their interpretation, the outcome of the interaction task might vary. This effect is clearly visible in the first and second experiments as the reference chosen (the sReal cube or sAR cube) determines the outcome of the task. In the same direction, visualization strategies should minimize inconsistencies between the AR and the real contents. However, if this is not possible, the interface designer must ensure that the visualization provides enough information to perform the task effectively.

The presented studies highlight the potential of evaluating registration errors in controlled VR simulations. Nevertheless, this paper has only focused on a particular subset of registration errors. Further studies should be conducted to evaluate other types of registration errors such as depth or lateral errors. This knowledge is paramount to better design AR applications and ensure they enable users to interact effectively and efficiently.

References

1. Azimi, E., Qian, L., Kazanzides, P., Navab, N.: Robust optical see-through head-mounted display calibration: taking anisotropic nature of user interaction errors into account. In: IEEE Virtual Reality, pp. 219–220 (2017). DOI: https://doi.org/10.1109/VR.2017.7892255

2. Azuma, R., Bishop, G.: Improving static and dynamic registration in an optical see-through HMD. In: ACM Annual Conference on Computer Graphics and Interactive Techniques, pp. 197–204 (1994). https://doi.org/10.1145/192161.192199

3. Azuma, R.T.: A survey of augmented reality. Presence: Teleoper. Virtual Environ. **6**(4), 355–385 (1997). https://doi.org/10.1162/pres.1997.6.4.355

4. Baričević, D., Lee, C., Turk, M., Höllerer, T., Bowman, D.A.: A hand-held AR magic lens with user-perspective rendering. In: IEEE International Symposium on Mixed and Augmented Reality, pp. 197–206 (2012). https://doi.org/10.1109/ISMAR.2012.6402557

5. Billinghurst, M., Clark, A., Lee, G.: A survey of augmented reality. foundations and trends®. Hum.-Comput. Interact. **8**(2–3), 73–272 (2015). https://doi.org/10.1561/1100000049

6. Ellis, S.R., Breant, F., Manges, B., Jacoby, R., Adelstein, B.D.: Factors influencing operator interaction with virtual objects viewed via head-mounted see-through displays: viewing conditions and rendering latency. In: IEEE Virtual Reality Annual International Symposium, pp. 138–145 (1997). https://doi.org/10.1109/VRAIS.1997.583063

7. Ellis, S.R., Menges, B.M.: Localization of virtual objects in the near visual field. Hum. Factors **40**(3), 415–431 (1998)

8. Furmanski, C., Azuma, R., Daily, M.: Augmented-reality visualizations guided by cognition: perceptual heuristics for combining visible and obscured information. In: Proceedings. International Symposium on Mixed and Augmented Reality, ISMAR 2002, pp. 215–320. IEEE (2002)

9. Holloway, R.L.: Registration error analysis for augmented reality. Presence: Teleoper. Virtual Environ. **6**(4), 413–432 (1997)

10. Holloway, R.L.: Registration errors in augmented reality systems. Ph.D. thesis, University of North Carolina at Chapel Hill (1995)

11. Klein, G., Murray, D.: Parallel tracking and mapping for small AR workspaces. In: ACM/IEEE International Symposium on Mixed and Augmented Reality, pp. 225–234 (2007). https://doi.org/10.1109/ISMAR.2007.4538852

12. Lee, C., Bonebrake, S., Bowman, D.A., Hollerer, T.: The role of latency in the validity of AR simulation. In: IEEE Virtual Reality, pp. 11–18 (2010). https://doi.org/10.1109/VR.2010.5444820

13. Lee, C., Bonebrake, S., Höllerer, T., Bowman, D.A.: A replication study testing the validity of AR simulation in VR for controlled experiments. In: IEEE International Symposium on Mixed and Augmented Reality, pp. 203–204 (2009). https://doi.org/10.1109/ISMAR.2009.5336464

14. Lee, C., Rincon, G.A., Meyer, G., Hollerer, T., Bowman, D.A.: The effects of visual realism on search tasks in mixed reality simulation. IEEE Trans. Visual. Comput. Graph. **19**(4), 547–556 (2013). https://doi.org/10.1109/TVCG.2013.41

15. Nabiyouni, M., Scerbo, S., Bowman, D.A., Höllerer, T.: Relative effects of real-world and virtual-world latency on an augmented reality training task: an AR simulation experiment. Front. ICT **3**, 13 (2017). https://doi.org/10.3389/fict.2016.00034

16. Ragan, E., Wilkes, C., Bowman, D.A., Höllerer, T.: Simulation of augmented reality systems in purely virtual environments. In: IEEE Virtual Reality, pp. 287–288 (2009). https://doi.org/10.1109/VR.2009.4811058

17. Ren, D., Goldschwendt, T., Chang, Y., Höllerer, T.: Evaluating wide-field-of-view augmented reality with mixed reality simulation. In: IEEE Virtual Reality, pp. 93–102 (2016). https://doi.org/10.1109/VR.2016.7504692

18. Renner, P., Pfeiffer, T.: Evaluation of attention guiding techniques for augmented reality-based assistance in picking and assembly tasks. In: ACM International Conference on Intelligent User Interfaces Companion, pp. 89–92 (2017). https://doi.org/10.1145/3030024.3040987

19. Zhou, F., Duh, H.B.L., Billinghurst, M.: Trends in augmented reality tracking, interaction and display: a review of ten years of ismar. In: IEEE/ACM International Symposium on Mixed and Augmented Reality, pp. 193–202 (2008). https://doi.org/10.1109/ISMAR.2008.4637362

Interactive Techniques and Use-Case Studies

Recreating Sheffield's Medieval Castle *In Situ* using Outdoor Augmented Reality

Matthew Leach[1]([⊠]) [iD], Steve Maddock[1] [iD], Dawn Hadley[1] [iD],
Carolyn Butterworth[1], John Moreland[1], Gareth Dean[1], Ralph Mackinder[1],
Kacper Pach[1], Nick Bax[2], Michaela Mckone[2], and Dan Fleetwood[2]

[1] University of Sheffield, Sheffield, UK
{mileach1,s.maddock,d.m.hadley,c.butterworth,
j.moreland,g.dean,r.mackinder,kpach1}@sheffield.ac.uk
[2] Human, Sheffield, UK
{nick,michaela,dan}@humanstudio.com

Abstract. Augmented Reality (AR) experiences generally function well indoors, inside buildings, where, typically, lighting conditions are stable, the scale of the environment is small and fixed, and markers can be easily placed. This is not the case for outdoor AR experiences. In this paper, we present practical solutions for an AR application that virtually restores Sheffield's medieval castle to the Castlegate area in Sheffield city centre where it once stood. A simplified 3D model of the area, together with sensor fusion, is used to support a user alignment process and subsequent orientation tracking. Rendering realism is improved by using directional lighting matching that of the sun, a virtual ground plane and depth masking based on the same model used in the alignment stage. The depth masking ensures the castle sits correctly in front of or behind real buildings, as necessary, thus addressing the occlusion problem. The *Unity* game engine is used for development and the resulting app runs in real-time on recent high-spec *Android* mobile phones.

Keywords: Augmented Reality · Outdoor augmented reality
Mobile augmented reality · Location-based augmented reality
Smartphones · Occlusion culling · Cultural heritage

1 Introduction

Sheffield's medieval castle is long gone, destroyed during the English Civil War in the mid-seventeenth century. However, the legacy of the castle endures in the landscape of the city: the location of the castle, Castlegate, was developed for industry and then for various markets. It now lies abandoned, after Castle Market was relocated in 2013, and awaits redevelopment. This paper presents research on using Augmented Reality (AR) to visualise a 3D model of medieval Sheffield Castle embedded in the Castlegate site.

© Springer Nature Switzerland AG 2018
P. Bourdot et al. (Eds.): EuroVR 2018, LNCS 11162, pp. 213–229, 2018.
https://doi.org/10.1007/978-3-030-01790-3_13

Outdoor AR experiences which attempt to embed 3D content into an environment are more complex than AR experiences inside buildings. Potential solutions are complicated by real world complexities such as dynamic environments (e.g. people and traffic movement and lighting changes) and solving the occlusion problem, i.e. showing a 3D model with some parts in front of and some parts behind different buildings. Specialist hardware, with depth cameras, can help, as can remote server power, but real-time SLAM (simultaneous localisation and mapping) is beyond consumer mobile phones for outdoor AR.

This paper presents a set of practical solutions to the challenges of producing an outdoor AR experience in a city centre site. The scale of the problem is constrained by using prior knowledge of the site, a user-controlled alignment process and the fusion of a range of sensor data. GPS is used to locate the user at one of a few set viewing points, which helps to optimise subsequent rendering speed for the 3D castle model. A virtual model of the 3D area is then overlaid on the mobile phone's video feed and the user aligns the model with the real world, giving a solid fix on position and orientation, before the virtual castle is displayed. The 3D model of the area is also used to address the occlusion problem. This knowledge-based depth masking process means that the castle sits in front of and behind different buildings, accordingly, based on user position. The mobile phone's sensors (GPS, gyroscope and accelerometers) are used to deal with continuous viewing changes; the compass sensor is also used as part of initial orientation setting. In addition, the sun's approximate position is used to change the lighting for the virtual castle, thus better integrating it into the real world environment. Whilst previous solutions have dealt with the occlusion problem for AR, our research work uses a virtual object (the castle) that is much bigger than its surrounding buildings, and, at the same time, deals with partial occlusion by those buildings in real-time on a consumer smartphone.

The remainder of this paper is organised as follows. Section 2 will consider related work, looking at the range of issues that affect outdoor AR experiences. Section 3 will present the system, covering the data required (models of the castle and the relevant area of the city and photographs of landmark buildings), the user processes (alignment and viewing) and rendering, including the approach for solving the occlusion problem. Section 4 will present the results and discussion. Finally, Sect. 5 presents conclusions.

2   Related Work

AR works best indoors, with various toolkits available to support the creation of indoor AR experiences: *ARToolKit*[1], *ARKit* and *ARKit 2*[2] [2], *ARCore*[3], *Vuforia*[4], and *Wikitude*[5]. Both marker-based and markerless tracking are supported,

---

[1] https://www.hitl.washington.edu/artoolkit/.
[2] https://developer.apple.com/arkit/.
[3] https://developers.google.com/ar/.
[4] https://www.vuforia.com/.
[5] https://www.wikitude.com/.

with ground plane detection being a key part of markerless solutions [15]. However, markerless tracking is difficult to achieve on outside scales, as the ground is often uneven and may have obstacles in the way which frustrate the detection process. Nonetheless, there has been successful outdoor AR work. Verykokou et al. [16] use a tablet PC in their computer-vision based work, but they only detect a specific almost-planar object in the scene before augmentation. Seo et al. [14] use an image registration technique but further work is needed for the method to be applicable to smartphones. The ideal solution for outdoor tracking is a process known as simultaneous localisation and mapping (SLAM) [4]. This family of methods uses computer vision to build a virtual map of the surroundings, in which features are detected and tracked to position and orientate the user. The approach is commonly used in robotics, but only works well with specialist hardware such as depth sensors and also requires complex computer vision processing, which would be too slow on a consumer grade mobile device.

Practical AR applications can be produced on consumer mobile devices, albeit with compromises. Perhaps the best known example of this is *Pokémon GO*[6], which became wildly popular across the UK and in many other countries after its release in 2016 [13]. This takes advantage of a multiscale approach, where the map view only uses GPS to roughly locate the user and then markerless detection is used to place a virtual Pokémon on the ground level in front of the user. As the locations are controlled and the Pokémon only appear near to the user, it is (reasonably) certain that the ground plane will be easy to detect and that there isn't much integration required to make the Pokémon appear as part of the scene.

Cirulis and Brigmanis [3] also make use of a phone's GPS. They compute the relative position of virtual buildings and display them based on the GPS location, however, with GPS results being relatively inaccurate this could easily cause alignment issues and jittering. Huang et al. [8] use a virtual model of an area with dedicated hardware to perform outdoor registration, but they compromise on precise tracking, instead focusing on information display. Vlahakis et al. [17] also use GPS, and enhance this with a Differential GPS beacon located at a known position to improve accuracy. CityViewAR [11] uses GPS for geolocation of city buildings. This works outdoors but is constrained by not dealing with anything in front of the virtual building.

Marker based techniques have been used in outdoor applications [10,12]. For example, Kim et al. [10] use the *Vuforia AR plugin*[7] for *Unity*[8] to provide information about three Korean cultural heritage sites. All of the sites have good features for marker based detection, although they are focusing on information display rather than augmenting the sites themselves. As such they only need to detect whether one of the sites is visible, rather than obtain any solid tracking information.

---

[6] https://www.pokemongo.com/.

[7] https://unity3d.com/partners/vuforia.

[8] https://unity3d.com/.

An issue common to many AR experiences is producing correct occlusion of virtual objects. Without depth information, even if a virtual object should appear behind a real world object, it will still appear in front of it. Techniques for obtaining depth information either rely on stereo/depth cameras, or using prior knowledge of the scene combined with location of the user in a virtual environment. At present, depth cameras have insubstantial range for outdoor use, and produce low resolution data. This requires further processing to construct an environment mesh from point cloud data. This can be done using traditional mesh reconstruction algorithms, although more recently neural network based approaches are being experimented with and producing promising results [7]. In outdoor applications, the prior knowledge approach is more commonly used [5,9]. We also use prior information, which is a 3D model of the environment that the virtual object is embedded into. The virtual object is a castle displayed at real scale. Occlusion with surrounding, smaller, real buildings is also addressed.

3   Data and Methods

Figure 1 shows the various components of our AR application and the data required for each stage. Stage 1 provides instructions to the user, including a map of the area and recommended viewing points. Stage 2 includes the alignment process where, after an initial coarse check on viewing position and direction using the GPS and compass sensors on the smartphone, the user aligns a virtual 3D model of the area containing various 'landmark buildings' with the real world view. Stage 3 is the viewing stage, where the castle is seen in situ using AR, correctly aligned and positioned relative to the user. Thereafter, tracking of orientation is done using the smartphone's gyroscope and accelerometer sensors. The app is developed using the *Unity* game engine and built for *Android*. The phone used for development and testing was a Motorola Moto Z (Snapdragon 820 processor, 1.8 GHz Quad-core CPU, Adreno 530 integrated GPU). The following subsections will describe the components of the system.

3.1   Data

The data required for the application consists of a model of the Castlegate area, photographs of the front of specific landmark buildings, and a model of the castle. The 3D model of the Castlegate area was produced by MArch students at The University of Sheffield's School of Architecture and is illustrated in Fig. 2 using *SketchUp*[9]. The model is made up of approx. 55,000 triangles. This relatively small memory footprint lessens the burden on the smartphone's processor and is sufficient to support the user alignment process and the depth masking aspects of the AR application. The initial model is untextured – it is the geometry that is important for the depth masking stage. However, to support the user alignment process (see later), photographs of the fronts of 'landmark buildings' (buildings that are easily distinguishable within the Castlegate area) are added to relevant parts of the model as texture maps, as illustrated in Figs. 3 and 4.

---

[9] https://www.sketchup.com/.

Program Flow (User Processes)	Data/Hardware Requirements
App Start (Press Continue)	– User Interface Icons
Alignment Screen (User lines up virtual landmark buildings with real world scene) (Press Aligned)	– GPS location – Landmark building photos – Known locations for landmark buildings – Gyroscope data – Accelerometer data
Landmark buildings hidden, castle displayed (UI options)	– Castle model – Gyroscope data – Accelerometer data

Fig. 1. An overview of the components of the system.

The model of Sheffield Castle (Fig. 5) was created by Human[10], a Sheffield-based creative agency. It is based on archaeological and historical evidence for what the castle was like, drawn from research on the unpublished archives from mid-twentieth-century excavations, with inspiration also drawn from surviving castles of similar type (Richmond, Helmsley and Barnard), for the architectural details. The castle is modelled as a set of distinct pieces as shown in Fig. 6 so as to support only rendering those that are visible during rendering. Each of the pieces is hidden or shown depending on the viewing location. The complete model

Fig. 2. The model of the Castlegate area viewed in *Sketchup*. Castlegate, which is where the castle was situated, is oulined in red. (Color figure online)

Fig. 3. Texture map of a landmark building in the scene.

---

[10] http://humanstudio.com/.

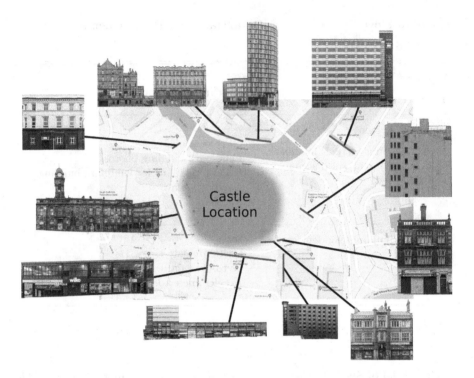

Fig. 4. The various landmark buildings and their locations. Map data ©2018 Google.

consists of 3100 triangles and uses 69 textures, 50 with resolution 2048×2048, 16 with resolution 1024×1024 and 3 with resolution 512×512. Figure 7 shows how the castle sits in the Castlegate model from Fig. 2. A key part of this stage is to make sure the ground level of the two models is aligned – this is important for later stages. The ground heights of each of the area and castle models follows the current land height for the Castlegate area, although the castle model includes a moat.

3.2   Alignment Processes

This section focusses on stage 2 in Fig. 1. An initial viewpoint is established using GPS, followed by a user alignment process between the model and the real world view. Orientation tracking is also required.

GPS for standard smartphones is only accurate to approx. 5–8.5 m in good conditions [19]. In an urban environment, particularly when the scene is being viewed from pavement level, tall buildings may be close to the user and lead to even worse performance. We solve this issue by defining specific viewpoints where the user should stand. The active viewpoint is chosen by selecting the viewpoint with the minimum Euclidean distance to the reported GPS location. This selection process takes place when the app is started, and every 10 s thereafter –

Fig. 5. The textured, full resolution model of the castle. The model includes a surrounding landscape and moat (in grey in this image).

Fig. 6. An exploded view of the separate parts of the castle.

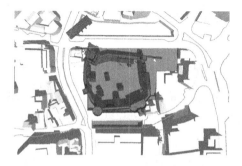

Fig. 7. The model of Sheffield Castle positioned at its historic location in the Castlegate model.

a continuous update would use unnecessary resources, both computationally and in terms of battery power on the user's device. A time of 10 s is considerably shorter than it would take to walk between any of the defined viewpoints, ensuring that when the user reaches such a point, the app will have updated their location.

Having established a viewpoint, the next step is a user alignment process. This involves detecting view orientation and the direction the user is facing. In theory, the compass could be used to detect the direction the user is facing. However, mobile device compasses are not particularly accurate, and are also affected by surrounding magnetic fields. During testing, the reported angle was often found to be up to twenty or thirty degrees away from the true angle. Thus an accurate bearing could not be found. However, it gave an initial guess for the orientation, which roughly aligns the viewpoint direction with the Castlegate model so that relevant landmark buildings are in view. Using this initial information, the landmark buildings can then be used to refine the alignment.

Figure 3 illustrates one of the landmark buildings, as described in Sect. 3.1. From the user's position, the landmark buildings are displayed in their correct position relative to the virtual Castlegate model – the white Castlegate area model is not visible, only the landmark buildings. The user can swipe on the screen to rotate the scene until the relevant virtual landmark buildings line up with the real ones, based on the current viewpoint position. The Castlegate model is now aligned with the real world from the user's viewpoint. However, other processes are happening in parallel – user orientation and perspective correction – which must be considered before the alignment process is complete.

The user's orientation is tracked so that the correct view of the castle model can be presented in relation to the real world view. The smartphone's gyroscope and accelerometer sensors are used for this. The gyroscope sensors give a very accurate reading for the angular velocity of the device around each of the main axes. By integrating this we can determine the total angle the device has moved through. An issue, however, is that error accumulation in the integration causes drift. Initial experiments used a Kalman filter [18] to mitigate this. This worked well for correcting pitch measurements, but absolute heading values from the compass were incorrect and, since the Kalman filter used these to update its state, the results were poor, converging to the wrong angle and producing jittery behaviour. Instead, a complementary filter [6] was used with a small timestep in the Euler integrator. Since only minor drift corrections were required, this worked well. In addition, the complementary filter has a lower performance impact than a Kalman filter requiring only a simple multiplication and addition, rather than an iterative matrix solve or approximation. This was two orders of magnitude faster in testing.

Camera perspective must also be considered. From the defined viewpoints process, the user's location is known. The roll, pitch and yaw of the smartphone are tracked by the user orientation process. The roll and pitch can be determined purely from the accelerometer and gyroscope data, whilst the user has completed the alignment process to ensure the correct yaw. These transformation values are applied to the *Unity* camera. With the real and virtual cameras' positions matching, the fields of view must be matched to ensure the same view is seen by both cameras. To match the field of view, the device camera's field of view and aspect ratio are queried. This combined with the aspect ratio of the screen is sufficient information to produce the correct perspective matrix. As the screen and camera aspect ratios do not match, the actual camera image is cropped which affects the field of view. For a screen of wider aspect ratio than camera, the updated field of view can be computed according to the following formula:

$$\theta_c \frac{(W_c/W_s)}{(H_c/H_s)} \tag{1}$$

where θ_c is the reported vertical camera field of view, W_c is the width of the image returned from the camera, W_s is the width of the screen, H_c is the height of the image returned from the camera and H_s is the height of the screen. For our test smartphone, the screen is 16:9, whilst the camera is 4:3, or 16:12. As such the vertical component is scaled by three quarters to match the 16:9 screen aspect. This also reduces the effective vertical field of view by 3/4. The device camera reports a 50° vertical field of view, so three quarters of this, 37.5, is used for the vertical field of view of the *Unity* camera.

Figure 8 shows the alignment process in progress. For the building on the right in Fig. 8a, both the virtual landmark building and its real counterpart are visible. The user then swipes to rotate the virtual scene until it matches the real scene as seen in Fig. 8b. The user is free to look around during this process to also compare other buildings for alignment. When the user is happy with the alignment, a tap on the smartphone screen reveals the virtual castle model correctly augmented into the real world scene. One final part of the alignment process worth noting is the slowest part of the whole process was using *Unity*'s WebCamTexture class to handle the video feed. Performance was improved significantly by using code to natively access the camera.

(a) pre-alignment   (b) post-alignment

Fig. 8. User alignment with the frontages of the Market Tavern and the building to its right.

3.3 Rendering

After user alignment, the virtual castle model is displayed. This involves three aspects. First, to give a real sense that the castle is augmenting the real world, real buildings that are behind the castle should not be seen, and real buildings in front of the castle should obscure the virtual model. Second, the ground planes of the virtual model and the real world should be aligned. Third, the lighting of the virtual model should consider the position of the sun in the real world, so as to better match the lighting of the surrounding real world buildings.

Correctly embedding the virtual 3D model into the real world required a process to detect what should be in front of, rather than behind, the virtual object. Standard smartphone cameras do not report any depth information. Our solution for the occlusion problem makes use of the user's location and orientation and knowing what the user's view should be in the real world, based on the earlier user alignment process between the virtual Castlegate model's landmark buildings and the real world. Since we have the full virtual Castlegate model aligned with the real world, and we know the castle's position within the Castlegate model, we can use the Castlegate model to create a depth mask to stop portions of the virtual castle from being drawn, making it appear hidden by buildings in the foreground. We call this location knowledge-based depth masking. It is similar in concept to the approach used in [5,9], but is extended to use 3D models. They are only interested in occluding small, ground height markers, however, for an object the size of a castle, only portions of it may be occluded, and it is larger than the occluding objects, so their ray based approach is not sufficient. Our method allows occlusion of only parts of objects.

Fig. 9. The Castlegate model buildings outlined in orange will act as a mask for the castle.

Fig. 10. The castle masked by the Castlegate model buildings.

A multi-pass rendering approach is used. Initially, the depth and colour buffers are cleared. In the first pass, the video feed is rendered full screen. This ensures that a full background is available. In the second pass, occluding buildings are rendered using a shader which writes only to the depth buffer. This masks out regions where the castle should not be drawn because buildings are present in front of it, as illustrated in Fig. 9, and the actual buildings will be displayed in the correct location in the video feed assuming the alignment process was carried out correctly. In the final pass, the castle is rendered, with any masked portions failing the depth test, essentially cutting a hole in the castle model, as illustrated in Fig. 10. Thus the castle will appear to be behind real foreground buildings.

Making AR objects appear as though they are correctly integrated with the ground is challenging. For small objects, a simple shadow surrounding it may be sufficient, but for a large object this is very difficult as correctly computing how the shadow should appear on the video feed is non-trivial. In addition, without proper depth information, even portions of the castle model that might be under the ground are rendered on top. To solve this, we use a virtual ground plane. The ground is modelled to match the layout of the real land. This approach means inclusion of the moat is trivial.

To further integrate the castle into the real world, the sun's position must be considered so that the lighting of the castle appears to better match that of the surrounding buildings. The sun's position can be computed from the date, time of day and longitude and latitude of the area. This calculation involves using astronomical formulae, based on those found in the *Astronomical Almanac*[11]. Initially, the date is converted to Julian days and centuries. From these, sidereal time is computed. Solar coordinates are determined from the results of the

---

[11] http://astro.ukho.gov.uk/nao/publicat/asa.html.

previous calculations, and these are used to calculate the right ascension and declination. Finally, these are transformed to Alt/Az coordinates. A more detailed explanation can be found in the Appendix.

The final aspect of rendering to consider is performance, since a mobile device has limited processing power. The castle is composed of individual pieces (Fig. 6) to help increase performance. Only those parts that are visible from the defined viewpoints in the application need to be rendered; those pieces that are entirely blocked by others do not need to be rendered. In addition, mipmapping and level of detail techniques are used to further reduce the rendering time.

4   Results and Discussion

Figures 11 and 12 show the view when the user is aligning the Old Town Hall landmark building texture with its real world counterpart. Once this is aligned, the virtual castle model is then displayed, as shown in Fig. 13. Note how the real old town hall building is seen beyond the virtual castle. The user can then rotate her mobile device to show other parts of the scene. Figure 14 shows the scene once the viewpoint is rotated to the right along the castle wall to show the main gate. The real Market Tavern (also one of the landmark buildings in the Castlegate model) is shown in front of the castle demonstrating the effect of the depth masking process. Figure 15 shows the occlusion when the camera is angled upwards. Another example of the alignment process is given in Figs. 16 and 17. Here, the Metropolitan hotel is used as the landmark building in the alignment process, and the user must then rotate her camera to see the castle (Fig. 18). Figures 19 and 20 demonstrate the dynamic lighting in the app. Variation is particularly noticeable on the buttresses supporting the wall, and on the tops of the crenellations.

Fig. 11. The view of the old town hall during the alignment process.

Fig. 12. The view of the old town hall after alignment. The row of shops on the left is also a landmark texture.

Over time, with continuous changes in orientation, some calculation drift can occur, since this is based on integration of gyroscope data. The virtual model and the real world can become slightly misaligned. In general, a misalignment of a few degrees is not an issue at this scale as the castle sits well within the area of

Fig. 13. The virtual castle viewed with the real old town hall in the background.

Fig. 14. The depth masking technique cuts a hole in the castle, leaving the image of the real Market Tavern showing from the video feed.

Fig. 15. Occlusion masking shows the castle appearing behind the Market Tavern.

Fig. 16. The Metropolitan hotel before alignment.

Fig. 17. The Metropolitan hotel after alignment.

Fig. 18. After user alignment with the Metropolitan hotel, the camera view is rotated to show the castle.

Fig. 19. A view of the castle from the north side taken in the morning. The sun is to the east (the left of the figure). The front face of the buttress supporting the wall is not receiving direct sunlight and appears 'flat'.

Fig. 20. A view of the castle from the north side taken shortly after midday. The sun is high in the sky. The front face of the buttress supporting the wall is brighter than in Fig. 19, as are the angled upper surfaces of the crenellated battlements.

Fig. 21. Over time, with continuous changes in orientation, calculation drift can occur, producing a slight misalignment between the virtual model and the real world, which affects the depth masking process.

Fig. 22. An enlarged view of the old town hall in Fig. 12

land – a small difference in location won't be noticed. The drift does, however, create some problems in conjunction with the depth masking. The cutout in the castle model for a foreground building requires a good alignment, or the wrong portion of the video feed can be displayed in the hole (Fig. 21). When this occurs, user alignment must be redone.

Figure 22 shows an enlarged portion of Fig. 12. As can be seen, representing landmark buildings as textured planes works well for the flat frontage of the building. However, the tower of the old town hall is set back from the building face and, as such, appears in the wrong place for alignment, since it has been projected forwards into the textured plane. An alternative solution could use multiple textured planes, but it is unclear if this extra complication would be of benefit, since the current alignment process, based on the building frontage, seems to work well.

5 Conclusions

A practical, working, outdoor AR system that runs on android phones with appropriate sensors has been presented. A user alignment process, together with the fusion of a range of sensors, produces a system that is stable and easy to use. The 3D model of the area is used both in the user alignment process and also as part of a depth masking process so that the 3D virtual castle is properly placed in the real world view. There are some drift issues over time, although these can be rectified by user re-alignment. Further work could consider how to retain the alignment for longer, perhaps using a lightweight version of SLAM, as well as how to remove the initial user alignment step.

Initial experiments have been done to add links to social media tools within the application, with the aim of allowing the general public to share their thoughts on the restored castle model (thus producing a reconstruction AR application, using Bekele's categorisation [1]). Also, since the Castlegate area will undergo redevelopment in the future, our intention is to be able to display the future 3D plans for the area as an alternative user option. We could also offer an option to display a model of the remaining underground chambers on the site which preserve some of the archaeological heritage. Both of these would be relatively straightforward since the models would be geolocated in the Castlegate model in the same way that the castle model was. This would give local people a chance to use an AR application to be involved in redevelopment of the site, and make their views known on both the future building plans and the site's cultural heritage.

Acknowledgements. This research was funded by a grant from the AHRC/EPSRC Immersive Experience scheme (grant no. AH/R009392/1). Research on the archaeological archives relating to Sheffield Castle was funded by the Pamela Staunton Bequest (University of Sheffield).

Appendix

All trigonometric functions listed operate in radians. Angles should be corrected to a range between 0 and 2π throughout unless otherwise noted.

Compute the number of Julian days and Julian centuries since J2000:

$$d_j = 367y - \left\lfloor \frac{7}{4}(y + \lfloor (m+9)/12 \rfloor) \right\rfloor + \left\lfloor \frac{275m}{9} \right\rfloor + d - 730531.5$$

$$C_j = \frac{d_j}{36525}$$

where d_j is the Julian day, y is the year, m is the month in numerical form, d is the day in numerical form and C_j is the Julian century.

Compute the sidereal time:

$$S_h = 6.6974 + 2400.0513C_j$$
$$S_{ut} = S_h + \frac{366.2422}{365.2422}h$$
$$S = 15S_{ut} + L_o$$

where S_h is the sidereal time in hours at midnight, S_{ut} is the sidereal time in hours including the current time, S is the local sidereal time and L_o is the longitude.

Update to fractional (including time of day) Julian days and centuries:

$$d_j = d_j + \frac{h}{24}c_j = \frac{d_j}{36525}$$

Compute solar coordinates:

$$G_{MeanLong} = \frac{2\pi}{360}(280.466 + 36000.77C_j)$$
$$G_{MeanAnom} = \frac{2\pi}{360}(357.529 + 35999.05C_j))$$
$$E_{cen} = \frac{2\pi}{360}((1.915 - 0.005C_j)\sin(G_{MeanAnom}) + 0.02\sin(2*G_{MeanAnom}))$$
$$L_{eliptic} = G_{MeanLong} + E_{cen}$$
$$O = \frac{2\pi}{360}(23.439 - 0.013C_j)$$

where $G_{MeanLong}$ is the mean solar longitude, $G_{MeanAnom}$ is the mean solar anomaly, $E + cen$ is the equation of center, $L_{eliptic}$ is the eliptical longitude and O is the obliquity.

Compute right ascension and declination:

$$R = \text{atan2}(\cos(O)\sin(L_{eliptic}), \cos(L_{eliptic}))$$
$$D = \arcsin(\sin(R)\sin(O))$$

where R is the right ascension and D is the declination.

Compute horizontal coordinates. The hour angle, H, should be brought into the range $-\pi$ to π.

$$H = \frac{2\pi}{360}S - R$$
$$Alt. = \arcsin(\sin(\frac{2\pi}{360}L_a)\sin(D) + \cos(\frac{2\pi}{360}L_a)\cos(D)\cos(H))$$

where H is the hour angle and $Alt.$ is the altitude.

Compute the azimuth angle:

$$Az. = \arctan\left(\frac{-\sin(H)}{\tan(D)\cos(\frac{2\pi}{360}L_a) - \sin(\frac{2\pi}{360}L_a)\cos(H)}\right)$$

where $Az.$ is the azimuth angle.

Finally, adjust the azimuth angle to the correct quadrant.

References

1. Bekele, M.K., Pierdicca, R., Frontoni, E., Malinverni, E.S., Gain, J.: A survey of augmented, virtual, and mixed reality for cultural heritage. J. Comput. Cult. Herit. **11**(2), 7:1–7:36 (2018). https://doi.org/10.1145/3145534

2. Buerli, M., Misslinger, S.: Introducing ARKit-augmented reality for iOS. In: Apple Worldwide Developers Conference (WWDC 2017), pp. 1–187 (2017)

3. Cirulis, A., Brigmanis, K.B.: 3D outdoor augmented reality for architecture and urban planning. Procedia Comput. Sci. **25**, 71–79 (2013). https://doi.org/10.1016/j.procs.2013.11.009

4. Durrant-Whyte, H., Bailey, T.: Simultaneous localization and mapping: part I. IEEE Robot. Autom. Mag. **13**(2), 99–110 (2006). https://doi.org/10.1109/MRA.2006.1638022

5. Galatis, P., Gavalas, D., Kasapakis, V., Pantziou, G., Zaroliagis, C.: Mobile augmented reality guides in cultural heritage. In: Proceedings of the 8th EAI International Conference on Mobile Computing, Applications and Services, pp. 11–19 (2016). https://doi.org/10.4108/eai.30-11-2016.2266954

6. Higgins, W.T.: A comparison of complementary and Kalman filtering. IEEE Trans. Aerosp. Electron. Syst. **3**, 321–325 (1975). https://doi.org/10.1109/TAES.1975.308081

7. Höft, N., Schulz, H., Behnke, S.: Fast semantic segmentation of RGB-D scenes with GPU-accelerated deep neural networks. In: Lutz, C., Thielscher, M. (eds.) KI 2014. LNCS (LNAI), vol. 8736, pp. 80–85. Springer, Cham (2014). https://doi.org/10.1007/978-3-319-11206-0_9

8. Huang, W., Sun, M., Li, S.: A 3D GIS-based interactive registration mechanism for outdoor augmented reality system. Expert Syst. Appl. **55**, 48–58 (2016). https://doi.org/10.1016/j.eswa.2016.01.037

9. Kasapakis, V., Gavalas, D.: Occlusion handling in outdoors augmented reality games. Multimed. Tools Appl. **76**(7), 9829–9854 (2017). https://doi.org/10.1007/s11042-016-3581-1

10. Kim, H., Matuszka, T., Kim, J.I., Kim, J., Woo, W.: An ontology-based augmented reality application exploring contextual data of cultural heritage sites. In: 2016 12th International Conference on Signal-Image Technology & Internet-Based Systems (SITIS), pp. 468–475. IEEE (2016). https://doi.org/10.1109/SITIS.2016.79

11. Lee, G.A., Dünser, A., Kim, S., Billinghurst, M.: CityViewAR: a mobile outdoor AR application for city visualization. In: 2012 IEEE International Symposium on Mixed and Augmented Reality (ISMAR-AMH), pp. 57–64. IEEE (2012). https://doi.org/10.1109/ISMAR-AMH.2012.6483989

12. Murru, G., Fratarcangeli, M., Empler, T.: Practical augmented visualization on handheld devices for cultural heritage. In: Proceedings of the 21st International Conference on Computer Graphics, Visualization and Computer Vision, pp. 97–103 (2013)

13. Paavilainen, J., Korhonen, H., Alha, K., Stenros, J., Koskinen, E., Mayra, F.: The Pokémon GO experience: a location-based augmented reality mobile game goes mainstream. In: Proceedings of the 2017 CHI Conference on Human Factors in Computing Systems, pp. 2493–2498. ACM (2017). https://doi.org/10.1145/3025453.3025871

14. Seo, B.K., Kim, K., Park, J., Park, J.I.: A tracking framework for augmented reality tours on cultural heritage sites. In: Proceedings of the 9th ACM SIGGRAPH Conference on Virtual-Reality Continuum and its Applications in Industry, pp. 169–174. ACM (2010). https://doi.org/10.1145/1900179.1900215

15. Simon, G., Fitzgibbon, A.W., Zisserman, A.: Markerless tracking using planar structures in the scene. In: 2000 Proceedings of the IEEE and ACM International Symposium on Augmented Reality (ISAR 2000), pp. 120–128. IEEE (2000). https://doi.org/10.1109/ISAR.2000.880935

16. Verykokou, S., Ioannidis, C., Kontogianni, G.: 3D visualization via augmented reality: the case of the middle stoa in the ancient agora of athens. In: Ioannides, M., Magnenat-Thalmann, N., Fink, E., Žarnić, R., Yen, A.-Y., Quak, E. (eds.) EuroMed 2014. LNCS, vol. 8740, pp. 279–289. Springer, Cham (2014). https://doi.org/10.1007/978-3-319-13695-0_27

17. Vlahakis, V., Ioannidis, M., Karigiannis, J., Tsotros, M., Gounaris, M., Stricker, D., Gleue, T., Daehne, P., Almeida, L.: Archeoguide: an augmented reality guide for archaeological sites. IEEE Comput. Graph. Appl. **22**(5), 52–60 (2002). https://doi.org/10.1109/MCG.2002.1028726

18. Welch, G., Bishop, G.: An introduction to the Kalman filter. In: Annual Conference on Computer Graphics & Interactive Techniques, SIGGRAPH 2001 Course 8 Computer Graphics, Los Angeles, CA, USA, 12–17 August 2001 (2001). https://sreal.ucf.edu/wp-content/uploads/2017/02/Welch2001.pdf

19. Zandbergen, P.A., Barbeau, S.J.: Positional accuracy of assisted GPS data from high-sensitivity GPS-enabled mobile phones. J. Navig. **64**(3), 381–399 (2011). https://doi.org/10.1017/S0373463311000051

Added Value of a 3D CAVE
Within Design Activities

Jean Basset and Frédéric Noël[✉]

Univ. Grenoble Alpes, CNRS, Grenoble INP,
(Institute of Engineering Univ. Grenoble Alpes), G-SCOP, 38000 Grenoble, France
`frederic.noel@grenoble-inp.fr`

Abstract. 3D stereoscopic based virtual reality reaches a good level of maturity. Many applications are proposed in many areas including professional tasks. Anyhow, whenever a new device appears, its added value remains an issue. In this article a CAVE with a desktop size is under focus. A manufactured product design task was selected to assess the added value of this new configuration. A panel of users were expected to achieve the task on a usual 2D desktop and within the CAVE. The experience demonstrates that the selected task takes a real advantage of the CAVE configuration.

Keywords: 3D CAVE · Stereoscopy · Virtual reality · Design task

1 Introduction

Virtual Reality is a research and development issue from many years now. The introduction of low cost head mounted displays (HMD) has boosted VR experiences in many area but still face some maturity issues (resolution, latency, etc.) and intrinsic bottlenecks (very closed vergence, dissociation between gaze perception and internal hear, etc.). These issues may lead to discomfort up to nausea for some individuals. The conditions of deployment of the HMD technology in professional applications remains unclear.

On the other hand, CAVES are the main second solution to experience 3D immersion. Due to its intrinsic size the distance from eye to the display is much higher than in HMDs. With Ultra High Resolution displays pixel size was recently improved and the size of the equipment allows to take advantage of a cluster of computers to reduce latency. But indeed the equipment size usually expects to invest in the building to install such an infrastructure. Its overall cost, including maintenance is also a brake to its deployment.

Observing these two issues, the G-SCOP laboratory specified and developed (with the support of BARCO and Immersion), a five faces CAVE at a desktop scale. It is called the Mihriad cave. The overall system is just two centimetres less than a standard office height (2.5 m) and has a $9\,\mathrm{m}^2$ footprint. Even using only full HD projectors it leads to a 0.3 mm pixel. The main objective is to create

© Springer Nature Switzerland AG 2018
P. Bourdot et al. (Eds.): EuroVR 2018, LNCS 11162, pp. 230–239, 2018.
https://doi.org/10.1007/978-3-030-01790-3_14

an environment that should be easily deployed in industry even within SMEs design office.

This type of CAVE is viewed as a specific component of the design office of the future. In this office many applications will still use monoscopic displays but specific tasks could take advantage of a 3D stereoscopic vision. This paper summarises an experience to assess the advantage of the CAVE beyond a usual 2D monoscopic display. It almost demonstrates that for very specific tasks the CAVE provides a real added value and opens a multi-modality vision of the design office where multiple devices and interaction tools are selected depending on the expected tasks.

2   Use Case Description

The experience is based on a use case selection. Many applications are considering VR to support gesture training [1–3] in various expertise task. Maintenance, assembly/disassembly task are often mentioned in papers [4–7]. The main idea is usually to repeat in a safe virtual word complex real activities. Here we are considering actions that could be rapidly applied with a direct added value in a design office. As early mentioned by Krueger [8], *"users want to focus on their tasks rather than on operating the computer"*. We could have selected a disassembly training process but we selected the process which prepares the disassembly instructions. That means that we do not directly support the end-user who will operate the process but the designer who explains the process he has in mind. Then the task should be a specific task along the design process and should be directly connected to usual tasks.

First rank industry already invested in 3D CAVEs but this infrastructure remains quite unique and must be planned in the industrial processes to let time for CAVE preparation but also because usage demand comes from many different services. The infrastructure must be shared. The Mihriad CAVE is expected to be a proximity device available for rapid usage. Design mainly uses CAD tools which are (up to now!) still based on traditional 2D graphic user interface. It is a real bottleneck also for these tools to identify the tasks performance respect to the rendering and interaction device. It may be more efficient to use traditional CAD graphic user interface than a 3D environment to sharply position a part with constraints: just select two faces, axes and constrain them for alignment. With disassembly the final position does not matter so much. Then the CAVE with gesture tracking may offer a more obvious added value.

While 3D interaction seems to be very natural, it was demonstrated risks of full 3D interaction [9]. 3D virtual free gestures may be tiresome and should be avoided for long term activities. It was also demonstrated the benefits of tangible interaction [10] which is less obvious with a mouse interaction.

Then we promote a design office organisation where various device may be seamless used depending on the expected task and the use case is used to assess the added value of a specific CAVE configuration and to analyse its potential integration within design offices. The use case considers the disassembly of a turning manufacturing machine as shown in Fig. 2.

3   Study Design

Then the goal of this study is to compare the performances of users for the same task between the Mihriad CAVE and a 2D computer screen. The results of the study will give a baseline for future work in the CAVE, by highlighting strengths or weaknesses over classic working environment. The study is based on two assumptions:

H1: Efficiency hypothesis: for a similar simple 3D object manipulation task, people will be more efficient and feel more comfortable using the CAVE than using a 2D screen.

H2: Operational hypothesis: in the CAVE, the subjects will be able to perform the task in a shorter time, and should report the task as easier than on the 2D screen.

3.1   Working Environment

The Mihriad CAVE is composed of five 70" screens; three walls (front, left, right), one "roof" (top), and one at desk level (bottom). The immersion and interaction in the virtual environment are done with tracked glasses and controller. The tracking depends on ten Optitrack cameras (Fig. 1) and reflective markers on tracked items. The Mihriad cave may be seen as an extension of a 3D workbench [8] with more immersion capacity due to extra displays.

The study protocol asked subjects to work both in virtual reality in the CAVE, and in 2D on a classic computer screen. Those environments will be named "CAVE condition" and "2D condition". The virtual prototype used in the study is a turning machine (See Fig. 2). No mechanical knowledge of the machine is necessary to perform the study.

Fig. 1. Aparatus, from the left: Mihriad CAVE, Optitrack camera, tracked glasses and controller

3.2   Procedure

Upon arrival, subjects were asked to fill a consent form and a demographic questionnaire. The researcher conducting the study then presents the research project, the equipment, and the virtual prototype used during the study. Then, subjects perform a same task on the virtual prototype, both in CAVE condition and 2D condition. The order of the condition is rotated between subjects to avoid impact of learning effects on the observations.

The task expects the manipulation of parts composing the virtual prototype. Their positions can be saved on demand. Subjects are guided by the researcher's instructions during the task. The subject is asked to dismantle several parts of the virtual prototype by removing them from their support, and to discard them by placing them on plane surfaces of the 3D model. The parts associated with the task are the work holding device (a 3-jaw chuck) and the tool post as shown in Fig. 2.

As soon as the task is achieved under a given condition, subjects fill a questionnaire concerning their subjective feelings about this experience. At the end of the study, subjects fill a last questionnaire, asking for their global feeling on the study. This create a first subjective feedback; the next section complete this feedback with objective observations.

Fig. 2. Right: The turning machine virtual prototype. Left: Manipulated pieces: The holding device (green box) and the tool post (red box) (Color figure online)

3.3   Collected Data

Measurements. During the study, several sub-activity times were recorded in each condition: the total time to achieve the condition, the part manipulation task duration, and the point of view manipulation task duration. The total time is split into part manipulation sub-activities, point of view manipulation sub-activities and pauses. We also counted the occasions where the subject cancelled an object's manipulation which is considered as a number of manipulation errors.

A technical tracking issue appeared which was not solved before the experience. In the CAVE, it creates image skips. Those skips are counted in order to control their impact on the results about the CAVE condition. The subjects are not given strong precision constraints regarding the position of the parts after disassembly.

Questionnaires. The consent form explained the context of the study and clarified the anonymity of the collected data, the known risks of VR (motion sickness) and the volunteer status of the subjects. The demographic form gathers data that may have an impact on the performances of subjects. Those data are the age of subjects, their guiding hand, and whether or not they had a previous experience with CAD software, HMD based virtual reality or CAVE systems.

The after task subjective questionnaire was composed of two main parts. First, the subjects filled a NASA-TLX [11] standard questionnaire, used to estimate the effort required to complete a given task: the subjects estimate their feeling for six items on a given scale (mental, physical and temporal exigence, effort, performance, and frustration). The addition of scores for these items gives the estimated workload score. In the second part of the subjective questionnaire, six affirmations are proposed to the subject (See Fig. 4), who indicates his level of approbation on a 7 level Likert [12] scale (From 1: "Completely disagree" to 7: "Fully agree").

Finally, the post-study questionnaire directly asks subjects the condition they preferred, and whether or not they felt discomfort linked to the image skips in the CAVE condition, i.e.: the CAVE (See Fig. 6. The question concerning subjects preferences is doubled in order to check for answer's consistency and to avoid influencing subjects in a direction or the other.

4   Study Results

4.1   Participants

A panel of 19 participants (13 men and 6 females) volunteered to take part in the study. The subjects were aged from 20 to 62 ($mean = 30 \pm 12$). All but one were right-handed, and all had normal or corrected to normal vision (the CAVE's glasses were wide enough to be worn on top of eyeglasses without consequent hindrance). 13 already had an experience with CAD softwares, 7 with HMD based virtual reality, and 3 with CAVE systems. 10 subjects started with the 2D modality, and 9 with the CAVE modality.

4.2   Data Analysis

Most of our collected data presents a non-normal distribution. Furthermore, the same subjects are measured over both conditions during the study, observations therefore are not independent. Thus, we mostly used Wilcoxon non-parametric tests to study our data. We chose a statistical level significance of 5%. All statistical tests were made using R (https://www.r-project.org/).

Manipulation Times. Figure 3 compares subjects' manipulation times between CAVE and 2D conditions. Normality of distribution and independence of observation being rejected, we used Wilcoxon tests.

- For total condition time: $p - value = 0.014$
- For pieces manipulation time: $p - value = 0.005$
- For point of view manipulation time: $p - value = 6.554e - 07$

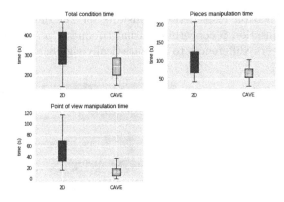

Fig. 3. Comparison of manipulation times

Then for the three measured times, Wilcoxon tests demonstrated the differences are significant. Times are longer in the 2D condition than in the CAVE.

Since a same subject tested the two conditions of work, we also checked the effect of subjects' condition order. Wilcoxon tests were also conducted leading to the following results:

- For total condition time: $p-value = 0.007$
- For parts manipulation time: $p-value = 0.027$
- For point of view manipulation time: $p-value = 0.954$

Here Wilcoxon tests showed that measures are significant (despite the subjects' condition order) for total condition time and for parts manipulation time but are not significant for the point of view manipulation time.

To complete these tests, we conducted two ways ANOVA explaining manipulation times by the condition and order. Like said before, the ANOVA's assumptions (normal distribution, independence of observation) are not respected. However the ANOVA is considered robust to rejection of its assumptions, and is the only test able to check for interactions between factors. The results (See Table 1) of these ANOVA is thus used as a complement for the Wilcoxon tests.

Table 1. Results of two-way ANOVA on manipulation times explained by the condition and the order ('*'= significant difference)

p-values	Condition	Order	Cond:Order
Total condition time	0.007 *	0.008 *	0.026 *
Parts manipulation time	0.001 *	0.039 *	0.119
Point of view manipulation time	0 *	0.391	0.093

Subjective Feelings. Figure 4 shows subjects' answers to the subjective questionnaire in both conditions. Once again, normal distribution is rejected.

We conducted Wilcoxon tests between answers for 2D and CAVE conditions. Apart from the question 6 concerning visual tiredness ($p - value = 0.51$), all tests showed answers' differences to be statistically significant.

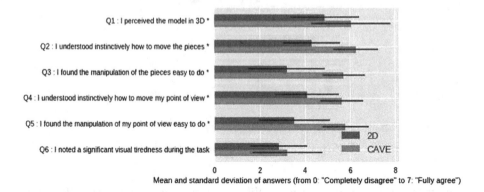

Fig. 4. Comparison of answers to the subjective questionnaire

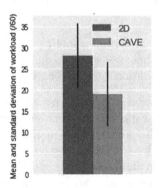

Fig. 5. Comparison of answers to the NASA-TLX

Figure 5 shows the estimated workload score of subjects between conditions. The 6 items of the NASA-TLX are rated by the subject on a 10 points scale, giving a workload score on 60. Mean score for CAVE condition is 18.89, and 28.10 for 2D condition, with for both condition a standard deviation close to 7.60. This difference is confirmed significant by a Wilcoxon test ($p - value = 0.001$).

Errors. Mean number of errors in 2D condition is 1.10, and 0.21 in CAVE condition. A Wilcoxon test proved this difference statistically significant ($p - value = 0.014$). The order of conditions did not create a significant difference in error number (Wilcoxon test, $p - value = 0.477$).

Post-study Questionnaire. Figure 6 presents the subjects' answers to the post-study questionnaire. The difference between the two questions concerning preferences is large enough to be considered significant without statistical tests.

Most subjects felt a nuisance linked to image skips in the CAVE (mean answer=
4.05 ± 1.72). This result is completed by the actual number of counted image
skips during the study's CAVE condition: 4.84 ± 3.11.

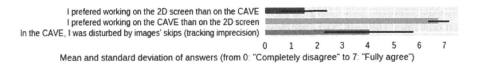

I prefered working on the 2D screen than on the CAVE
I prefered working on the CAVE than on the 2D screen
In the CAVE, I was disturbed by images' skips (tracking imprecision)

0   1   2   3   4   5   6   7
Mean and standard deviation of answers (from 0: "Completely disagree" to 7: "Fully agree")

Fig. 6. Answers to the post-study questionnaire

Demographic Data. No link could be made between the demographic data of
the subjects (age, guiding hand, experience) and their performances and feelings
during the study (times, questionnaires).

4.3   Study Conclusion

The results of the study showed that users were faster performing the task in the
CAVE condition than in the 2D condition. It is clearly highlighted by both the
total task duration and the object manipulation time. The time to manipulate
the parts, is not affected as much by the order than the total condition time;
for both, interactions between order and condition are rejected. Point of view
manipulation time is not even affected by the order of the condition. The time
differences between CAVE and 2D conditions is therefore not just an effect of the
order. Also, the subjects also made significantly more errors in the 2D condition;
they cancelled action significantly more often than in the CAVE. Then the CAVE
condition appears to reach higher performance for this activity.

The subjective questionnaire shows that subject were more comfortable at
perceiving the third dimension of the prototype in the CAVE than in 2D (The
contrary would have been an issue !). In the CAVE, they also better understood
how to manipulate the environment, and found it easier to practice afterwards.
Finally, subjects didn't feel a significantly higher visual tiredness in the CAVE
condition. This question is not sharp enough to conclude about visual tiredness,
but it can be claimed that the users did not fill major inconvenience for a short
time usage.

The NASA-TLX shows that subjects felt a significantly less important workload in the CAVE condition than in 2D. Also the final questionnaire shows
that subjects unanimously preferred working in the CAVE than in 2D. This
result is to handle with care; indeed most subjects never had an experience with
CAVE systems (16/19), or even with virtual reality (12/19). Their answer is thus
hardly separated from the enthusiasm of using a novel technology. Nonetheless
this result shows that subjects felt more comfortable in the CAVE than in 2D.
Moreover, subjects considered image skips in the CAVE as a nuisance: their
preference for the CAVE, as well as their better performances, are significant
despite this additional nuisance.

Those results confirm the veracity of our operational hypothesis: *H2: In the CAVE, the subjects will be able to perform the task in a shorter time, and will report the task as easier.* Thus we can confirm that people are more efficient and feel more comfortable using the CAVE than a 2D screen for a disassembly sequence creation task (**H1**). This result is only valid for the expected task but it demonstrates that a CAVE provides a real added value, almost for well selected tasks.

5   Discussion and Conclusion

Added Value of the CAVE: The study showed that subjects are more efficient objectively (faster, fewer errors) and subjectively (better comprehension, lower felt workload, preference) in the CAVE system than in 2D to perform the given virtual prototype manipulation task. The task concerned the use-case described in part 2, i.e. the design of a disassembly sequence by an operator. The results of the study highlighted the strong potential of the Mihriad CAVE for this use-case, and therefore for its usage in future design offices.

More deeply, the study focused on basic 3D objects manipulation. The good results of the subjects showed the CAVE's potential over a 2D screen concerning the manipulation of virtual prototypes. This promising result suggests that further work on the CAVE will be likely to extend our use-case to other design tasks concerning virtual prototyping. This study can then be considered a first step toward the integration of the Mihriad like CAVE in future design office.

Points of Attention and Perspectives: The technical solution should be also upgraded. It will improve the CAVE experience. Some extra features should enhance the ergonomics and precision of the system: collision detection between objects, "magnet" function [4], etc. Work is still in progress to enhance its usability. More important the duration of the task was rather short (<5 min in average). Our measurements of subjects tiredness (through the NASA-TLX) might thus be underestimated, as suggested by Bérard et al. [9]. Currently the CAVE must be promoted as a complementary tool within the design office for short session usage.

At last, this study was not built to draw any conclusion from the demographic data of the subjects. Subjects were recruited with no restriction within the students and staff of the university. Further study should be designed to check the effect of demographic data such as age, guiding hand, or experience with virtual reality.

Acknowledgements. G-SCOP laboratory is member of Persyval Laboratory Of Excellence (French labex) and participates to the Authoring Augmented Reality research action where this study takes place.

References

1. Chedmail, P., Maille, B., Ramstein, E.: Accessibility and ergonomics study with virtual reality, a state of the art. Méc. Ind. **3**, 147–152 (2002)
2. Mujber, T., Szecsi, T., Hashmi, M.: Virtual reality applications in manufacturing process simulation. J. Mater. Process. Technol. **155–156**, 1834–1838 (2004)
3. Krassi, B., D'Cruz, M., Vink, P., Kantola, P.: ManuVAR: a framework for improving manual work through virtual and augmented reality. In: Advances in Occupational, Social, and Organizational Ergonomics, Proceedings of the 3rd International Conference on Applied Human Factors and Ergonomics, Miami, Florida, USA, 17–20 July 2010, 10 p (2010). ISBN-13: 978-0-9796435-4-5
4. Chryssolouris, G., Mavrikios, D., Karabatsou, V., Fragos, D., Sarris, I., Mourtzis, D.: A virtual reality based approach for the verification of human related factors in assembly and maintenance processes. In: Computer-Aided Ergonomics and Safety Conference (1999)
5. de Sa, A.G., Zachmann, G.: Virtual reality as a tool for verification of assembly and maintenance processes. Comput. Graph. **23**(3), 389–403 (1999)
6. Tching, L., Dumont, G., Perret, J.: Haptic assembly of CAD models using virtual constraint guidance. In: ASME Conference Proceedings, ASME 2010, pp. 11–19 (2010)
7. Seth, A., Vance, J.M., Oliver, J.H.: Virtual reality for assembly methods prototyping: a review. Virtual Real. **15**, 5–20 (2010). https://doi.org/10.1007/s10055-009-0153-y
8. Krueger, W., Froehlich, B.: The responsive workbench. IEEE Comput. Graph. Appl. **14**, 12–15 (1994)
9. Bérard, F., Ip, J., Benovoy, M., El-Shimy, D., Blum, J.R., Cooperstock, J.R.: Did "minority report" get it wrong? Superiority of the mouse over 3D input devices in a 3D placement task. In: Gross, T. (ed.) INTERACT 2009. LNCS, vol. 5727, pp. 400–414. Springer, Heidelberg (2009). https://doi.org/10.1007/978-3-642-03658-3_45
10. Grosskopf, A., Edelman, J., Weske, M.: Tangible business process modeling – methodology and experiment design. In: Rinderle-Ma, S., Sadiq, S., Leymann, F. (eds.) BPM 2009. LNBIP, vol. 43, pp. 489–500. Springer, Heidelberg (2010). https://doi.org/10.1007/978-3-642-12186-9_46
11. Hart, S.G., Staveland, L.E.: Development of NASA-TLX (Task Load Index): results of empirical and theoretical research. In: Advances in Psychology, vol. 52, pp. 139–183. Elsevier, San Jose State University, San Jose (1988)
12. Likert, R.: A technique for the measurement of attitudes. In: Archives of Psychology, vol. 140, pp. 1–55. The Science Press, Columbia University, New York (1932)

Anchored Multiperspective Visualization for Efficient VR Navigation

Meng-Lin Wu$^{(\boxtimes)}$ and Voicu Popescu

Purdue University, West Lafayette, IN 47907, USA
wu223@purdue.edu

Abstract. This paper presents a novel multiperspective visualization (MPV) approach designed to improve navigation efficiency in Virtual Reality applications. The MPV is continuous and non-redundant, it shows the near part of the scene with a conventional, first-person visualization to anchor the user, and it is controlled with user head translations and rotations reminiscent of natural motion. Three types of anchored MPV are introduced, one that provides a lateral disocclusion effect, allowing the user to see around occluders and through side portals, one that provides a vertical disocclusion effect, allowing the user to see over and on top of occluders, and one that provides teleportation, allowing the user to relocate. The VR navigation efficiency benefits of the anchored MPV have been analyzed in a user study. Significant improvements were achieved in the metrics of number of teleportations and total distance traveled. In these metrics, large or greater Cohen's d effect sizes were observed at p-values below 0.05 in a first VR scene, while medium effect sizes at p-values of 0.1 or better were observed in a second VR scene.

Keywords: Virtual Reality · Visualization techniques · Rendering

1 Introduction

In Virtual Reality (VR) applications, a head-mounted display (HMD) tracked with six degrees of freedom supports using real walking for natural navigation, where there is an identity mapping between the user's physical and virtual motion. The user selects the desired view intuitively, by walking to translate the viewpoint, and by rotating their head to change view direction. However, real walking navigation presents several challenges. One challenge is the fact that the real world space hosting the VR application is typically smaller and of a different shape compared to the virtual space, which can prevent the user from reaching some desired viewpoints. For example, a desired viewpoint might coincide with real-world furniture, it might be beyond the walls of the real world room, or it might be high up, on a higher level of a multistory virtual world that is hard to reach.

Another challenge is that in complex virtual world scenes occlusions limit how much the user can see from any given viewpoint. Comprehensive exploration

© Springer Nature Switzerland AG 2018
P. Bourdot et al. (Eds.): EuroVR 2018, LNCS 11162, pp. 240–259, 2018.
https://doi.org/10.1007/978-3-030-01790-3_15

Fig. 1. Top: lateral disocclusion effect. The side corridor is occluded in a conventional visualization (left), and visible in our anchored multiperspective visualization (MPV) (right). The disocclusion effect was deployed by the user with a small left translation of their head. The MPV shows the near part of the scene conventionally, anchoring the user. Bottom: vertical disocclusion effect. A conventional visualization does not show on top of the ledge (left), whereas our anchored MPV does (right). The disocclusion effect was deployed by the user with a small upward translation of their head achieved by getting up on their tiptoes. The MPV shows the ledge and the walls in front of the ledge conventionally, anchoring the user.

requires translating the viewpoint to circumvent occluders and to gain line of sight to all potential regions of interest (ROIs). When a potential ROI turns out to be of no interest, the user has to retrace their path and to explore the next one. Such sequential scene exploration is inefficient. Furthermore, when scene understanding depends on seeing several ROIs simultaneously, or on visualizing dynamic, possibly evading targets, sequential scene exploration is ineffective.

Another reason why real walking might not always be desirable is based on ergonomics considerations. For some applications, the user might prefer not to expend the energy needed to navigate the VR world by always walking and rotating their head in the real world. In other words, for applications where the experience of actual physical locomotion is not essential, users might prefer navigation interface constructs that allow them to see more with less physical effort in a shorter amount of time.

Many approaches have been investigated for overcoming these challenges of using real walking for navigation in VR. One promising approach is based on multiperspective visualization (MPV), which relies on images that integrate samples captured from multiple viewpoints. Consider a virtual scene with two corridors intersecting at a right angle. Using a conventional visualization, a user has to translate the viewpoint up to the intersection to examine the side corridors in search of an ROI. If, on the other hand, an MPV shows not only the main corridor but also the side corridors, the user can examine the side corridors from their current location, which avoids the unnecessary navigation to the intersection when the side corridors turn out to be empty. Similarly, MPV can let the user see distant parts of the scene, without having to move beyond the walls of the real world space hosting the VR application. An MPV can also let the user examine two potential ROIs simultaneously, in parallel, even when no conventional visualization can show both ROIs at the same time.

Harvesting these potential advantages of MPV in the context of VR navigation requires solving two problems: (1) to design an MPV that is effective, i.e. that has the high information payload needed for navigation efficiency, but that remains easy to interpret by the user, and that does not induce user disorientation or motion sickness; (2) to devise navigation interface elements that allow the user to invoke their MPV superpower intuitively, in order to benefit from the additional perspective quickly and to the fullest extent.

In this paper we present anchored multiperspective visualization, a novel multiperspective visualization method designed to improve VR navigation efficiency. Our method was designed based on the following principles: (1) the MPV image should be continuous and non-redundant; (2) the MPV should show the near part of the scene with a conventional first-person visualization controlled through natural motion, anchoring the user; and (3) the MPV effect should be controlled with user motions reminiscent of natural motion, by tethering the secondary perspective selection to the user's head rotations and translations.

We have designed three types of anchored MPV. The first type allows the user to achieve a lateral disocclusion effect (Fig. 1, top) The user cannot see down the right side corridor with a conventional visualization (left). The MPV (right) integrates a secondary perspective into the main user's perspective, allowing the user to see down the right side corridor. The secondary perspective is controlled by the user translating their head to the left as if to look around a corner. The small head translation is amplified and applied to a secondary viewpoint that swings into place to reveal the side corridor. The user view change is used directly, without amplification, to render the nearby geometry, which remains in agreement with the user's proprioception to anchor the user.

The second type of anchored MPV allows the user to achieve a vertical disocclusion effect (Fig. 1, bottom). The user cannot see on top of the ledge in a conventional visualization (left). The MPV (right) integrates an additional perspective, with a high up viewpoint, to reveal the object on the ledge. The secondary perspective is controlled by the user by getting up on their tiptoes as if to examine a tall shelf above eye level. The small vertical user viewpoint translation is amplified and applied to a secondary viewpoint that translates up the necessary amount to see on top of the ledge.

The third type of anchored MPV allows the user to teleport from one location to another. MPV disoccludes parts of the scene not visible from the main user viewpoint, but it does not and should not produce a visualization that shows the entire scene. Consequently, the need to quickly move directly to a distant location of the scene remains even in MPV navigation. We have designed an anchored MPV teleportation method that proceeds in two stages, evocative of how a caterpillar moves (Fig. 2). First, the secondary viewpoint moves forward, getting closer to the far part of the scene, translating from the origin to the destination, while the primary viewpoint doesn't move, remaining at the origin. Second, the primary viewpoint moves forward to the secondary viewpoint, while the secondary viewpoint doesn't move.

We have conducted a user study to detect and quantify any VR navigation efficiency benefits brought by our anchored MPV method. 16 participants were divided evenly in a control group, who used conventional visualization, and an experiment group, who used our anchored MPV. Each participant performed a searching task and a matching task in each of two virtual environments: a single-story area of connected rooms, and a larger room with walkways suspended from the periphery walls, high above the room floor. For the first environment the experiment group participants had available our lateral disocclusion anchored MPV, and for the second environment they had available our vertical disocclusion anchored MPV. In all cases, all participants had the ability to teleport to any scene location to which they had line of sight. The experiment group used our MPV teleportation. The experiment group performed significantly better than the control group in the first virtual environment, achieving improvements in the metrics of distance traveled and number of teleportations. Cohen's d effect size of large and greater was observed with p-values below 0.05. In the more complex second virtual environment, the experiment group achieved improvements of medium Cohen's d effect size at p-values of 0.1 and less. Experiment group participants also reported improvements in spatial awareness and perceived navigation efficiency.

In summary, our paper makes the following contributions: (1) a set of principles for designing VR navigation methods based on multiperspective visualization, (2) three anchored multiperspective visualization based on our design principles, one for lateral disocclusion, one for vertical disocclusion, and one for teleportation, and (3) a user study confirming the potential of our anchored MPV to improve VR navigation efficiency.

2   Prior Work

In VR, a preferred scene navigation modality is actual user locomotion in the physical space, which is translated to matching view changes in the virtual world. However, the physical space typically differs considerably from the virtual space. Due to this mismatch, some virtual viewpoints become inaccessible. In Sect. 2.1, we discuss this challenge and prior work aimed at alleviating it. Another challenge arises from the reduction in visualization efficiency due to occlusions of ROIs by scene geometry, forcing the user to search for an unobstructed line of sight through extensive viewpoint navigation. In Sect. 2.2 we review prior work for improving VR navigation efficiency using the multiperspective occlusion management approach.

Fig. 2. Two-stage MPV teleportation concept. In the first stage (top two images), the primary perspective stays locked on the origin, anchoring the user, while the secondary perspective translates to the destination. In the second half (bottom two images), the secondary perspective stays fixed, anchoring the user, while the primary perspective moves to assume the secondary perspective.

2.1 VR Navigation Challenges

The most intuitive VR navigation is an identity mapping between physical and virtual motion [20,25]. One common problem is that the physical space is considerably different than the virtual space. Usually the physical space is more restricted than the virtual world.

To fully explore the virtual world, the real and virtual locomotion must purposefully diverge to allow sufficient virtual motion while limiting physical motion. One approach is teleportation, which allows the user to designate a destination in the virtual world, and then to instantly relocate to that destination [1]. The visualization is discontinuous as the user changes location instantaneously, without any indication of the position of the destination relative to the origin. Therefore, the user needs some time to reorient themselves after arriving at the destination. A technique to reduce this discontinuity is to translate the user from the origin to the destination along a straight path [9]. However, a slow translation might cause nausea, as the user's viewpoint changes without any perceived acceleration, while a fast translation does not resolve the visualization discontinuity issue. In practice, a visual "blink", i.e. fade-out followed by fade-in, is applied as the viewpoint translates, to minimize nausea while providing some visual connection between the origin and the destination [4].

Another approach is artificial, or free, locomotion, where the user relies on input devices such as joysticks or keyboards to navigate the view beyond the tracked head pose. The divergence between virtual and physical motion is thus directly controlled by user input. This method preserves visualization continuity, so spatial awareness is not compromised. However, due to the detachment of the user's virtual movement from their physical movement, the artificial locomotion method induces more motion sickness compared with teleportation-based methods [5]. Specifically, the visual and physical senses of acceleration are out of sync. One technique for alleviating nausea is to limit the user to discrete artificial locomotion steps, which are enacted abruptly to break the sensation of artificial acceleration. However, larger steps impact spatial awareness, while smaller steps incur frequent visual discontinuity [4].

Other approaches hide the mismatch between the physical and the virtual worlds by deviating from the tracking data, for example by making the user cover long straight lines in the virtual world by walking in circles in the physical world [18,19], by resetting user pose [27], and by modifying input gain [17,30]. Another approach is to distort the virtual world to pack it tightly in the limited confines of the physical world [24]. An approach that blends physical and artificial locomotion is the treadmill approach, or the smart platform approach, where the user actually walks, but without covering large distances in the physical world [23]. The shortcomings of the approach are confusing motion divergences, tethering the user, and reliance on expensive and bulky hardware.

2.2 Multiperspective Visualization in VR

MPV is a class of visualization techniques that integrate multiple perspectives into the main user perspective. MPV originated in the visual arts, e.g. Picasso's Cubism, and is applied to achieving comprehensive visualization, such as a ski trail map showing simultaneously trails not all visible from a single viewpoint.

Earlier research work focused on relaxing the single center of projection constraint, but the sampling rays remain linear [6,16,31]. More recent work introduced piecewise linear or even curved sampling rays that provide the flexibility needed to go around occluders to reach distant ROIs [3,11,15]. While relaxation of the constraints opened up more degrees of freedom in the camera model used to render the visualization, the camera model generalization also created the need for automatic and interactive constructors that provide the application with the desired disocclusion effect [28].

In VR occlusion management, MPV is also found to be an effective technique [29], while conventional desktop occlusion management techniques such as transparency and explosion visualizations face various challenges. Transparency techniques introduce visual clutter that scale with scene complexity [7], whereas the MPV approach does not introduce additional geometry and does not violate pictorial depth cues. Explosion techniques disturb scene geometry [10], which impact the user's spatial awareness in VR, whereas the MPV approach does not disturb surface connectivity.

Portal-based visualization is a technique closely related to MPV. It composites additional views of the scene within the main view in a picture-in-picture fashion [8]. In VR applications, it supports teleportation navigation where the user teleports to destinations revealed through the portal [14]. However, the teleportation destination, as viewed through the portal, is beyond the vista space [13]. The user is therefore unable to trace the path of teleportation.

Our MPV method increases scene exploration efficiency by giving the user a preview of ROIs that are occluded in a conventional visualization. Compared with portal-based visualization, our MPV incorporates disoccluded ROIs into the vista space, avoiding disorientation due to untraceable teleportation [26]. Compared with the prior work in MPV navigation [29], our MPV supports both lateral and vertical disocclusion. It provides more versatile and at the same time more intuitive ways of controlling the additional perspectives, and it allows the user to assume seamlessly any additional perspective revealed by MPV using teleportation. The user's spatial awareness is further increased by visually anchoring the user in the scene as the additional perspectives are deployed and retracted, and during teleportation.

3   Anchored Multiperspective Visualization

In this section, we first discuss in more detail our three principles for the design of effective multiperspective visualization for VR navigation, and then we present our three methods for anchored MPV.

3.1   Design Principles for Effective Multiperspective Visualization in VR

(1) *MPV image continuity and non-redundancy*
This first principle encapsulates general concerns for achieving effective MPV, irrespective of the VR context. An MPV has to be continuous, i.e. points that are close in 3D should project to nearby image locations. This concern disqualifies MPVs obtained through a discontinuous collage of individual perspectives, or

through parallel visualization with multiple disconnected rectangular images. An MPV also has to be non-redundant, i.e. it should not show a part of the scene multiple times. Continuity and non-redundancy are necessary conditions for obtaining an MPV that can be parsed by the user without the disadvantage of a significant cognitive load, which is particularly important in the VR navigation context.

(2) *Primary perspective MPV anchoring*

This second principle ensures that, as the conventional visualization morphs into an MPV, and as the MPV parameters are changed interactively, there is always a significant part of the image that is unaffected by the MPV effect, and that the unaffected part of the image corresponds to the space surrounding the user. The user's visual system relies on this primary visualization of nearby geometry, in sync with their own primary perspective, to remain in agreement with the motion perceived by the user, and to dissociate from the distant parts of the scene that move incongruently with the perceived motion, both of which contribute to preventing disorientation and motion sickness.

(3) *Natural secondary perspective navigation*

An MPV has a significantly higher number of degrees of freedom than a conventional visualization, with each additional perspective introducing six more extrinsic parameters. This third principle prohibits complex navigation interfaces that ask the user to manipulate a high number of degrees of freedom individually, and mandates allowing the user to control the secondary perspectives with natural motions similar to the ones used to control the main user perspective in conventional VR.

3.2   Anchored MPV for Lateral Disocclusion

A frequently needed disocclusion effect is to see around an occluder, e.g. to see around a tree, or to see through a side opening, e.g. through a window in a

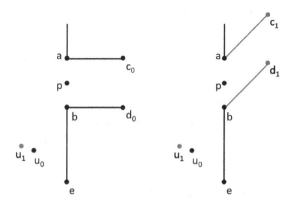

Fig. 3. Lateral disocclusion through anchored MPV. A conventional visualization from viewpoint u_0 does not show the side corridor (left). A small left translation of the head from u_0 to u_1 deploys a disocclusion effect that shows inside the side corridor (right).

house facade. Such a lateral disocclusion effect can be provided by integrating a secondary perspective from a viewpoint that has line of sight around the tree or through the window. We provide a lateral disocclusion effect as follows.

Given a virtual scene, we define a set of vertical rectangles in the scene to serve as portals to guide the lateral disocclusion effect. The portals are defined where the user is likely to benefit from disocclusion, e.g. at the doorways that connect various sections of the scene, or between an occluder and nearby walls, such as a column in a middle of a room. The portals are not rendered, but when a user exploring the scene with a VR HMD sees the geometry spanned by a portal, the geometry changes color to indicate the availability of a disocclusion effect. The user activates the disocclusion effect with a controller button. The activation itself does not change the visualization to an MPV. After activation, lateral translations of the user's head as recorded by the HMD will deploy a secondary perspective that sees through the portal.

In Fig. 3 the user's initial viewpoint is u_0, looking at portal ab. In the conventional visualization (left), the user cannot see deep inside the portal from u_0. Once the user activates the disocclusion effect of the portal, a subsequent left translation of the user viewpoint rotates the geometry behind the portal plane about the pivot point p, which is the center of the portal rectangle. The rotation gives the user line of sight perpendicularly through the portal, e.g. swinging the side corridor wall vertices c_0, d_0 to c_1, d_1, respectively (right). The rotation angle is proportional to the user's lateral head translation, and the gain is tuned such that a small amount of translation $u_1 u_0$ (e.g. 20 cm) is sufficient to see down the portal. The small translation wouldn't have been sufficient to see down the portal with a conventional visualization, i.e. the user would see only marginally more inside the portal from u_1 as compared to u_0 (left). The small translation is amplified by our lateral MPV disocclusion effect to introduce the necessary second perspective on the geometry beyond the portal plane.

The rotation angle is capped to the value needed to the see down the portal. Any geometry vertices or fragments that cross the portal plane when rotated are discarded (i.e. they are not drawn), which does not create artifacts as this geometry wouldn't have been visible anyway due to the side corridor walls. Vertex projection is continuous and non-redundant, which enforces the first design principle. Nearby geometry, i.e. the part of the eb wall seen by the user, is drawn conventionally, from the primary perspective, which anchors the user, enforcing the second principle. The additional perspective is deployed by the user translating their head to the left, and by slightly panning the view to the right in order to keep the portal in the center of the image, which is the natural motion the user would make if they were close to point b and wanted to look inside the portal, so the interface is in agreement with the third principle.

3.3 Anchored MPV for Vertical Disocclusion

In addition to lateral disocclusion, an explorer of a 3D virtual scene might also want to be able to see on top of horizontal surfaces that are suspended above the user's eye sight. Given a virtual scene, we define a set of ledge edges. Like in the case of portals, when a VR explorer has a predefined ledge edge into view, a highlight alerts them to the availability of a vertical disocclusion effect, and the user can activate the effect with a controller button.

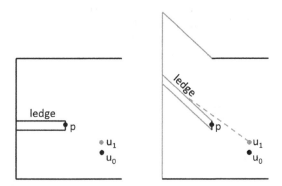

Fig. 4. Vertical disocclusion through anchored MPV. A conventional visualization does not show on top of the ledge (left). The user tiptoes to generate a small upward head translation from u_0 to u_1 that deploys a disocclusion effect that shows on top of the ledge (right).

Figure 4 shows the conventional visualization of a scene with a ledge (left) and the same scene with our vertical disocclusion MPV effect (right). The initial user viewpoint u_0 is too low to see on the ledge. A small vertical translation of the user viewpoint to u_1 brings in an additional perspective that sees on the ledge. The disocclusion effect is implemented as a rotation of the geometry beyond and above the ledge, such that the new viewpoint u_1 is above the ledge plane, disoccluding the ledge. The viewpoint u_1 wouldn't have been high enough to disocclude the ledge in a conventional visualization (left). The small translation u_0u_1 is amplified to achieve the vertical disocclusion effect.

Like in the case of lateral disocclusion, the vertex projection is continuous and non-redundant, and the user's view of the floor and of the ledge edge doesn't change, anchoring the user. Finally, the vertical up and down translation is controlled by the user's tracked HMD, who gets up on their tiptoes up to see atop the ledge, and back down to revert to a conventional visualization.

3.4   Anchored MPV for Teleportation

We allow the user to teleport between an origin and a destination viewpoint, as needed to change floors, rooms, and, in general, to overcome the constraints of the real world and of the tracking system. Teleportation is a rapid transition between the two viewpoints, which can induce user motion sickness because the user moves, i.e. "flies", without actually engaging in locomotion. Prior work suggests that the safest teleportation is a very abrupt one, but that is also the teleportation that disorients the user the most.

We have developed a teleportation that aims to alleviate these disadvantages. The user selects the destination with the cursor, which is always placed at the intersection between the view direction and the scene geometry. Therefore, the destination is selected with the HMD by changing view direction. The destination viewpoint is the point on the vertical through the cursor that is at the user's height above the ground. If this initial destination viewpoint is too close to a wall, the destination viewpoint is pulled back away from the wall to provide a meaningful view once teleportation is complete. The user triggers teleportation with a controller button.

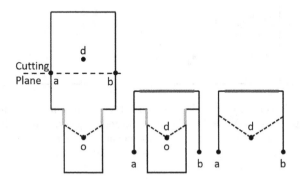

Fig. 5. Anchored MPV teleportation. The viewpoint moves from o to d in two phases: first the part of the scene beyond the cutting plane is brought down, anchoring the user with the near part of the scene (green, from left to middle), and then the cutting plane is brought down, anchoring the user with the far part of the scene (red, from middle to right) (Color figure online)

Our anchored teleportation method is illustrated in Fig. 5. The origin and destination viewpoints are o and d. During the first phase (i.e. transition from left to middle in Fig. 5), the far perspective is brought closer, by translating the scene geometry beyond the cutting plane with vector od. The cutting plane is positioned between the two viewpoints, splitting the distance between them at a fixed ratio. This first phase brings the far part of the scene closer, to be as close as it will be when the viewpoint is at d, but without pushing away the near part of the scene. The visualization of the near part of the scene (green) remains unchanged, which anchors the first phase of the teleportation. During the second phase, the cut plane is translated along the vector do, which makes the nearby geometry disappear from view. The visualization of the far part of the scene (red) remains unchanged in this second phase, which maintains uninterrupted anchoring.

Figure 5 illustrates teleportation along a straight line, but the same procedure is followed if the user chooses to teleport using a lateral or vertical disocclusion MPV. The only difference is that once the second phase is complete, any residual distortion of geometry is gradually eliminated. Geometry is distorted only close to the portal or ledge planes, and typically the user desires to teleport deeply through the portal or beyond the ledge, so the geometry is undistorted off screen. Figure 2, left, shows frames from a "straight line" teleportation. Figure 2, right, illustrates teleportation into a side corridor, starting from the lateral disocclusion effect.

4 User Study

In order to evaluate the effect of our multiperspective visualization technique on VR navigation efficiency, we conducted a randomized user study, with the approval of our Institutional Review Board. Each participant performed three tasks in VR, and their actions were logged for subsequent analysis. After task completion, the users responded to a questionnaire that provided their subjective evaluation of task performance.

The participant wore a VR HMD (i.e. Windows Mixed Reality headset [12]). The VR HMD performs six degree of freedom SLAM-based tracking of the pose of the participant's head. In addition, the participant used a motion-tracked hand-held controller to enable interactions with the virtual world through actions such as pointing and clicking buttons. The HMD displays stereoscopic image pairs rendered from viewpoints offset by the interpupillary distance to provide stereoscopic depth perception.

4.1 Participants

A total of 16 participants (14 male) completed our study. The participants were graduate students of ages between 23 and 37. They were randomly assigned to experiment and control groups of 8 participants each. Participants in the control group performed all tasks using only conventional, single-perspective visualization, while the participants in the experiment group performed all tasks using our anchored MPV.

The between-group design was chosen over the within-subject design to avoid any learning effect when repeating tasks from one condition to the next. Another reason is to mitigate the fatigue factor that can affect performance in extended task performance in VR environments–with the between-group design a participant's involvement time is reduced in half. However, the effect of prolonged usage of MPV navigation is an important avenue for future research, which is discussed further in Sect. 5.

4.2 Tasks and Evaluation

The participants performed tasks that required extensive virtual locomotion in two VR scenes using environments adapted from the Quake 3 Arena [22]. The first VR scene (Scene 1) is a single-story indoors area consisting of a set of rooms connected by corridors (Fig. 6, left). Two of the rooms contain cylindrical pillars in the center, which partially occlude the interior of the rooms regardless of the participant's current viewpoint. The second VR scene (Scene 2) is a large 3-story

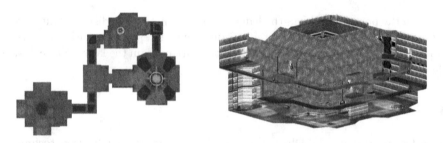

Fig. 6. VR scenes used in the user study. Left: Scene 1 is a set of rooms connected by corridors. Right: Scene 2 is a 3-story building with multi-level walkways.

building where the center is an inaccessible tower, while the levels are connected by walkways attached to the perimeter walls (Fig. 6, right).

Each participant was required to perform 3 tasks: two search tasks, each in a different VR scene, and one pair matching task. Before beginning each task, the participant completed a short warm-up exercise which is similar to the actual task, but differs in content and is much shorter. This warm-up period ensured that the participant correctly operated the HMD and the hand-held controller, and that the test procedures were clear. Participants received no other training beyond this warm-up period.

The participant's performance was evaluated from recorded data using objective metrics, which were unknown to the participants. During the performance of each task, the participant's tracked physical HMD pose was logged, along with any interaction events such as initiating teleportation, acquiring a target object, or matching a pair of target objects. The logs were processed to extract metrics of interest. Additionally, each participant was asked to respond to a questionnaire after completion of the tasks. The questionnaire recorded subjective evaluation of performance and comfort.

4.3   User Interface for Locomotion and Anchored MPV

In both Scene 1 and Scene 2, the user was free to employ real walking by moving within a 2 m by 2 m physical space. To navigate beyond the limits of the physical space, the user employed teleportation. The user pointed the hand-held controller at the intended destination, and then clicked the controller button to initiate the teleportation. (Fig. 7, left). In Scene 2, the user could additionally access higher floor walkways by designating the walkway edges as a teleportation destination. As the user points the hand-held controller at a walkway edge, the edge is highlighted to indicate that the edge is a valid destination (Fig. 7, right). The user can also select any visible lower floor surface. As the controller button is clicked, the virtual viewpoint is teleported to the destination. The teleportation is not completed instantly, but the virtual viewpoint is translated to the destination at a fast 40 m/s straight line velocity. During the translation, participants in the control group experienced the conventional "blink" visual effect,

Fig. 7. The user selects the teleportation destination using a hand-held controller. Left: In both VR scenes, the user teleports by pointing a "laser" beam at the destination and clicking using the controller. Right: In the second VR scene, the walkway edges that are eligible as teleportation destinations are highlighted in blue when swiped with the laser beam.

whereas participants in the experiment group experienced the anchored MPV teleportation described in Sect. 3.4.

Our lateral disocclusion anchored MPV (Fig. 1, top) was accessible to experiment group participants performing tasks in Scene 1. The anchored MPV is activated automatically as the user gazes at virtual portals defined by corridor archways or connecting cylindrical pillars to side walls. The available archways and pillars in Scene 1 are predetermined prior to the study. Once the MPV is activated, the user moves laterally in small amounts to rotate the secondary perspective horizontally.

Our vertical disocclusion anchored MPV (Fig. 1, bottom) was accessible to experiment group participants performing tasks in Scene 2. The vertical disocclusion anchored MPV is manually activated. First, the user designates a walkway edge on a different floor by pointing with the hand-held controller and holding down the button. Then, with the button held, the user tiptoes or crouches a small amount to raise or lower the secondary viewpoint. Due to the need to hold down the button for activating the anchored MPV, the user of the MPV is required to double-click the controller button in order to initiate teleportation in Scene 2. Any new area revealed by the anchored MPV is also a valid destination for teleportation.

Search Tasks (Search 1 and Search 2). The search tasks Search 1 and Search 2 were performed in Scene 1 and Scene 2 respectively. In both search tasks, the participant was asked to find target objects in the form of gold coins placed in the VR scene. There were 6 coins that appeared one after another. Their locations were unknown to the participant, but were identical for all participants. A coin disappeared once it was found and collected by the participant by getting within $1m$ of the coin, either through real walking or through teleportation. An audio cue was triggered at the collection of a coin to notify the participant. The task was complete when all coins are collected.

Pair Matching Tasks (Match). The pair matching task (Match) was performed in Scene 1. In this task, the participant was asked to identify target objects in the form of colorful mushrooms, of identical color pattern. There were 8 objects in 4 distinct color patterns, whose placement was identical for all participants. The participant first pointed to one visible target object and selected it by clicking a button. When the participant clicked on the second object of identical pattern, the pair was considered matched and it disappeared from the scene, with an audio cue. The task was complete when no targets remained.

Post-performance Questionnaire. Each participant was asked to respond to a questionnaire after completing the three tasks. The purpose of the questionnaire was to evaluate the participant's perception of their own performance and of our MPV technique. The participant responded to each of three statements "You always felt present in the virtual world", "Your spatial awareness was maintained while moving around", and "You could reach any intended destination efficiently", by choosing an answer on a 1 to 5 scale, with 1 meaning "Not at all" and 5 points meaning "Very much".

4.4   Results and Discussion

We analyzed each participant's recorded logs to measure performance along several metrics. The most relevant metrics for this study are the metrics for navigation efficiency: (1) the number of times the participant initiated teleportation, (2) the accumulated teleportation distance, and (3) the time required to complete a task. These metrics were not revealed to the participants.

These metrics are evaluated for their effect sizes using Cohen's d [2], where qualifiers "small", "medium", and "large" are applied to cases where $d > 0.2$, $d > 0.5$, and $d > 0.8$, respectively. The qualifiers are extended to include "very small", "very large", and "huge" for $d < 0.01$, $d > 1.2$, and $d > 2.0$, respectively [21]. Statistical significance is evaluated using the two-sample t-test. We report the p-value to identify measurements that were due to chance.

Finally, we report the aggregate results of the questionnaire responses for discussion of subjective metrics which cannot be extracted from the task logs.

Number of Teleportations. Each teleportation incurs a discontinuity in the user's mental localization in the virtual world, after which the user must re-orient themselves. Therefore, it is desirable to minimize the number of teleportations. Furthermore, the ill-effects of teleportation can be reduced by improving visualization during teleportation.

Table 1. Average number of teleportations per participant.

Task	Control	Experiment	Diff.	p	d	Effect size
Search 1	83.4 ± 48.9	21.6 ± 18.5	61.8	<0.01	1.7	Very large
Match	51.8 ± 24.8	27.6 ± 22.7	24.1	0.03	1.0	Large
Search 2	98.3 ± 71.5	50.3 ± 31.5	48.0	0.06	0.9	Medium

We expect our anchored MPV to reduce the number of teleportations for two reasons. First, our MPV disoccludes ROIs and allows the user to plan their path more efficiently. Therefore, the user is able to avoid teleportating to destination only to find that it is not of interest. The second reason is that our anchored MPV extends the set of possible teleportation destinations to those areas newly disoccluded by the visualization. As the user is not limited to teleporting only to destinations with a line of sight, they are able to traverse at once a path that might require multiple teleportations using conventional visualization. Table 1 shows the result for the metric of number of teleportations. In Search 1 and Match tasks, which are both performed in the single-floor Scene 1, our anchored MPV significantly reduced the number of teleportations required to complete the tasks, with the p-value well below 0.05. The effect sizes are very large and large for tasks Search 1 and Match respectively. In the Search 2 task, which is performed in the more complex 3-story Scene 2, the results are positive with a medium effect, although with a higher p-value of 0.06.

Table 2. Average distance traveled per participant, in meters.

Task	Control	Experiment	Diff.	p	d	Effect size
Search 1	464 ± 135	222 ± 90	242	<0.01	2.1	Huge
Match	326 ± 103	228 ± 86	99	0.03	1.0	Large
Search 2	677 ± 306	527 ± 236	150	0.1	0.5	Medium

Accumulated Teleportation Distance. We analyze the accumulated teleportation distance because the majority of locomotion that is conducted in our VR scenes is through teleportation, therefore it is representative of the total amount of virtual viewpoint travel. We expect users of our anchored MPV to accumulate less traveled distance. This is due to the increased path planning efficiency as discussed in Sect. 4.4. Table 2 lists the average per participant distance traveled for each task. Significant improvements of huge and large Cohen d's effect sizes were observed for both Search 1 and Match tasks performed in Scene 1. This is in line with our expectation that the user is able to explore maps effectively with less required virtual locomotion. The result for task Search 2 performed in the more complex Scene 2 also shows an improvement of medium effect size. The statistical significance at $p = 0.1$ is not as strong as with tasks performed in Scene 1. However, the positive effect size suggests a more significant result is possible with more user study participants.

Task Completion Time. Table 3 reports the time our participants took to complete the three tasks. The experiment group had a statistically significant advantage for the first task. For the second task, the experiment group was faster, but the advantage was not statistically significant. For the third task, the average completion time for the experiment group was longer than for the control group. From our observation of the participants during the experiment, we explain this based on a longer time the participant needed to engage the MPV interface. As shown in Table 1, the number of jumps is significantly lower for the experiment group even for the third task, indicating that the MPV is effective, except that using it takes longer. A direction of immediate future work is to improve the time effectiveness in which the vertical disocclusion MPV is used, by suggesting to the user the availability of the effect in a more salient way during training (the blue highlight is sometimes easy to miss), and then by suggesting the tiptoeing mechanism that actually implements the MPV.

Table 3. Task completion time, in seconds.

Task	Control	Experiment	Diff.	p	d	Effect size
Search 1	113 ± 45	56 ± 29	57	<0.01	1.5	Very large
Match	89 ± 25	78 ± 25	11	0.2	0.4	Small
Search 2	157 ± 71	175 ± 88	(18)	0.7	0.2	Small

Questionnaire Responses. The final metric we used to compare the two participant groups was a compilation of the self-evaluation questionnaire responses (Table 4). The experiment group self-reported higher spatial awareness and higher navigation efficiency, while they reported a lower sense of actual presence in the virtual environment. It comes as no surprise that the experiment group had better spatial awareness than the control group as the MPV essentially provides a preview of the scene, without as much disorienting backtracking as required by the sequential exploration with a conventional visualization. Furthermore, our MPV was designed to anchor the user at all times, so the additional information presented did not come at the cost of confusing the user. Similarly, the improvement of navigation efficiency is a reasonable hypothesis based on the same arguments. We explain the decreased sense of presence by the fact that, like any MPV, our method upgrades the user from an uninterrupted immersive first-person view of the scene to an occasional second or even third-person monitoring of the scene. The user shifts fluidly viewpoint and their association with a specific location in the scene, and the consequent decrease in sense of presence is a reasonable trade-off towards gaining navigation efficiency.

Table 4. Overall subjective evaluation.

	Control	Experiment	Diff.	d	Effect size
Spatial awareness	3.3 ± 1.3	4.3 ± 1.0	1.0	0.7	Medium
Efficiency	4.1 ± 1.5	4.6 ± 0.5	0.5	0.4	Small
Presence	4.0 ± 1.1	3.5 ± 1.1	(0.5)	0.4	Small

5   Conclusions and Future Work

We have presented a novel method for multiperspective visualization for Virtual Reality that promises to improve navigation efficiency. Our method visualizes the scene with images that show more than what is visible from a single viewpoint, by integrating additional perspective continuously and non-redundantly. Another goal of our MPV is to always anchor the user by showing part of the scene geometry conventionally, from the user's first-person view. Finally, MPV navigation should remain as intuitive as possible, by allowing the user to control the additional perspectives through the tracked HMD. We describe anchored MPV techniques for lateral disocclusion, for vertical disocclusion, and for teleportation. The MPV benefits have been confirmed in a user study.

Additional user studies should be conducted to explore in depth the subjective effects of MPV navigation. Our post-performance questionnaire provided preliminary insights to the users' perceptions, but the study is not tailored to measure subjective effects such as visual quality, cognitive effort, and user comfort. Especially, tasks which require prolonged usage of MPV navigation should be designed to examine any cumulative effect of simulator sickness, even though no test participant expressed discomfort at any point during the study. At the same time, these longer tasks allow examination of any training effects as participants become familiar with the user interface.

One direction of future work is to find automatically the places in the scene where disocclusion effects are useful. This is in view of the limitation that the virtual portals needed to be manually marked in Scene 1 of our user study. One option is to preprocess the scene, and another option is to decide on the potential for disocclusion on the fly, based on the current frame.

Another direction of future work is to investigate the anchored MPV benefits in the context of dynamic, and even evading targets, which place even more stringent requirements on the quality of the disocclusion effect and on the intuitiveness of the interface for deploying it. These requirements are particularly relevant to gaming applications, where targets could follow complex strategies, or they could be other humans. Furthermore, there is interplay between leveraging visualization to facilitate navigation, and designing visualization for game mechanics. It is worth studying how to optimize for both sets of goals in the design space for VR visualization. As VR interfaces strive to become mainstream and to move beyond entertainment and into day to day use, a scenario that requires special attention is the sit at desk scenario, for which multiperspective visualization might be particularly well suited.

References

1. Bozgeyikli, E., Raij, A., Katkoori, S., Dubey, R.: Point & teleport locomotion technique for virtual reality. In: Proceedings of the 2016 Annual Symposium on Computer-Human Interaction in Play, CHI PLAY 2016, pp. 205–216. ACM, New York (2016)
2. Cohen, J.: Statistical Power Analysis for the Behavioral Sciences. Psychology Press, London (2009)
3. Cui, J., Rosen, P., Popescu, V., Hoffmann, C.: A curved ray camera for handling occlusions through continuous multiperspective visualization. IEEE Trans. Vis. Comput. Graph. **16**(6), 1235–1242 (2010)
4. Davis, S., Nesbitt, K., Nalivaiko, E.: A systematic review of cybersickness. In: Proceedings of the 2014 Conference on Interactive Entertainment, IE 2014, pp. 8:1–8:9. ACM, New York (2014)
5. Habgood, J., Moore, D., Wilson, D., Alapont, S.: Rapid, continuous movement between nodes as an accessible virtual reality locomotion technique. In: Proceedings of the 25th IEEE Conference on Virtual Reality and 3D User Interfaces, VR 2018, Reutlingen, Germany (2018)
6. Hartley, R.I., Gupta, R.: Linear pushbroom cameras. In: Eklundh, J.-O. (ed.) ECCV 1994. LNCS, vol. 800, pp. 555–566. Springer, Heidelberg (1994). https://doi.org/10.1007/3-540-57956-7_63
7. Kameda, Y., Takemasa, T., Ohta, Y.: Outdoor see-through vision utilizing surveillance cameras. In: Third IEEE and ACM International Symposium on Mixed and Augmented Reality, pp. 151–160, November 2004
8. Kunert, A., Kulik, A., Beck, S., Froehlich, B.: Photoportals: shared references in space and time. In: Proceedings of the 17th ACM Conference on Computer Supported Cooperative Work & Social Computing, CSCW 2014, pp. 1388–1399. ACM, New York (2014)
9. Laviola, J.J.: A discussion of cybersickness in virtual environments. SIGCHI Bull. **32**, 47–56 (2000)
10. Li, W., Agrawala, M., Curless, B., Salesin, D.: Automated generation of interactive 3D exploded view diagrams. ACM Trans. Graph. **27**(3), 101:1–101:7 (2008)
11. Mei, C., Popescu, V., Sacks, E.: The occlusion camera. In: Computer Graphics Forum (2005)
12. Microsoft: Windows mixed reality. http://www.microsoft.com/
13. Montello, D.R.: Scale and multiple psychologies of space. In: Frank, A.U., Campari, I. (eds.) COSIT 1993. LNCS, vol. 716, pp. 312–321. Springer, Heidelberg (1993). https://doi.org/10.1007/3-540-57207-4_21
14. Neat Corporation: Budget cuts (2018). http://neatcorporation.com/
15. Popescu, V., Rosen, P., Adamo-Villani, N.: The graph camera. ACM Trans. Graph. **28**(5), 158:1–158:8 (2009)
16. Rademacher, P., Bishop, G.: Multiple-center-of-projection images. In: Proceedings of the 25th Annual Conference on Computer Graphics and Interactive Techniques, SIGGRAPH 1998, pp. 199–206. ACM, New York (1998)
17. Ragan, E.D., Scerbo, S., Bacim, F., Bowman, D.A.: Amplified head rotation in virtual reality and the effects on 3D search, training transfer, and spatial orientation. IEEE Trans. Vis. Comput. Graph. **23**(8), 1880–1895 (2017)
18. Razzaque, S., Kohn, Z., Whitton, M.C.: Redirected walking. In: Eurographics 2001 - Short Presentations. Eurographics Association (2001)

19. Razzaque, S., Swapp, D., Slater, M., Whitton, M.C., Steed, A.: Redirected walking in place. In: Proceedings of the Workshop on Virtual Environments 2002, EGVE 2002, pp. 123–130. Eurographics Association, Aire-la-Ville (2002)
20. Ruddle, R.A., Lessels, S.: The benefits of using a walking interface to navigate virtual environments. ACM Trans. Comput.-Hum. Interact. **16**(1), 5:1–5:18 (2009)
21. Sawilowsky, S.S.: New effect size rules of thumb. J. Mod. Appl. Stat. Methods **8**(2), 597–599 (2009)
22. id Software: Quake 3 Arena (1999)
23. Souman, J.L.: CyberWalk: enabling unconstrained omnidirectional walking through virtual environments. ACM Trans. Appl. Percept. **8**(4), 25:1–25:22 (2008)
24. Sun, Q., Wei, L.Y., Kaufman, A.: Mapping virtual and physical reality. ACM Trans. Graph. **35**(4), 64:1–64:12 (2016)
25. Usoh, M., et al.: Walking > walking-in-place > flying, in virtual environments. In: Proceedings of the 26th Annual Conference on Computer Graphics and Interactive Techniques, SIGGRAPH 1999, pp. 359–364. ACM Press/Addison-Wesley Publishing Co., New York (1999)
26. Weissker, T., Kunert, A., Froehlich, B., Kulik, A.: Spatial updating and simulator sickness during steering and jumping in immersive virtual environments. In: Proceedings of the 25th IEEE Conference on Virtual Reality and 3D User Interfaces, VR 2018, Reutlingen, Germany (2018)
27. Williams, B., et al.: Exploring large virtual environments with an HMD when physical space is limited. In: Proceedings of the 4th Symposium on Applied Perception in Graphics and Visualization, APGV 2007, pp. 41–48. ACM, New York (2007)
28. Wu, M.L., Popescu, V.: Multiperspective focus+context visualization. IEEE Trans. Vis. Comput. Graph. **22**(5), 1555–1567 (2016)
29. Wu, M.L., Popescu, V.: Efficient VR and AR navigation through multiperspective occlusion management. IEEE Trans. Vis. Comput. Graph. (2017). https://doi.org/10.1109/TVCG.2017.2778249
30. Xie, X., et al.: A system for exploring large virtual environments that combines scaled translational gain and interventions. In: Proceedings of the 7th Symposium on Applied Perception in Graphics and Visualization, APGV 2010, pp. 65–72. ACM, New York (2010)
31. Yu, J., McMillan, L.: General linear cameras. In: Pajdla, T., Matas, J. (eds.) ECCV 2004. LNCS, vol. 3022, pp. 14–27. Springer, Heidelberg (2004). https://doi.org/10.1007/978-3-540-24671-8_2

Author Index